Quality Social Work

Also by Robert Adams

A Measure of Diversion: Case Studies in IT (with S. Allard, J. Baldwin and J. Thomas)

Problem-Solving Through Self-Help Groups (with G. Lindenfield)

Protests by Pupils: Empowerment, Schooling and the State

Prison Riots in Britain and the USA

Social Work and Empowerment

The Abuses of Punishment

The Personal Social Services: Clients, Consumers or Citizens?

Quality Social Work

Robert Adams

Consultant editor: Jo Campling

MACMILLAN

First published 1998 by
MACMILLAN PRESS LTD
Houndmills, Basingstoke, Hampshire RG21 6XS
and London
Companies and representatives
throughout the world

ISBN 0–333–63693–7

A catalogue record for this book is available
from the British Library.

10   9   8   7   6   5   4   3   2   1
07 06 05 04 03 02 01 00 99 98

Copy-edited and typeset by Povey–Edmondson
Tavistock and Rochdale, England

Printed in Malaysia

For James George Adams, my father, who needed quality services in his last illness

Contents

CHAPTER NINE

List of Tables

Acknowledgements

I am grateful to Ann James, Keith Pringle and Alan Tuckman for making critical comments on earlier drafts of Chapters 1 and 2 and for various discussions with many practitioners over the years. Mal Blackburn has supplied material for Chapter 7. Additionally, I appreciate conversations with Sylvia Grimes, Malcolm Jordan, Terence O'Sullivan and students and various colleagues at Humberside university and Anglia polytechnic university. Giles Darvill, Mike Lauerman, John Paley, Euan Henderson and Bob Sang, though they are probably unaware of it, have provided me with insights into the Health and Social Services Management programme. I want also to thank many colleagues in the Standing Conference of Heads of Social Work Courses (SCHOC) and the Social Work Education Committee (SWEC) of the Joint Universities Council (JUC), in whose meetings and other activities I have participated over the years, and which have informed in particular the discussion in Chapter 4. Hugh MacPherson, Principal of the Northern College of Acupuncture, has enabled me to develop a view of the 'new quality' in social work. Kwame Ocloo of the Institute of Employment Rights, Lucy Vickers of Oxford Brookes University and Nicholas Rose of Public Concern at Work (Lincoln's Inn House, 42 Kingsway, London WC2B 6EN) have provided much useful information about whistleblowing, public audit and the law. As ever, I appreciate the help of Jo Campling, and the patience of Catherine Gray.

Finally, I have to acknowledge that in spite of the efforts of all the above people, and the boundless enthusiasm of Pat in debating quality, all deficiencies in the quality of this book remain my responsibility alone.

ROBERT ADAMS

Introduction

This book argues that the current shortcomings of social work need addressing by adopting an approach based on quality maximisation. All too often, quality assurance is based on the adoption of basic or minimum standards. Quality maximisation necessitates an authentic process of empowering service users, their carers, practitioners and managers. Initiatives concerning quality assurance, if they are framed only as a response to particular government initiatives, or specific scandals or inquiries, may compound rather than resolve problems of social work practice, and the multiple, conflicting and even contradictory nature of expectations upon workers in the personal social services. The analysis of contributory factors to quality in social work should not simply be error-driven. Thus, this book is not intended as a comprehensive discussion of all the inquiries which have taken place into the shortcomings of social work. It draws on those inquiries which contribute to the examination of quality. There is a need to appreciate, but look beyond, perceived shortcomings and responses to these in particular aspects of practice, in order to develop a quality social work. In brief, that is the intention of this book.

I suggested in *Social Work and Empowerment* (Adams, 1996b) that the paradigm shift to empowerment-in-practice would require a reconceptualisation of a great part of the social work literature. This current book has resulted from applying this notion to contemporary approaches to assuring quality in social work. In order to address and transcend the problems and issues associated with quality in social work, an already empowered practice needs to face the challenge of 'the new quality' in social work.

Much of the literature on quality assurance, like the plethora of guidelines, packages and procedures of the 'how to do it' school, shares two features. First, much is product-driven, in the sense that the authors take for granted the process and are also convergent in their atheoretical focus on whatever goal they presume to set for themselves, or claim is set for them. Second, many authors do not seem to regard quality in itself as problematic.

In contrast, this book starts from the reality of the contemporary crisis in the human services, reflected in uncertainties, insecurities, resource-starvation, anxieties and even fears about the future – contributing to concerns about workers, service users and carers – in which health and personal social services are purchased and delivered in the 1990s. The term 'crisis' refers to the widely perceived view that the human services are not meeting people's needs: that the welfare state has created needs which cannot be met; that the state cannot bear the costs of providing sufficient services to meet these needs (Oliver, 1990, pp. 95–6); that workers are experiencing deskilling, low morale, stress and burn-out; that service users are feeling unempowered, that educators are feeling marginalised and researchers are excluded from funding to carry out critical research. Additionally, particularly in consequence of the above points, there is a crisis in social work, in how it is located in policy terms, understood – not least, by some key political figures in the last Conservative government – and in how it is organised, managed, resourced and delivered.

The high profile of debates and prescriptions concerning quality in social work attests to features of social work itself. The claim of social workers to professional status could be viewed as seriously compromised by the constraints and uncertainties of their working environment and the lack of substantive progress towards empowering service users. If that is where social workers practise, then the preoccupations of their managers are altogether different. Viewed from outside the profession of social work, its short-comings may be viewed as largely due to the failings of social workers themselves. Thus, quality assurance is purveyed as a management device for rectifying the failings of social work. Unsurprisingly, given this widespread view, the bulk of the literature on quality assurance is atheoretical and concerned with the techniques of its application.

In contrast, this book argues that quality is a concept appropriated by politicians and managers, in part to further the managerialist agenda of curbing professional expertise. So, this book uses studies of quality in particular areas of social work as the stimulus for a discussion of the components of an approach to quality maximisation in social work. The data have been accumulated gradually, for almost as long as the score of years during which I have puzzled about this subject.

Though this book is about quality, it inevitably considers the failings of social work. It addresses the question: despite major reforms in the law, and in the procedures governing practice, how have social workers and their colleagues in the health and personal social services allowed the very people whom their authorities and agencies exist to serve, to be deprived of care, put at risk of harm or even abused?

The last two decades of the twentieth century have witnessed an unprecedented wave of scandals and inquiries into the shortcomings of social work. Ironically, the same period is unique for the effort which governments, through the Audit Commission and Social Services Inspectorate, and professional bodies such as the Central Council for Education and Training in Social Work (CCETSW) have devoted to setting up and implementing measures to assure the quality of social work in particular and the personal social services in general.

The quest for quality in social work is prone to being addressed as part of a technically, and even technologically, driven agenda concerning the imperatives of change in organisations where social work is practised. But quality assurance is no more about techniques than social work is solely concerned with skills. The drive for quality needs to be understood in the wider context of changes occurring in the public services – at the level of social policy and the state, as well as in the local authorities.

It also needs locating in the context of concepts and theories informing successive reorganisations of local authority personal social services, notably the changes brought about following the Seebohm Report (1968) in the early 1970s and those involving the creation of quasi-markets in the human services from the end of the 1980s onwards.

Structure and contents of the book

The book is laid out so that examples and case studies are interwoven through the chapters. Chapter 1 introduces problematic features of the concept of quality assurance. The range of different approaches to quality assurance deployed in the personal social services are examined in Chapter 2. Chapter 3 discusses the deployment of managerialism and ways of challenging it. Chapter

4 deals with factors affecting changes in social work education and ways of furthering the struggle for quality.

The next part of the book (Chapters 5 to 8) integrates discussion of three key components of quality assurance – standard setting; auditing; and monitoring and evaluation – with the examination of criminal justice, mental health, child care and community care.

Finally, Chapter 9 brings together the implications of the foregoing material and sets out what would be involved in adopting strategies based on a quality maximisation approach.

The book applies the term 'social worker' with varying degrees of precision at different points; sometimes, it applies only to workers holding a social work qualification; at other times, it applies to all those working with people in particular settings in the personal social services.

1

Quality Assurance in Social Work

Concern about delivering quality in social work has moved from a marginal to a central position during the final quarter of the twentieth century. The widespread adoption of methods of quality assurance in social work since the 1980s has taken place in the context of major changes in policies, structures, organisational and managerial arrangements for delivering personal social services. This chapter examines those ideas about quality which accompany these trends and maps some of the main contributors to the processes by which quality has assumed prominence on the social work agenda.

Quality assurance: problematic concepts and practices

EXAMPLE 1.1

Shona is social work manager in a voluntary agency with block contracts for children's services with three neighbouring local authority social services departments. She would like to introduce quality assurance, ideally in the form of an 'off the peg' set of purchased procedures which she can speedily fit over existing practices.

EXAMPLE 1.2

Jacob is a social worker who has received a telephoned complaint from a carer for an older person, that the urgent assessment he requested three weeks ago in order to get her into a residential home, still has not been carried out.

Neeti is a care assistant who has been asked by a young person leaving care to listen to her account of abuse by a former care assistant, but not to take official action.

Beyond error-driven and procedurally-based approaches

The first example suggests a manager whose view of the short-comings of practice is that the template for quality assurance can be obtained from elsewhere and superimposed as a 'quick fix' onto the work situation. The second example raises many issues and questions, among which the following are crucial: What should the worker do, immediately and subsequently? Clearly, there is a priority in the second situation to act on a complaint, in accord with the employer's complaints procedure. But the second situation raises the person's right to services. How adequate are these services? What shortcomings in them can be identified? How should these failings be addressed, by agencies, by individual practitioners, service users, carers and others? What policies and procedures need to be put in place to prevent such failures reccurring? What are the implications for quality of such incidents, and the responses to them? The third example raises questions and dilemmas about how staff should set limits to confidentiality when working with people. In response to all three examples, it is necessary to state that organisations delivering personal social services will have recognised, and probably published, procedures for dealing with complaints about quality and accusations about the conduct of staff, and that professional staff will have received training in responding to disclosures about abuse. Each example would repay discussion between staff, service users and carers about how the questions specified above, and many others which may be identified, should be addressed.

But the purpose of this book is to reach beyond the grasp of immediate 'solutions'. It develops the argument that quality social work is best developed on sound principles of quality maximisation, rather than from the pressure to remedy specific mistakes. Excellence in social work is unlikely to proceed from a framework for quality assurance which is error-driven. Unfortunately, on the one hand, many local authority staff and professional social work providers regard quality assurance as rather a foreign body – more relevant to the commercial sector, or at any rate the private provider of personal social services than to the statutory authority. On the other hand, there are immense political and public pressures for immediate 'solutions' to symptoms of defects in the quality of practice (Golding and Middleton, 1982). These are evident in a series of critical inquiry reports dating from the mid-1970s when social work took on a generic character and became higher profile (Colwell, 1974; Meurs, 1975; Howlett, 1976). They are also evident in the massive growth in coverage of social work scandals in the mass media (Franklin and Parton, 1991; Social Worker 2 in the Lucie Gates case, 1983; Phillips, 1979; Young, 1979; Andrews, 1974; Mawby, Fisher and Hale, 1979; Mawby, Fisher and Park, 1979; Walker, 1976; Roberts, 1980; Hill, 1980; Aldridge, 1994).

Increasingly, from the late 1980s, the personal social services has taken on the mantle of quality assurance processes and procedures (Cassam and Gupta, 1992). But, the wider context of change in the personal social services has had a great impact on quality assurance in social work. Social policy since the early 1970s has led to major changes in the organisation and scope of local government. These have accompanied the growing preoccupation of managers and practitioners in the personal social services with various aspects of quality. Quality assurance is a key plank in the responses of central and local government to the accelerating changes and uncertainties which pervade the personal social services in the 1990s and seem likely to, in the forseeable future. The concept of quality has come into its own in the 1990s, its significance has been enhanced by the prominence of quality assurance mechanisms, procedures and structures in the personal social services. At times, concerns about quality have been heightened by complaints about shortcomings in practice; on other occasions, mechanisms such as inspection and complaints procedures, whilst relevant to quality assurance are no substitute for it, and have been instituted by legislation such as the NHS and Community Care Act 1990; the government and the staff who manage the personal social services have also taken measures to implement quality assurance. These measures may be regarded as means by which politicians and employers rein in such autonomy as social workers possess, controlling them and curbing their professional power. The rationale for that strategy has been partly the belief that quality assurance is a technical activity based on a value-neutral concept of quality which works simultaneously on behalf of the interests of all stakeholders in the personal social services.

Concepts and approaches associated with quality assurance have been developed over half a century to a high level of sophistication in commerce and industry (Ernst and Young, 1993; Omachonu and Ross, 1994). Their transfer to the human services may be advocated as though this is unproblematic, as Clifford and colleagues imply (Clifford, Leiper, Lavender and Pilling, 1989, p. 14), rather than their significance and functions being viewed critically. The assuring of quality, dealt with in publications such as Freeman (1993) and Sale (1990), may be presented as a technical set of procedures, or in the form of a package (Casson and George, 1995; Kerruish and Smith, 1993) whose application will achieve quality services that can be transferred easily from the commercial sector and applied with minimal adaptation to the public services. The literature on quality assurance is overwhelmingly oriented to the commercial rather than the care sector; it is replete with methods and approaches, whose take-up may not in itself improve quality.

Quality assurance procedures may provide a measure of reassurance to managers and practitioners alike, that some aspects of their constrained and uncertain work, at least, can be controlled and made predictable. Their presence implies that providers can guarantee the standards of services, even though the human, financial and physical resources may not be available to extend their quantity and scope and maximise their quality. There is accumulating evidence from practice that procedures and quality standards *of themselves* do not bring about quality. The experience of staff introducing quality assurance in the London Borough of Newham, for example, indicates that the development of written policies and procedures was no guarantee that quality would improve and practice become more consistent (Manning, 1996, p. 6).

The context in which the judgement is made about whether a particular service is high quality or not, shapes the judgement itself. The quality of practice is affected not only by the interaction between the people involved, but also by historical and social factors, and by structures which maintain social differences and inequalities.

Quality assurance cannot be depoliticised, deproblematised and made uncontroversial. The fact that the realities of quality assurance in the personal social services are complex and challenging is shown in the collection of essays edited by Kelly and Warr (1992). In reality, the term 'quality' has many meanings and applications; it may refer to a standard, a process, or a stage in a process. Quality is problematic also in the sense that the word may signify different things in different circumstances – and sometimes in similar circumstances! – depending on who uses it and for what purposes. Within social work, the increasing use of quality assurance mechanisms may be viewed superficially as a grasping after greater effectiveness. But the many stakeholders in quality include politicians and managers as well as professionals and service users. Thus, responses to issues concerning quality social work may direct attention to debates over standards in social work, as well as the interplay between the agendas of different groups in central and local government. In contrast, a service user may *experience* changes in the name of quality as simply reduced, rather than better, services. This is not surprising since, as Chapter 3 shows, dominant approaches to quality assurance tend to serve the interests of managers rather than those of service users and carers.

Quality: panacea or problematic?

Imposed quality control rather than quality maximisation (see Chapter 2), offers management a ready-made aerosol which can be applied wholesale to the organisation in a top-down fashion, so as in the short term to hide fissures and irregularities; it creates the appearance of homogeneity and adherence to given standards of performance and fends off attacks by critics such as the mass media or dissatisfied or unsatisfied service users.

Debates about the quality of services take place over assumptions about the goodness or desirability of particular models of provision, and approaches to organising, managing and delivering services, based on different value positions. For example, the concept of quality as a technical 'solution' springs from rationality, and the appeal rooted in the wider faith in the certainty of technical knowledge (Oakeshott, 1962). In the 1990s, terms associated with quality have assumed an iconic significance, notably in areas such as community care, where new legislation has affected practice. A variety of practices deployed under such banners as quality control, quality assurance and so on, seek to address the complex and deep-seated problems of the personal social services, allegedly addressing people's needs in settings where resources are ever more scarce and where the means to satisfy people's demands depend increasingly on rationing services rather than supplying them as of right.

Assuring quality: a moral and political activity

Quality assurance in social work is not just a technical but a political and moral enterprise. Staff involved in quality assurance necessarily encounter moral and ethical choices of a similar order to those faced by other social work practitioners. Quality assurance is linked in a complementary relationship with the conceptualisation of the market economy espoused by the government, exemplified in the quasi-markets of community care services.

The separate commissioning, purchasing and provision of quality products is integral to the very creation and sustaining of quality, according to the market approach to competing for quality. It involves negotiating, or competing, sometimes with erstwhile colleagues, to secure contracts in the marketplace. It has assumed a prominent position on the agenda of the purchasers and providers of social work services, at a time when their quality content has been subject to widespread criticism; the fact that this has happened partly through a number of scandals and inquiries, is a conundrum, whose explanation lies in the discrepancies between the relatively great power exercised by politicians, managers and professionals, in contrast with service users.

EXAMPLE 1.4

Thus, for example, approaches to assuring quality in child protection have been responses to crisis and management-led, rather than emanating from, and having as their core, the participation of service users. A number of factors since the mid-1970s have raised the profile of child abuse as a problem, and at the same time led to child protection being dealt with on a firefighting basis, rather than prioritising the best long-term interests of those involved, and the child in particular (Thorpe, 1994). It follows, therefore, that a critical appreciation of quality assurance needs to stand outside not only its technicalised, proceduralised forms in a commodified social work, but also its function as the strong arm of managerialist local, if not central, government control over the workforce. Parton notes that since the late nineteenth century, social work came to occupy a somewhat ambiguous and newly defined space, with allegiances both to civil society – individuals and families – and to the state – particularly through the court and statutory responsibilities (Parton, 1991, pp. 13–14). But a more complex map of contributing factors includes more than simply those emanating from the state and the clients or service users. Considerable power is exercised by experts and by managers and part of the reality, and the responsibilities, of social workers reflects their location as employees in commissioning, purchasing and providing agencies – which before the 1990s could have been referred to in more simplified terms as the local state (Corrigan and Leonard, 1978; Cockburn, 1978). To the lack of homogeneity within each of these areas – leading to a plurality of voices rather than consensus, on occasions – can be added the activities of the media, organisations in the independent sector and pressure groups, including the activities of service users, such as the parents of children of whom abuse has been alleged. These different contributors to concerns about quality are located in the broader context of the preoccupations with quality of politicians and policymakers which have emerged since the 1970s, in the human services generally and in social work in particular.

Quality assurance in the human services

As the human services – this term includes education, health, housing, penal, social work and social services – have changed, so the requirements for managing them have become more suited to the dominant economic, political and professional ideology of managerialism in the marketplace of the provision of services. The preoccupation with quality of organisations in the commercial and public sectors in the UK is a feature of the period since the 1970s. This is not to debunk assertions that quality was an issue in Britain as long ago as the Middle Ages (Drummond, 1993, p. 1). But what is understood by quality has changed so much in the score of years since the mid-1970s, let alone over a longer period, as to render general references to conceptualisations of quality before the mid twentieth century as only of historical relevance. Claims by companies in the commercial sector that they are committed to providing quality goods and services, as well as by agencies in the human services, not surprisingly attract general approval from employers, employees, consumers, service users and the public. The spread of movements towards quality assurance in the personal social services has been hastened by the split between purchasers and providers and the requirement to issue service specifications when contracts are issued.

The move towards quality assurance has been somewhat uneven in the personal social services, partly because of differences between authorities. Some social services and social work departments in unitary authorities have central units and sections devoted to quality whilst others devolve responsibility for quality to individual providers. Partly also, the take-up of quality in different service sectors varies greatly. The publication of standards for residential care for older people and the development of quality assurance in this sector has been associated with legislative requirements for the registration of homes (Registered Homes Act 1984; Registration of Homes (Amendment) Act 1991). The lack of any such requirement for domiciliary care means that home care tends not to be the subject of quality assessment, though in at least one unitary authority known to the author, the independent inspection unit in Social Services has been contracted by the Quality Unit to carry out an inspection of home care services, as an early stage in the process of introducing quality assurance to this area.

Quality assurance in general may be associated with a number of different goals, such as the attempt to increase output, improve effectiveness, remedy general weaknesses or respond to specific criticisms or shortcomings. In other words, quality assurance procedures may be viewed as opportunities to enhance the performance of an organisation, or the means by which to tackle problems, whether these are located within or outside it.

Whilst these attempts to grapple with quality assurance as an objective are unexceptionable, it is doubtful whether quality as one aspect, no matter how central to the performance of an organisation, is capable even of addressing the range and variety of problems identified above, let alone solving them. After all, the existence of diverse rationales for adopting the delivery of quality services as a goal, renders problematic the nature of that goal and the methods used to address it. This confirms the need for critical scrutiny, not only of the fact that quality assurance may be a means of assessing performance, but that it appraises the *status quo* rather than fundamentally reshaping it.

The starting point for a more realistic assessment of the contribution quality assurance mechanisms may make to the performance of an organisation or agency in delivering a service, is to clarify what is meant by the concepts of quality and quality assurance. Further, the interests of the different stakeholders of the process of the work of the human services differ. Hence, the meanings and expectations attached to the term 'quality assurance' by, say, managers, practitioners and service users in a human services organisation are likely to vary widely.

Quality in social work: distinctive features

The preoccupation with quality in social work is distinctive in six major ways. First, the personal social services differ significantly from the commercial sector. The product of industry – in traditional manufacturing more concerned with output of things rather than service-based – has been displaced during this process by an emphasis on person-based service. But the shift in values implied in this change requires a complex readjustment rather than a simple, smooth transition. It affects managers, workers, service users and carers. The personal social services have become commercial purchasers of services provided by a growing number of independent – voluntary and private – providers. More service users – older people, parents, people with impairments, children – take a fuller part in the discussions about their own assessments and service planning than ever before. There are more professional links between social workers and other professionals than ever before. Multi-disciplinary, multi-professional working is part and parcel of child care and community care practice. The education and training of social workers is becoming more flexible and overlapping with ongoing employment. Employment based paid and volunteer workers have greater opportunities than a generation ago of training in the workplace. There are prospects of joint qualifying and postqualifying programmes with other professionals, notably in healthcare.

Second, the value bases of staff in the personal social services – as specified in CCETSW Paper 30 (1996) and Unit 0 of the Standards for Caring (Care Sector Consortium, 1992) – assert that people are intrinsically valued, and are not regarded merely as units of supply or demand, production and consumption; outcomes are sought with people, not simply as outputs or products; relationships, in what is done, feelings and experiences are valued at least as highly as 'facts'. Hence there is ideological conflict, when commercial values collide with or invade the personal social services. Third, the personal social services are distinctive within the human services in that they cater for the problems experienced by some people, rather than education and health services, which serve all the population.

Fourth, the value base of the personal social services involves a recognition that the individual service user may be part of a group, family, network, neighbourhood or community, which experiences inequalities and/or oppression, such as that associated with gender, ethnicity, age, social class, disability, sexuality or religion. Legislation may exist with the aim of redressing such inequalities, for example, in the area of disability and equal opportunities (Disability Discrimination Act 1995, Fair Employment [Northern Ireland] Act 1989 or Race Relations Act 1976). The goal of the personal social services is the betterment of the service user through meeting his or her needs, whereas that of the commercial organisation is to make a profit, through satisfying the customer. The personal social services deal with people who are individuals, who may also be part of stigmatised groups. So, social workers fulfil a difficult role, simultaneously acting on behalf of the state and the individual, and also meeting personal needs in the context of the categories by which the person is defined, including the groups, families, networks, neighbourhoods and communities to which they relate or belong. Fifth, the creation of quasi-markets in the personal social services in the 1990s has, in effect, played a major part in commodifying previously decommodified relations – a point implicit in the critique of the move towards a competence-based Diploma in Social Work (see Timms, 1991, and discussion in Chapter 4). Rather than simply accepting these changes at face value, it is important to understand them and to interpret them in relation to these wider changes occurring in the human services. Sixth, widespread concern about serious shortcomings in the quality of social work services has been triggered by specific incidents in the postwar period, and from the late 1980s these have been generalised from particular failures to questions about the credibility of social work in general. The next section of this chapter examines some of these concerns.

The welfare state in the 1990s comprises, as it did in the 1940s, an amalgam of public, voluntary, private and informal arrangements for securing the welfare of people. What have changed dramatically in the creation of market-based service provision are the local government structures and processes for achieving this and the balance of responsibility between local authorities as managers and other agencies and groups as providers of services. Again, whilst social work as a profession has been repositioned by these changes, this does not mean that they have been universally embraced. Consequently, not only does the contract culture of the marketplace for delivering services in the 1990s contain a great many more heterogenous and fragmented providers than formerly; it also presents a fissured, rather than a smooth surface.

Practice is not just diverse, but is riven with debate and contradiction. It is marked by contested concepts and issues, rather than consensus. Two examples which are characteristic of the field are, firstly, the problems associated with, rather than what critics argue are largely resource-led services. Community care in the 1990s is a notable example. The NHS and Community Care Act 1990 represents an unprecedented off-loading by the State of responsibility for health and social care provision, to newly-created self-managed units for residential, day and domiciliary care. Thus, the quasi-market created by the Act retains State control of key areas such as resources, whilst it 'places SSDs in the crucial role of planning to meet need and to ration demand by need assessment. The market is not allowed to allocate resources, providers will compete, but users will not. Whether a user gets a service will be determined by regulated need assessment by a case-manager' (Kelly, 1991, p. 185) The rhetoric of care planning suggests that services are needs-led. But the reality is that 'the case-manager's budget will be determined by a more global analysis of likely demands based on both demographic and service usage data' (Kelly, 1991, p. 185), and, of course, the total supply of resources is capped by the government, so the role of first line managers and practitioners tends to be to prioritise needs and devise strategies for integrating assessment and care planning with the rationing process.

Secondly, inherent tensions are created by the paradigm shift in social work since the 1970s from treatment to empowerment, overlaid by the consumerism which gathered momentum in the policies of the 1979–97 Conservative government from the late 1980s. This latter situation is complicated by the ways in which different stakeholders in the personal social services have taken up the empowerment paradigm, and have attempted to use it to fulfil their own interests (Adams, 1996a, pp. 22–3). Thus, its ascendancy has become more absolute in social work education than in some provider agencies. In the field of community care, a version of user empowerment has been set out in official guidance on the implementation of the NHS and Community Care Act 1990, which may be interpreted in a radical way to signify a commitment to user participation, but also which can be reconciled with the consumerist assumptions of the quasi-market philosophy on which the Act is based. At the same time, a user-led discourse of empowerment exists, which is critical of those very assumptions. The fact that these positions are in conflict, and have not been reconciled in official discourse about practice, is one contributory factor in the confused and uncertain circumstances in which first line managers and practitioners work.

A further complication is the deployment of a bewildering variety of terms in approaches to assuring quality. The next part of this chapter examines the main definitions of quality likely to be encountered in the personal social services.

Defining quality

The use of the word 'quality' in the professional context should be distinguished from its everyday usage. The *Oxford English Dictionary* definition of quality refers to the twin notions of comparison with other things of the same kind and the degree or grade of excellence of something; in the literature on quality assurance in the personal social services, the term 'quality' may have a meaning restricted to the physical, measurable, aspects of 'fitness for purpose' of the particular product or service being evaluated. Quality can also refer to the ability of a product or service to meet the needs of the customer at an affordable price. An International Standard (British Standard BS EN ISO 8402: 1995, p. 3) defines quality as 'the totality of characteristics of an entity that bear on its ability to satisfy stated and implied needs'. However, this Standard recognises that quality may be used to refer on the one hand to conformity to requirements and on the other hand to a degree of excellence (British Standard BS EN ISO 8402: 1995, p. 3). The British Standard (British Standard BS 4778: Part 2: 1991a, 4.1.1, p. 5) gives an identical definition of quality, but distinguishes three main usages of the term mentioned above: to compare degrees of excellence between products, to assess the quantitative level of quality and to assess the 'fitness-for-purpose' of a product or service (British Standard BS 4778: Part 2: 1991, 4.1, p. 5).

The significance of the term 'quality' changes with its user and the context in which it is used. Thus, the injection of the term 'quality' into community care in the 1990s, for example, coincides with the requirement that the internal market is sustained by, and sustains, the mixed economy of public, voluntary and private providers. It contributes to making the system – the commissioning, contracts, the purchase and provision of services, the monitoring and the evaluation of services delivered – function effectively. There is a problem in determining whether quality refers only to those circumstances where the products or services are delivered at a price the customer can afford. How do we judge what is an acceptable standard or price? The concept of quality has been identified above as playing a key role in the significant changes in the personal social services brought about since the 1970s. It would be a mistake to view these changes as revolutionary, in the sense that they do not overturn and completely replace what went before.

James (1992) defines quality in social services as 'the totality of features and characteristics of a product or service that bear on its ability to satisfy a given need' and argues that the Social Services Inspectorate (SSI) definition of quality assurance 'needs to be broadened beyond a description of service delivery processes to include the centrality of users' views on defining quality'. The British Quality Association's Social Care Agencies Sector Committe has published guidelines for social care agencies on how to interpret BS5750, which is the British quality standard for services and products (British Standards Institute (BSI), 1987, a–f).

According to the Department of Health (DH, 1992a, p. 26), quality assurance approaches is a catch-all term, including quality control, quality assurance systems and generic quality or total quality. Quality assurance concerns 'all activities and functions concerned with the attainment of quality'. The Social Services

Inspectorate published a 'purchase of service' practice guide for England and Wales (SSI, 1991a). This states that 'quality assurance is used to refer to those processes which aim to ensure that concern for quality is designed and built into services. It implies commitment on the part of local authority social services committee members and senior managers to a systematic approach to the pursuit of quality and will be demonstrated by an explicit statement of policy, setting out agency expectations and standards' (p. 30).

The Scottish Office Social Work Services Group published a discussion paper (Scottish Office, 1991), which contrasts with Leckie's view that high quality activity may grow upwards (Leckie, 1994, p. 135). It prescribed a top-down approach defined by management, in which 'quality assurance needs to be developed from senior management, with freedom to develop and experiment at unit level. Quality assurance systems include quantitative techniques such as check lists, schedules, procedures, but they also focus on qualitative aspects such as relationships between staff and management, between staff and users, team building, and so on. There are already being developed systems which can be used by social work departments either on a department-wide basis or for aspects of service delivery' (Scottish Office, 1991). Leckie (1994, p. 131) identifies three examples which he suggests are successful, of the application of the British Standards Institution 1986 standards BS5750 to social care agencies in Britain, whole social services departments in Norfolk and Gloucester and a single residential establishment in Napier House, Newcastle, a residential home for older people. He notes doubts about whether BS5750 can be applied to social work, 'because its requirement for a quality policy and clearly defined procedures throughout all the processes of an organisation has major resource implications, and may in any case not lead to improvements in outcome in services for users' (Leckie, 1994, p. 131). These features – increased reliance on standards such as BS5750, the involvement of users and the joint development of standards between health and social care/social work agencies – offer ways forward. However, the shift from a managerially-imposed approach to quality to a genuinely total quality – maximisation – approach (see Chapter 2 for discussion of this distinction) remains more problematic in the light of the current resource priorities rather than quality assurance, emphasised by a government commitment to market approaches.

The Social Services Inspectorate defines quality control as an approach which 'refers to those processes of verification, and will include systematic monitoring, including statistical and other management information, recurring and one-off audits and inspection activity designed to establish whether standards are being achieved. Quality control is one aspect of quality assurance. It should provide objective feedback to line managers who have continuing responsibility for quality, about what is actually being achieved' (quoted in Leckie, 1994, p. 127).

It is difficult to envisage a single definition of quality in social work which would achieve recognition by all stakeholders – managers, practitioners, service users, educators, researchers and others. Nevertheless, it seems reasonable that discussion of how to achieve quality social work should be based on such a definition. As becomes clearer in the next chapter, this book is based on the principle of maximising quality in social work, rather than adopting a basic standard, enshrined in a 'minimalist' statement of what consistutes 'good enough' social work. So, the following working definition is proposed: *Excellent social work is social work which guarantees people access to high quality services which ensure their needs are met.* This presumes that excellent social workers demonstrate a range of expertises, the 'official' list of which has been published by the Central Council for Education and Training in Social Work (CCETSW) in Paper 30 (CCETSW, 1996), which despite its breadth, provides a minimal statement of standards of the kind referred to above.

Managerialism and the quality agenda in the human services

The Conservative government moved in the 1980s towards the use of quality as a tool of management control over a social work/ social services workforce which had grown rapidly in size and, in social work, vociferousness about the shortcomings of social policy in an unequal society. Quality maintenance was also employed as a key means of controlling the quasi-markets being set up in the health and social services, by the early 1990s (James, 1992, pp. 41–2). Prominent among the bearers of the 'new' mission of quality from the 1980s were the Audit Commission and the Social Services Inspectorate. Yet the origins of managerialism lay much earlier, in theories and practices associated with scientific management, articulated by Frederick Taylor, early in the twentieth century (see Chapter 3). The concern with quality was appropriately ambiguous. It appealed to the Right, since it fulfilled the contradictory requirements of New Right quasi-classical economic and social policy theory and practice and managerialism and the centralisation of control. It also coincided superficially – but conveniently for politicians, managers and activists alike – with the more radical advocacy of service user participation, growing professionalism and the importation into the health and social services of progressive ideas about management development; some of these were from the commercial sector but some of them grew out of research and consultancy within the sector.

By the early 1990s, the NHS and Community Care Act 1990 had legitimated the notion of quality assured health and social care services. Section 46 of this Act required each local authority to prepare a community care plan, specifying how the needs of the local population would be assessed and met. The separation of purchaser, commissioner and provider roles was seen partly as a means by which to 'improve the quality of services through explicitness about standards' and 'improve monitoring and review in terms of quality of services and outcomes for clients' (Department of Health, 1991a, para 10, p. 7).

The last two sections of this chapter bring together the problematic features of social work and the concept of quality, and also identify the main contributors to concerns about quality in social work.

Some problems of quality in social work

The issue of quality has become an important contributor to controversies surrounding social work since the 1980s, such as whether social work is necessary, marginal, or simply irrelevant in the enterprise culture of the post-welfare state. It is unfortunate, perhaps, that the scandals around social work have exacerbated its proneness to criticisms. Additionally, the fact that the subject matter of social work is intrinsically problematic and its prevalent values of openness and self-critical scrutiny leading to the profession baring its soul in public, have exacerbated its proneness to criticisms. Also, these factors have intensified the struggle between advocates and critics of social work as a profession whose subject matter is intrinsically problematic. This is partly because of the diverse ways in which approaches to quality may be applied to social workers' activities.

For other reasons as well, social work is an embattled profession. It scrabbles for a somewhat precarious foothold as a semi-profession in contrast with the 'real' professions of the law and medicine. Its focus on the problematic aspects of people's lives contributes to its contested nature. Since the 1940s, much of the growing criticism of many aspects of the work of the personal social services has been laid, fairly or unfairly, at the doors of social workers. This has been accentuated by an increasing tendency towards criticisms – for example, through formal inquiries, or through the mass media, or both – of aspects of the work of the personal social services. There is also a tendency for social work to be subjected to ideologically based criticisms. The oil crisis in the Middle East in the winter of 1973–4 did nothing to allay fears among politicians of both the right and the left that increased public spending on education, health and social services could not be afforded indefinitely. Direct attacks on the personal social services in general and social work in particular from the political supporters of Thatcherism were a feature of the decade from 1979. These were based on economic and ideological grounds. Economic criticisms were grounded in the wider scepticism about the ever-growing cost of welfare in general in the welfare state and widespread 'scroungerphobia' (Golding and Middleton, 1982). The 1990s saw an emphasis on political activities transcending party politics, involving embedding the market philosophy and contract culture throughout the management and delivery of local health and social care services. The arrangements for the organisation and management of social work came under scrutiny as well as social work itself. Ideological attacks on the social services, implicating social work, came from some conservative politicians (Clarke, 1993, pp. 72–4).

Criticisms of social work fall into six categories: First , there is a view that there are practical shortcomings in skills linked with criticisms of training. Second, there is the simplistic argument that social work has over-reached itself. Brewer and Lait (1980) have written as though the failings of social work are manifest, since its claims to a distinctive, autonomous professional identity are spurious. This is simplistic and erroneous, since the very centrality, and contested subject matter, of social work in society in part accounts for the vitriolic criticisms it attracts. A spirited debate about whether British social work has a future was conducted in the British Association of Social Workers' (BASW) journal *Professional Social Work* (*PSW*, February 1994; *PSW*, May 1994). One correspondent resurrected the argument that the identity of social work as a profession would be strengthened by a practice involving contracted services independent of the local authority (letter from Maurice Phillips, *PSW*, May 1994, p. 7). One would expect there to be an inverse correlation between the status of a profession and the extent to which quality assurance procedures are imposed on it from outside. Thus, in theory it is more likely that social workers will experience this, rather than medical consultants. In practice, however, the introduction of charters for service users in pursuance of the Conservative government's Citizen's Charter (Prime Minister's Office, 1991) produced measures to monitor standards which cut across these relationships, based on four components of public services: quality, choice, standards enforced against a stated code of practice and value for money.

Third, criticism from key politicians in the last Conservative government and from employers focused on what is regarded as an excessive emphasis in qualifying social work courses on aspects such as sociology and social policy and anti-oppressive practice, at the expense of basic skills. Critics of social work in the 1980s and 1990s, not exclusively right-wing or government-based, have attacked the commitment of practitioners to anti-oppressive practice and to adopting the 'ologies' as providing theoretical bases for critiques of divisions and inequalities in existing society.

Fourth, there is the denigrating view that social work training should be competence-based, alongside, and not above, vocational skills. According to this view, social work should be located at N/SVQ levels 3 and 4, rather than being accessed through a diploma-based, or even degree-based higher education qualifying programme. Sixth, there is the stereotypical argument taken for granted in much mass media coverage of scandals, investigations and inquiries, that social workers are misguided at best and incompetent at worst. This view is based on a patronising image of social workers as, somehow, a distinctive, inadequate group of people, drawn to the activity because of personal weaknesses or beliefs and equivalent to incompetent people.

Such criticisms illustrate the ambiguous location of social work as a profession, rather than confirming its weaknesses. In particular, they highlight the vulnerability of the social dimension of the personal social services.

Personalism/individualism: the vulnerability of 'the social'

Chapters 6 to 9 in particular refer to aspects of the vulnerability of *the social* in the way scandals and mass media treatment of inquiries focus attention on individuals and particular situations – whether blaming a social worker, highlighting the plight of a victim, or drawing attention to the shortcomings of a single set of local circumstances. One consequence of the marketisation of the greater part of the personal social services has been to intensify those features of social policy which individualise both the identification of the problem and the response by the state and professionals who act as its agents. *The social* is a term which is difficult to encapsulate in a word or simple phrase. It is part of the public domain, in contrast with that which is private, held to the individual. 'Any description of the social must begin by observing that it involves the relaxation of the general prohibitions which govern social relations. 'Normal' everyday life represses deep emotions. Work and community life provide few opportunities for people to communicate their deepest fears and anxieties directly to strangers. The social recognises this. It encourages the exchange of repression for openness and tolerance (Rojek, Peacock and Collins, 1988, p. 147). But *the social* in the personal social services, and in social work, also conveys the notion of collectivity. It embodies the idea that the problems of individuals, taken *en bloc*, may offer significance, and suggest responses, which transcend the problems of the individual (see, for instance, the theoretical analysis and practical examples given by Corrigan and Leonard, 1978).

Thus, in social work the social is the opposite of individualism. The term 'personalism' captures the tendency towards individualisation within social work, since it is little enough used for us to attach to it an ambiguity in meaning of the phrase 'needs-led services', intended to be a feature of community care provision in the 1990s. For the focus on providing personalised services is both advantageous, in that it offers the promise of meeting individual needs, yet potentially dangerous, in that it risks restricting the assessment of needs to a number of individuals, rather than developing an analysis of, and a collective response to, the social dimension of those needs (Adams, 1996a, p. 12).

The cumulative impact on social work of these trends has been to intensify the crisis around quality, by bringing to the foreground questions about the rationale for, and the nature of, practice, and the implications for what should be prescribed as best practice, of the marketisation of the personal social services. Whose interests did, and should, social workers serve: those of their managers, their professional peers, their clients – the service users – the clients' families or carers? Whilst professional values dictate an obvious response to this, for reasons locked into the complexity of the multiple accountabilities of social workers to all the interests listed above, its practice remains problematic.

Proceduralism and legalism

In child care, concerns about quality have led to extended and intensified legalistic and proceduralistic trends in the regulation of social work practice (see Chapter 6). Yet more generally, there is a lack of statutory, that is legislative, force backing up many aspects of the treatment of people for whom the personal social services are provided. For example, there is a lack of guidance on the inspection of home care services and services for people with physical and learning impairments, comparable to that contained in the section on the rights of older people, in the Department of Health report, *Homes are for Living In* (1989b). One way to raise standards is to institute unannounced inspections at sufficient frequency to deter malpractice – say, twice a year – and in any case at similar frequencies across all settings – statutory, voluntary or private – where people receive personal social services.

Contributors to concerns about quality in social work

The spur for concerns about quality in social work to be addressed comes from different directions: the government, management, academic, research, professional, media interests, procedures such as complaints, a disaster such as a scandal over a particular setting, or the user.

Several of these may be influential, particularly in a complex situation, perhaps when an issue is taken up first by one interest and then another. It is not uncommon for the media to raise a concern which then is taken up by professionals and by politicians. Sometimes, professionals voice concern and the media and politicians pick up an issue subsequently. Contemporary concerns are not necessarily those which history records as significant, and in retrospect history may be rewritten, as different stakeholders lay claim to decisive influence over the outcome of a particular initiative. On the whole, managers of the personal social services – and, in effect, this means largely male managers – have not contributed as significantly to quality services as have campaigns by service users and carers themselves.

Thus, different contributions are likely to be made from a variety of perspectives by the main stakeholders to concerns about quality in social work. Hall and colleagues have identified factors which contribute to social policy maintenance and change (Hall, Land, Parker and Webb, 1975), and wider questions associated with factors contributing to, or militating against social policy development and change are relevant to the impact of interests, organisations and groups on social work. From the early 1970s, the quality of generic social work was regulated increasingly by professional bodies such as the Central Council for Education and Training in Social Work (CCETSW) and central government, through social services boards in Northern Ireland, through the Scottish Office in Scotland and through the social work service of the DHSS, and latterly the Social Services Inspectorate, in England and Wales.

In the process of implementing measures to assure quality, tensions between a pragmatic, performance-driven view of what social workers do, and, for example, a value-driven, critically reflective, anti-oppressive practice, become visible and more intense. One reason why concerns about quality are near the heart of this conflict is because quality is a matter of concern to many stakeholders in social work – politicians, civil servants in the Department of Health, members of the Social Services Inspectorate, local authority managers, councillors, practitioners, service users and carers, educators and trainers, researchers, reporters in the mass media – though the nature of this concern may differ considerably from different vantage points. For example, there is a notable distance between the perspective adopted by the paper concerning the review of the performance of staff laid out by two senior officers in the Social Services Inspectorate (Mitchell and Tolan, 1994, pp. 20–30) and maximisation approaches to quality assurance.

In an ideal situation, the maximisation of quality could best be attempted where the participation of all stakeholders in social work practice – commissioners, purchasers, providers, service users, carers and others – is maximised and where the setting nurtures this.

Conclusions

This chapter has argued that it is inadequate for quality assurance to be regarded as a technical set of activities governed by procedures which ensure that everybody with a stake in social work benefits from whatever assurance is undertaken. It is clear from this chapter that there is no guarantee of the neutrality of quality assurance procedures. The next three chapters build on this argument. They show how the spread of managerialism in the personal social services and concomitant changes taking place in the education and training of social workers, should lead to great caution being exercised over any quality assurance activity which is not driven by a quality maximisation approach.

2

Approaches to Quality Assurance in Social Work

The first chapter of this book has shown that the concept of quality cannot be defined in simple, unambiguous terms; its use is complicated by many other problems besetting social work, not least, criticisms of the work social workers do, as well as questions about how well they do it. Also, many ingredients contribute to the raising of concerns about quality, and these operate in different ways for the variety of stakeholders involved in policy and practice.

Approaches to quality assurance are often discussed as though there is a single agreed meaning for the term; but there are many. A lack of clarity about which one is being referred to in a particular setting may be exploited by any stakeholders, but particularly by managers (see Chapter 3), who along with politicians have a major influence on restructuring the public sector in general and the organisation of the personal social services in particular.

This chapter provides a context for the closer examination of how issues concerning quality surface in different aspects of social work. It develops a conceptual framework for the application to social work of the major approaches to quality and discusses the approaches which form the backbone of the discussion of specific areas of practice in Chapters 5 to 8.

Changing approaches to quality

Chapter 1 drew attention to the tendency for the concept of quality assurance to be discussed merely as a technical fix for any actual or potential shortcomings in the organisation and its products or services. The use of quality assurance procedures may be restricted to the application of techniques rather than a theoretically grounded methodology. Alan Clarke (1994, p. 176) illustrates this with reference to the review of quality systems by Ziethaml and colleagues (1990, p. 74). They comment: 'Many companies believe they are committed to service quality but their commitment is to quality from the company's own internal, technical perspective. Service quality in many firms means meeting the company's self-defined productivity or efficiency standards, many of which the customers do not notice or desire.'

Discussion of 'how to achieve' quality assurance often obscures rather than critically highlighting its ideological functions in serving managerialist goals rather than those of the entire workforce, service users and the community. The roots of contemporary approaches to management in the personal social services lie in a mixture of scientific management and human relations perspectives. One way of charting this complex territory is to pose the question as to where the power lies in different approaches to quality assurance, and what the reference points are for these overarching perspectives. In this regard, Everitt (1990) links both scientific management and human relations approaches to management with the primacy of the role of experts, control in both approaches resting with top managers. At the same time, the perspective of participants changes, in the latter approach, for example, requiring of managers an understanding of the motivations and other factors influencing people's behaviour.

If the dominant metaphor of scientific management is the organisation as a machine, and that of the human relations approach is the organisation as a group or, in some cases, a family (Everitt, 1990, p. 143), the dominant image of local government, and within it the post-Seebohm social services department in the corporate era of the 1970s, was the office, the bureaucracy in Weber's classical use of the term (Gerth and Mills, 1946, pp. 196–244). That period of enthusiasm for corporate, almost Gothic in scale, local government responses to problems of managing local services, including the personal social services, can be underplayed. Everitt locates the innovation of teams of workers, post NHS and Community Care Act 1990, in the context of the enterprise which supplanted the earlier scientific and psychoanalytic models of management culture:

> People in organizations became increasingly aware that both scientific and psychoanalytic models of management served to place management control firmly in the province of experts, thus ensuring that organizational decision-making and prioritizing remained technical and did not become political. Things were becoming dangerous: something was needed to stop the tide. Enterprise, supported and promoted through the training agency, has come to the rescue. The 'enterprise culture' combines enhanced professionalism of management with corporate identity and loyalty achieved through interpersonal and team skills development. It divorces power and responsibility. Teams of workers, be they NHS units, schools, or Griffiths-style teams in social services, know that they are responsible for the continued effectiveness, even survival, of their service. Power is centralized. Women are accorded a particular place in this humanized and enterprising organizational culture . . . The new wave of enterprise incorporates women more firmly into management: after all, interpersonal skills are their very *raison d'être* . . . Potential conflict is thwarted before it arises. Enterprise confirms the professionalization of a political activity and is rapidly sweeping into the public sector. Social work organizations are permeable to such change in that they are imbued with notions of people-centredness and profess skills in interpersonal relations. (Everitt, 1990, pp. 143–4)

In the 1990s, quality assurance has come to play a leading role in the search for a reconciliation between commercialism and the people-based goals of the human services. Even where, or especially where, there is conflict, the response is to avoid challenging the dominant commercialism of the quasi-market and apportion professional autonomy and service user empowerment alike according to a similar rationing process as operates in the gatekeeping of services. Everything is contingent on resources, rather than upon authentic responses to human need informed by continual critical reflection on professional activity.

This section considers the theoretical reference points for the more detailed examination of quality issues in the personal social services in general and social work in particular.

Modulating and enhancing

Phillips, Palfrey and Thomas (1994, p. 6) distinguish modulating and enhancing standards of service (see Table 2.1). Modulating approaches are typified by quality control rather than quality improvement. They are mechanistic and procedural and refer to criteria such as staffing levels, staff–service user ratios, client throughput, waiting times for assessments and services delivered. Enhancing approaches are based on the quality of the work process itself and the effect of intervention as perceived by different participants in the process.

Going one stage further: empowering workers and service users

Although service users and workers are stakeholders in the work, neither modulating nor enhancing approaches put the empowerment of the service user and the agency and/or worker delivering human services at the centre of the activities. The centrality in social work in the 1990s of debates about empowering service users makes it desirable to incorporate this aspect in any framework for examining different perspectives on quality assurance. In this regard, Coote's analysis of the development of different models

Table 2.1 Modulating and enhancing approaches to quality

| | Approaches to quality | |
	Modulating	Enhancing
Goals	Good enough services	Better services
Key questions	How can we bring services up to standard?	How can we improve on the standard of services?
Typical processes	Inspection, review, audit, performance indicator, satisfaction survey	Formal evaluation/ appraisal

Source: Based on ideas drawn from Phillips, Palfrey and Thomas, 1994, pp. 7–16.

of quality assurance illustrates the boundaries of rhetoric about service user participation in the personal social services (Coote, 1994). Since the Second World War, in terms of their relative powerlessness, users have remain marginal to the personal social services, whilst experts, professionals and managers have retained their relative centrality. Coote argues that following the implementation of the NHS and Community Care Act 1990, the policy of asking service users for their views appears to involve users in the shaping, delivering and evaluation of services, but in reality maintains the power of professionals.

Approaches to assuring quality

The remainder of this chapter takes Anna Coote's analysis of different approaches to quality assurance as the basis for developing a typology which incorporates user empowerment into the process of assuring quality. Coote's argument is that of four major approaches to quality assurance in the second half of the twentieth century, the first three – scientific management, managerialism and consumerism – have retained dominance, and the fourth, concerned with empowering service users, has not been tried. Each of these approaches generates distinctive criteria for judging the effectiveness of the service or product. For example, the satisfaction of managers may be sought with the cost of a service, or practitioners with its outcomes; or, the emphasis may be upon the impact on service users. There are associated questions of the appropriateness and robustness of the methods used to gather evidence, their reliability and validity, their flexibility and applicability for a variety of uses in different settings. Table 2.2 illustrates the four approaches.

Management approaches

Scientific management Scientific managment, or Taylorism, is buttressed by consumer charters, offering the consumer the opportunity of complaining if services are not adequate. Chapter 3 examines the impact of Taylorism on the organisation and management of local authority services. Scientific management

Table 2.2   Four approaches to quality

Dominant approach to management	Dominant process	Person holding power	Approach to quality
Scientific management	oppression	expert	maintenance
Commercial managerialist	control	manager	rectification
Consumerist managerialist	consumer satisfaction	professional	enhancement
Democratic	empowerment	service user and worker	maximisation

Sources: Adapted from work of Phillips, Palfrey and Thomas, 1994, pp. 7–16; and Coote, 1994.

offers the appearance of objectivity in judgements by experts, sustains their power and maintains the relative powerlessness of the service user.

Commercial managerialist A managerialist approach involves gathering users' views about services they require and surveying their satisfaction with services provided. But the strategy of asking service users to express their views at certain points during the process of care management does nothing more than maintain the professionals in positions of power, whilst creating the appearance of user involvement in the shaping, delivering and evaluation of services.

Consumerist managerialist Consumerism involves offering customers a choice from competing services and a procedure for complaining if services are not adequate. The consumerist approach has widespread currency in health and social care in England, Scotland and Wales, since the NHS and Community Care Act 1990 was implemented. There are major problems of reconciling market-based approaches; and also, services provided by financially led agencies, with the meeting of service users' needs; with making human services into commodities; and with locating the service user 'across the counter' from the service provider, thus giving choice at the point of consumption rather than at the point of product/service development or production.

Additionally, Coote (1994, p. 192) notes two major weaknesses of this approach. First, service users of personal health or social care services do not act as isolated individuals, but as members of groups, neighbourhoods and communities. Thus, their needs and wants should be located in their social context and services regarded as social goods. Second, the alleged choice of services may be fictional if consumers are unable to shop around, for reasons of lack of mobility, or whatever.

Democratic The alternative approach proposed by Coote involves reclaiming concepts from the discourse of scientific management, managerialism and consumerism and shaping them into a democratic approach. This attempts to empower service users and address the structural inequalities affecting their circumstances.

Enabling service users as stakeholders in the personal social services to participate in shaping, delivering and evaluating their own services in this way, implies that they should have the option to become involved in theorising the politicised processes involved. Actions associated with the democratic approach to quality assurance are thereby necessarily self-consciously theorised and politicised by stakeholders in the process. This involves professionals articulating a non-oppressive practice concerned not just with counteracting the power of the managers and the evaluators, but also empowering themselves. The task of professionals in this situation is to ensure that service users are empowered and that the power of experts, managers, and the professionals' own power, is not perpetuated. Finally, of course, the fourth approach is vulnerable to undermining by managerialism, since, as has been noted elsewhere (Adams, 1996b, pp. 12–24), empowerment is largely portrayed in terms of benefits to individuals, rather than to people collectively, whether in groups, organisations or the community.

Four approaches to assuring quality in social work

Now we are in a position to set out the four main approaches of quality maintenance, quality rectification, quality enhancement and quality maximisation. In many ways, these occupy a continuum from error-driven problem rectification at one extreme to ideal-driven maximisation at the other, and from imposing quality to achieving it through maximising participation by all stakeholders in it. The correspondence is not exact, though, since quality rectification and quality maintenance overlap, as do quality enhancement and quality maximisation. A closer parallel may be drawn between controlling, even punitive, practices consistent with quality maintenance, between some forms of quality control and notions of remedying attitudes and actions, between quality enhancement approaches and the choices permitted to people in the consumerist marketplace of the work setting and approaches informed by the paradigm of empowerment, which aspires to maximise quality and radically change the culture of the organisation. Such points of comparison, however, should not be regarded as automatic or necessary. Situations may arise where approaches to quality conflict with dominant ideologies of practice.

Quality maintenance

Quality maintenance tends to be standards-driven. In these approaches (see Chapter 5), quality standards are determined wholly or largely by 'experts'. If other stakeholders such as service users are consulted, it is subsequently. Quality is assumed by managers to be owned exclusively by them and, by and large, imposed on a workforce which in extreme circumstances may be assumed to be indifferent or even resistant to change.

Standard setting in social work all too often is concerned with minima rather than ideals. A characteristic of maintenance is that a body will publish a set of standards; it is then possible for agencies to work to that minimum, rather than setting goals associated with quality maxima. For example, universities may adopt the occupational standards for social workers published by CCETSW (CCETSW, 1996a) as operating guides, rather than minima. Another example is the use of child protection procedures as the substitute for striving for excellence in practice, thus not addressing in a preventive way the causes which may lead to similar criticisms being made of social workers in successive child abuse inquiries.

Quality rectification

Quality rectification is the term used here for error-driven approaches, using the impetus provided, for example, by complaints procedures, whistleblowing and various forms of investigation and inquiry. (This does not mean that such elements as complaints procedures cannot contribute to other approaches.) The focus, inevitably, given this basis for action, is largely or wholly on curbing or eliminating shortcomings in services (see Chapter 6). The most widely used rectification approach to quality is quality control. This is a term referring to an approach which became popular in the 1940s in factories employing mass production processes, and supplying components for mass production, such as armaments, to wartime governments. As with quality maintenance, quality control approaches often implicitly take the rectification of poor quality as their starting point, rather than adopting a positive approach to quality enhancement. They tend to assume that the production and delivery processes are imperfect and inevitably lead to errors and flaws in the output. Quality control refers to mechanisms designed to identify these defects and to enable inspectors and managers to remedy them.

Thus, quality control is viewed in terms of the elimination of unsatisfactory performance (British Standard BS 4778: Part 2: 1991, 6.1.1, p. 8). In these terms, inspection is referred to in terms of its role in judging the extent to which products and services conform to specified requirements (British Standard BS 4778: Part 2: 1991, 7.1, p. 9). The preferred use of inspection is to detect shortcomings in processing rather than in products, in other words as fault prevention rather than as fault detection (British Standard BS 4778: Part 2: 1991, 7.1, p. 9).

Quality control is described in Social Services Inspectorate (SSI) guidelines as an aspect of quality assurance. It commonly describes procedures for checking the extent to which standards required in a particular area are adhered to. Quality control 'refers to those processes and verification, and will include systematic monitoring, including statistical and other management information, recurring and one-off audits and inspection activity designed to establish whether standards are being achieved. . . . It should provide objective feedback to line managers who have continuing responsibility for quality, about what is actually being achieved' (SSI, 1991a, p. 30).

Quality control involves essentially disciplining and boundary-maintenance functions, based on negative perspectives of the production and delivery process. It suffers from the additional problem that it relies on inspection of the product or service and the identification of shortcomings at a late stage. In many service-based organisations, whether in commerce or social work, it is too late to identify flaws at the point of delivery, since by then the service user will have been adversely affected and remedies are difficult to apply. It would be preferable to develop an approach to quality assurance which prevented, say, a ruined holiday or a failed placement of a child, rather than relying on quality control retrospectively to identify weaknesses in the service.

Quality enhancement

The enhancement of quality tends to be achieved through various forms of audit, such as the auditing of professional activity (see Chapter 7) and monitoring and evaluation (Chapter 8). Enhancement approaches to quality go quite a long way towards fulfilling the goals of different stakeholders in services. However, they take the status quo of the setting as given. They do not regard reality in the here and now as problematic. They do not address structural power differentials between workers and users as stakeholders; they take them as given. But they do tend to take on board much of the language of user participation and total quality approaches, within the parameters of existing power relations. Quality management and total quality management are examples of such approaches.

Quality management   Quality management describes approaches to quality which, rather than determining a minimum standard, set a goal which stakeholders strive for. Commonly, such approaches involve attempts to grasp the entire context of managing and providing goods and services. The SSI describes quality management as 'the overall system which an organisation uses to ensure the products or outcomes of its activities are those required or expected. It includes the processes of planning and setting goals, of putting goals into effect, of checking routinely on the outcomes and of development and problem-solving' (DHSSI, 1988a, p. 17).

There are commonly four key features of quality enhancement approaches: they demonstrate a commitment to improving standards; key stakeholders participate in the process; stakeholders, by and large, contribute to their own goals of raising standards, but individually rather than collectively; service users do not play the determining role in shaping, sharing and working towards these goals with other stakeholders.

Total quality management Total quality management (TQM) is a general principle concerning enabling change and continuous improvement, which also applies to TQM itself, thus making its simple definition impossible. TQM appears in different guises in Japanese and Western countries, notably Britain and the USA It may be used as a means of quality enhancement or quality maximisation (Ciampa, 1991).

Under quality enhancement, for example, TQM may be implemented through continuous direct control by management, embedding it within the practice of each worker who reports at intervals direct to the line manager, through the individual and collective professional supervision of the worker. Under quality maximisation, it may be achieved through a democratisation of the entire process involving workers, service users and carers.

The dominant ideologies of quality maintenance or enhancement rather than quality maximisation can be justified by reference to market assumptions rather than service users' expectations and sustained by the concepts and language informing them.

Quality maximisation

Quality maximisation (see Chapter 9) involves an acknowledgement that there is no neat solution to the problematic of quality assurance. The response to the question as to who governs total quality management – managers and professionals or service users – determines whether total quality management (TQM) is located in the enhancement or maximising category. Rather than total quality management being a concept managers and professionals wield in trying to develop a culture of quality, quality maximisation involves all stakeholders: citizens, gatekeepers of decisions, service purchasers, service providers; all are joint shareholders in the organisation and services provided.

Total quality management: enhancing or maximising quality? Although TQM was imported to the USA and to Britain as a Japanese product in the 1980s, its origins lay in earlier work on the improvement of quality in companies in the USA. Deming (1986, pp. 22–3), one of the prophets of the move to capitalise on the Japanese enthusiasm for quality, refers to the way Japanese engineers in the late 1940s studied the work of W. A. Shewhart on statistical methods of process control in the Bell Telephone Laboratories, in the research division of the Western Electric Company. They were looking for the best ways to use sampling to check for variations from standardised equipment. These statistical approaches had become established through their application by the Statistical Research Group to mass production during the Second World War (Tuckman, 1992, p. 8). Thus, from the 1980s the bringing of quality assurance mechanisms into the foreground converged with the the push towards establishing internal markets in service provision as well as manufacturing, independent as well as public sectors. In the 1980s, the concept of total quality management was justified very largely with reference to its function 'as both the secret of Japan's success and the means to halt decline in the West' (Tuckman, 1992, p. 13).

References to the need to emulate, and if possible outdo, Japanese approaches, abound in textbooks on total quality management in business organisations (see, for instance, Ciampa, 1991, pp. 9–13; Deming, 1986, pp. 2–6; Drummond, 1993, pp. 16–19). At that stage, TQM provided 'a prescription to change in the west . . . a 'culture change" which covers both the devolving of quality inspection from specialist to operator in the move from firefighting to TQM, as well as the more fundamental subjective acceptance of the customer–supplier chain as the only means of achieving quality. That one dimension of the culture change by TQM is the internalisation of an idealised market' (Tuckman, 1992, p. 13). The White Paper *Competing for Quality* (HM Treasury, 1991, p. 2) presents the case for such a culture change. Thus, the introduction of TQM, associated with moves to induce workers to adopt a business approach, may 'reinforce drives to cut down on levels of hierarchy through such things as increased use of work teams' (Tuckman, 1992, p. 15). Thus, the payoff for more junior staff who take on the ethos of the market approach in their work is that they may experience empowerment, but on condition that they do not challenge this global culture.

It is possible that the version of TQM exported first from the USA to Japan and then to Europe from Japan, is less team-oriented and more individualistic and competitive because of contrasts between Western and Japanese commercial culture rather than reflecting inherent features in TQM. This is illustrated in the tendency in the West to combine TQM with such features as performance related pay and staff appraisal.

Deming's concept of TQM differs from the notions of quality control and quality assurance. The latter approaches rely on experts and managers to institute and maintain quality, whereas Deming emphasises the need to develop a culture of quality in the organisation which capitalises on the motivation of staff and induces quality through the work group itself.

A problem arises over whether methods such as TQM have been colonised by professionals so far as to preclude them being genuinely empowering for service users and carers. Total quality management is merely one manifestation of the managerialist ideal of bringing the entire working environment under control, directing it towards fulfilment of the corporate purpose. Whilst the goals of TQM may be presented as every customer's dream, from the viewpoint of the worker they may simply be a set of unattainable standards, used perpetually as goads to greater efforts. A total quality management approach based on continuous managerial oversight minimises the opportunities for professionals to exercise and develop an autonomous culture of quality in the workplace. Devolving responsibility to the individual worker may seem, superficially, to offer benefits, but in practice also bypasses the professionalism of the workers collectively. An approach reliant mainly or exclusively on the professionalism of staff, individually or collectively, offers opportunities to develop an alternative set of beliefs and practices focusing on quality. However, it is only through a maximising approach that the other major stakeholders – service users and carers, individually and collectively – are brought into the centre of the work process.

Excellence in practice is sought rather than the maintenance of a minimum standard. This may entail what Peters and Austin refer to as having a passion for excellence (Peters and Austin, 1985). Quality maximisation represents an open-ended commitment to the ideal of excellence, held not just by those with managerial or professional power, in the total process of quality assurance, from defining the goals, through communicating and sharing them, to implementing, monitoring and evaluating practice. Quality maximisation approaches derive from traditions of popular protest and community action, which assume that significant initiatives are made by service users, rather than as part of processes shaped by service providers and professionals. Thus, maximisation of quality necessitates the worker and the service user being engaged side by side in complementary activities contributing to this task. Their relationship is as nearly symmetrical, and their influence over the process as near equivalent, as possible. Features of this process include the shared value base between *all* stakeholders and the joint identification of needs, purposes and services required. It is not only the concept of quality which matters, but also the way it is operationalised.

'Old' and 'new' quality assurance

The discourse associated with these four approaches, and theories embedded in them in one sense, illustrate positions on a continuum between oppressive and empowering activity. In another sense, there is a fundamental break between some approaches – notably between Eastern and Western approaches to maximisation. It is useful to engage with the oriental ideas on quality which have influenced, and have been influenced by, Western commercial practice. Berman refers to the work of Mary Caroline Richards, in his discussion of the somatic experience which is likely to underlie the form creativity will take in the arts in the next historical epoch (Berman, 1984, p. 340). Richards uses the expression 'the new quality' in a brief reference to this transition. If we import this notion into social work, and take on board the major differences between modernist Western concepts underlying creativity and what Berman terms traditional ones, some of the points of contrast between the 'new quality' and managerialist quality can be set out (Table 2.3). In charting these, the irony has to be appreciated that the word 'new' is being attached here to what Berman asserts is 'traditional'. However, this postmodernist feature is consistent with Oriental thought, which bypasses Western notions of evolution.

The synthesis of Oriental and Western philosophies inherent in practice implicit in quality maximisation approaches as outlined above is pursued in Chapter 9. In summary, the approach is holistic, that is, embracing theory, practice and research. The expertise resides in the interaction between the reflective practitioner, as practitioner/researcher, and the service user. It is non-divisive, non-hierarchical and practitioners, researchers and users are not segregated and ordered hierarchically by differing discourses of research, practice and academia.

The four approaches: variety in practice

Many systems concerning quality, whether based on maintenance, rectification, enhancement or maximisation, are concerned with achieving quality on more than an individualised basis. However, quality maximisation approaches are holistic, in that they involve engendering shared commitment to a common goal. Whereas quality maximisation occurs where all stakeholders – staff and service users – are empowered, approaches based on quality maintenance or enhancement may be associated with tokenism. In this sense, quality assurance forms part of the broader goal of

Table 2.3   Managerialist quality assurance and the new quality

Managerialist quality assurance	The new quality
In, or out of, mind	No mind
Opacity	Transparency
Struggle to ascend	Circularity
Working against or through	Working beyond
Schismogenic	Non-schismogenic (synonym: holistic)
Fragmented	Together
Modernist	Post-modernist
Self-expression	Expressing unity as universal
Creative	Decreative
Search for unity	Unity already attained

achieving quality, which in itself contributes to the aspiration of total quality in a setting or organisation (Oakland, 1989; Ciampa, 1991).

Conclusions

In discussing four distinctive approaches to assuring quality in the personal social services, this chapter has noted that each of the four approaches to quality proceeds from different assumptions about what makes for quality, emphasises the key role of particular participants in the process of quality assurance and adopts different strategies to achieve it. However, the variety of practice makes it unlikely that particular settings will adopt a single approach. Local reality is more complex, as is demonstrated through the examination below of a number of key areas. Chapters 5 to 8 consider aspects of social work with a view to identifying their shortcomings and specifying key indicators to enable them to address the goal of quality maximisation. The next chapter considers the links between ideas and styles of management.

3

Challenging Managerialism in Assuring Social Work Quality

Changes in the ideology of management in social work have occurred in the wake of the growth of a diversity of managerialisms in the personal social services from the 1970s. Such measures as performance indicators have been monitored by government bodies such as the Audit Commission and the Social Services Inspectorate. Concepts such as performance audits, and bodies such as the Audit Commission and the Social Services Inspectorate which ouotain them, play key roles in maintaining central government control over the nature of practice in the personal social services. At its worst, managerialism constrains professional autonomy and limits or undermines effectiveness. Of course, not all organisations providing social work services have these negative characteristics. The practitioner has to devise ways of making the best of the organisational context in which she or he works. In order for service quality to be maximised, these diverse forms of managerialism need to be understood and challenged in the workplace. This chapter locates key features of social work management arising from these changes in relation to the importation of notions of quality assurance from manufacturing industry.

Shortcomings in social services management

EXAMPLE 3.1

Concerns about quality have preoccupied social services departments since their creation in the early 1970s. A compendium of such concerns is illustrated by the findings of the inquiry report into the Pindown regime in Staffordshire children's homes. This found that 'management in the social services in Staffordshire was inadequate for its task and lacked many of the essential characteristics required to ensure good services to the public' (Levy and Kahan, 1991, ch. 17.4, p. 151). At all levels there were staff who worked extremely hard, 'in some cases much harder than was desirable for them or for the people they were serving. Vision, leadership, commitment to quality services, and recognition of the need for adequate knowledge, training and skill in the care of children were all seriously lacking' (ibid, ch. 17.5, p. 151).

The most senior managers were too remote from their subordinates (ch. 17.6, p. 151). They lacked involvement with other staff and with service users and they failed to provide adequate support for other staff (ch. 17.7, p. 151). They tended to make decisions in isolation, without adequate consultation (ch. 17.8, p. 151). Consequently, other managers had tasks imposed on them, and they imposed tasks and responsibilities on other staff (ch. 17.8, p. 152).

A letter from eighteen team managers written to the director of social services on 5 November 1990 concluded: 'The Team Managers wish to express their complete lack of confidence in the senior managers of the department' (ch. 17.12, p. 152).

It detailed the following areas of great concern: '(a) lack of structure, direction or any coherent philosophy within the department; (b) inability to follow child protection procedures because of insufficient staffing; (c) lack of resources to carry out effective work with families; (d) apparent lack of communication at senior management level; (e) inadequate training offered to staff dealing with 'this complex area of work'; (f) extremely low level of morale . . . across all districts/disciplines. Staff are left feeling totally unsupported by our senior managers' (ch. 17.11, p. 152). The catalogue of management failures included the difficulties of staff attempting to communicate – past the barrier of middle management – with senior managers (ch. 17.14, p. 152); the absence of a system for recording complaints and, until September 1988, the lack of a written complaints procedure (ch. 17.15,

p. 152); failure to respond to identification by staff of 'poor physical standards, lack of essential resources, and shortage of staff, and by their unwillingness to confront the reality of unmet need . . . Unqualified social workers were carrying not only heavy caseloads but also a high proportion of cases such as child abuse, or adoptions, which required a much higher level of skill than they possessed. There was no departmental guidance on workload management' (ch. 17.18, p. 153). 'Social services department management appeared to be related more to crises than careful and well-informed planning. There was little sense of direction and little evidence of professional aspirations. More than once we heard evidence of a dismissiveness towards training and research' (ch. 17.21, p. 153) There was 'excessive tinkering with the structure' between 1983 and 1989 (ch. 17.25, p. 154). Many reorganisations had taken place, 'largely in relation to cost cutting' (ch. 17.23, p. 154). 'Open debate and opportunities for staff to meet informally were not encouraged' (ch. 17.27, p. 154). There was 'resistance to experience and ideas from outside' and 'members of staff who expresssed aspirations to high standards were terms 'naive' (ch. 17.27, p. 154).

Interpreting the critique: putting management failures in context

There is a need to locate such criticisms of managements – the observations made on Staffordshire in the example above could be replicated in other inquiries – in a broader, critical understanding of the management of social services since the 1970s.

Management: dominant ideas Predominant ideas about management, and the knowledges informing the concepts surrounding it, are not neutral. How management is defined depends on how work changes and how different kinds of work are valued. Management

> is based on a body of knowledge that developed in the context of male-controlled organizations (the military, factories, the civil service). It was written about and encoded into 'theories' principally by men, and the research which has established the norms of managerial practice has mainly been based on male subjects. Its concepts and images are predominantly drawn from

the domains of order, hierarchy and rationality. Its goals are the
control of the internal world of the organization and mastery of
the external environment. (Newman, 1994, p. 185)

But it is a particularly *macho* form of masculinity which has
dominated management theory and practice, rather than men.
This is characterised by a lack of openness, lack of means for
communication upwards and a lack of democratisation in relations
between senior and subordinate staff and between staff and service
users.

Whilst the effectiveness of some aspects – as illustrated in the
above example – has not increased, the physical size of the
management sector of the personal social services has increased
significantly since the 1970s. However, following the creation of
new social services departments in the early 1970s there was a
dramatic decrease in the proportion of *qualified* social workers in
some of the children's departments (see Chapter 5). Management,
support and ancillary staff in headquarters or area offices increased
from 11 per cent to 16 per cent of the workforce – 24,000 to 38,000
– between 1983–4 and 1993–4. During the same period, there was
only a marginal 2 per cent increase from 11 to 13 per cent, in social
work staff in the workforce – 24,000 to 31,000. These figures take
account of the overall increase of 23,000 in the workforce – from
210,000 to 233,000 – during the same period (SSI, 1995, p. 90).

*Management and managerialism in social work and the social
services*   There is much debate about the extent to which general
principles and practices of management apply to the very wide
range of activities involved in particular sectors of, for instance, the
health and social services and within these, to social work. At the
most general level, it seems reasonable to distinguish between work
settings where the primary purpose is profit and those whose
primary goal is the benefit of people. But whilst this distinguishes
the factory producing goods from the statutory social services
agency, it leaves two areas unclear: boundaries between, say, the
service sector, including leisure, holidays, hotels, and the private
sector of housing, residential and nursing care for older people;
further, the distinction between former public sector and current
quasi-market provision of personal social services, needs further
clarification.

The concept of social work management embodies both the notion of the management *of* social workers and the use of management approaches *in* social work. The distinction between these is not altogether clearcut. Nevertheless, the former refers in part to the ways the operations of practitioners are managed by other people, notably line managers, and thereby to the organisational context in which practice takes place. The latter may refer to social work managers as a distinct category of staff, but also introduces the notion of management as a thread through practice itself.

Management conventionally has been thought of as being carried out by managers, whereas other work is carried out by non-managers. However, in the human services – notably health, penal and social services – senior professional workers have often carried management responsibilities. For example, in the early 1970s Seebohm and local government reorganisation produced an influx of social workers as incipient career managers of the newly genericised social services department; and in the NHS, as Walby and Greenwell note (1994, p. 59), planned systems were introduced in 1974 (DHSS, 1972), and a number of other factors (see Chapter 7) contributed to creating a strong managerial cadre, well before the Griffiths report of 1983.

Managerialism contributes to the lack of autonomy of the social worker, who often must practise in complex organisational settings, meet procedural demands and work within comprehensive guidelines which constrain professional decision-making (Barclay, 1982). Examples of such bureaucratic boundaries to professional autonomy include checklists and criteria governing people's eligibility for services and the prioritisation of their circumstances where resources are limited, and the allocation of resources – for example, for the placement of an older person in residential care.

Dominelli (1996) notes that the introduction of competence-based approaches in social work has undermined the professionalism of social work and reduced the scope for autonomous reflective practice. Social work in the statutory sector is likely to offer only very limited opportunities for anti-oppressive work which challenges practices embedded within the culture of the organisation. Also, the practice of community care will probably require the social worker to manage tensions between legal duties and powers, agency policies, the Community Care Plan, local procedural requirements such as the charter for service users and carers, local custom and practice of colleagues in social work and allied professions, as well as personal and professional values concerning empowering and anti-oppressive work.

Spread of managerialisms in social work organisations

Managerialism in this context refers to convergent management and professional activities, often involving managers exerting increased control over the field of professional endeavour. The growth and spread of managerialism in the personal social services was buttressed by changes in the education and training of staff. The granting to colleges of further education and former colleges of higher education and polytechnics of corporate status and independent status, no longer subject to control from local govenment, was accompanied by an extension and intensification of direct controls by central government over the college and new university sector. This impacted on the personal social services through the review of the Diploma in Social Work initiated by Virginia Bottomley at the Department of Health 1994–6. This led to the adoption by all qualifying programmes for social workers of a set of occupational standards and requirements which were competence-based; it was reflected also in the move in the 1980s by the Home Office towards developing national standards of probation work and, in the mid-1990s, imposing the segregation of qualifying programmes for probation officers from the Diploma in Social Work and shifting their centre of gravity from higher education to the workplace (see Chapter 4). Managerialism is the thread linking the mobilisation and control of large workforces of mass production industry – as in Henry Ford's car factory in Detroit in the early decades of the twentieth century (Beynon, 1975) – with the operation of quasi-markets in the human services, in the last two decades of the century.

Clarke *et al.* (1994a, pp. 6–7) put a stark view of managerialism when they argue that whilst professional ideology pushes practice towards empowering service users, managerialist strategies locate professionals and service users, as consumers, in a commercial relationship controlled by managers. This resonates with the classic analysis of Doray, who described how under scientific management, workers became slaves to the machine and the production process (Doray, 1988, p. 2). But, as Clarke *et al.* (1994a, p. 4) are at pains to point out, there is not one version of managerialism; there are managerialisms. The nature of these managerialisms continually changes, according to the setting and the task in hand. It is far from the truth that all managerialisms simply express uniformly powerful opposition to the values of professional social work. In fact, a notable feature of managerialism in the personal social services is the close interweaving with professional work achieved by some government-sponsored managerialist initiatives. The Social Services Inspectorate (SSI), for example, works between State policies, the operations of local authorities and professional practice of social work. For example, the SSI has continued a working style evolved in the former Social Work Service of the Department of Health and Social Security in the 1970s. This, though charged with the brief of implementing government policy, is sensitive to the issues affecting practice in local settings, informed by the profile of experience of many newer recruits to the ranks of inspectors. This influence can be seen in the publications offering advice, for example, to practitioners on the implementation of community care (DH/SSI, 1991c). At the same time, the tight parameters of managerial control amounted to an unambiguous curbing of professional autonomy, in which, as Shaw (1995, p. 132) notes, the Chief Inspector supports a shift to a working style where 'no individual fieldworker should be regarded as self-sufficient' (SSI, 1992, p. 13).

Also, the region, and locality in which personal social services are located, contribute an unavoidably political, as well as an economic, dimension. Thus, for example, the interface between this context and senior managers in the social services department of a local authority is shaped by local strategies for the area which lie beyond the personal social services. Thus, in a region with great difficulties of social deprivation, there may may be a strong pressure for the prioritising of economic development over what are perceived as social services goals.

From Taylorism to human relations management Just as the significance of quality lies in a set of sustaining beliefs underlying and inherent in practice, so managerialism involves ideologies and approaches embodying theories and concepts, rather than simply a toolkit of techniques. Everitt identifies two principal schools of management: scientific management as propounded by the Harvard Business School in the tradition of Frederick Taylor, and human relations management linked with the Tavistock Institute in London (Everitt, 1990, p. 143). These are represented in the history of the personal social services in the second half of the twentieth century. The restructuring of different aspects of the human services has engendered distinctive forms of managerialism, apposite to each. But managerialism involves more than social policy change, a shift of resources and a changed organisational shape. The former reflects an ideology given an unprecedented impetus by the work of Frederick Taylor in the early years of the twentieth century and still apparent in the closing years of the century, despite the popularity of many other subsequent approaches to management. Notably, human relations management exemplifies a number of distinctive streams of activity, which relate to different approaches to assuring quality.

Taylorism is the word often used to describe approaches based on Frederick Taylor's 'scientific management'. This relied on the tight, continuous control of the work process by managers, on the assumption that employees are inherently workshy and require constant supervision. Subsequently, a range of different conceptualisations of management developed, one of the most important reference points for these being the human relations movement. This relied on a more optimistic view of the attitudes of the workforce and on insights from psychology, social psychology and sociology to encourage management styles which tried to free up and harness the creativity and productivity of the workforce.

The restructuring of local authority and personal social services in the 1970s (Local Authorities Social Services Act 1970 and Local Government Act 1972) and the creation of quasi-markets in the 1990s (NHS and Community Care Act 1990) were associated with assumptions about the goodness and desirability of an ideology of the ideal relationship between production and technology and the shape of public service organisations, or technocracies. These were already burgeoning in C. P. Snow's novels, in relation both to technological changes (Snow, 1954) and changes in the neighbouring infrastructures of academia and the civil service (Snow, 1964) by the time of Harold Wilson's Labour government in the 1960s. A positive relationship between people and new technologies was anticipated. Seebohm was heir to a view of departmental organisation with its roots in Taylorism, based on the assumption that workers are basically extensions of the machine, informed by experience – epitomised in the production lines of Henry Ford in Detroit (Beynon, 1975) – of mass production in industry rather than the complexities of meeting human needs in a service-based organisation (James, 1994, p. 47). The new technologies spawned Post-Fordist doctrines, moving on from situating the worker on the factory production line of a mass-production industry, to a dispersed environment where fragmented responsibilities for contracted-out portions of the product were farmed out to a dispersed network of piece-workers.

Post-Fordism refers to this shift from the application of mass-production, mass-marketing and the maintenance of high demand and relatively full employment through state expenditure, to batch production in small units of production using flexible technology and niche marketing. This operates in a fragmented culture, where the welfare system is oriented towards making the workforce more flexible and sustaining competitiveness through keeping wages down, staff re-training or economic restructuring.

Fragmentation into small units: controlling purchasers and providers   The adoption of measures of quality assurance which act as fixed parameters, disciplining measures for the maintenance of the market approach, ensures that the dismantling of the public sector and the disaggregation of its services can take place without threats to its sustaining rationale in New Right ideology. The mixed economy of welfare involves a radical departure from the centrality of the social work/social services department as the provider, to a situation where it becomes the facilitator of provision largely by independent – that is, voluntary and private – producers. In less than a decade from their introduction, quality assurance mechanisms such as TQM assumed a central role in enabling the virtual public sector monopoly of local authority provision, in effect to be denationalised, that is, dispersed into the fragmented variety of independent providers, with the risks that carries for the quality of staff training, support and practice (Ollier, 1991). What is beyond dispute is the role of TQM, 'as – among other things – a mode of legitimating the very commodification of relations both inside hierarchy as well as, more recently, between hierarchies and

individual consumers of services'. This amounts to 'the commodification of sets of previously decommodified relations in such areas
as health, welfare and education' (Tuckman, 1992, p. 6). In effect,
TQM fulfils a similar function to other regulating mechanisms,
ensuring that the mixed economy is a managed quasi-market rather
than a free market.

Other measures to enhance remote control of local practice by the
'centre' The Thatcher government aspired 'to transform the
delivery of public sector services by improving economy, efficiency
and effectiveness in the bureaucracy' (Carter, 1989, p. 208), by
decentralising the delivery of services. Cuts in the numbers of civil
servants proposed in 1979 were anticipated to secure a 15 per cent
cut between 1979 and 1985; civil service pay was detached from pay
in the private sector and the Civil Service Department was
abolished. The Financial Management Initiative (FMI) which
was intended to promote decentralisation was countered by trends
during the 1980s *towards* centralisation, through reductions in
local authority block grants, cash limits on spending and rate-
capping (Carter, 1989, p. 209). The establishment of a new
Efficiency Unit led by Lord Rayner from Marks & Spencer was
linked with the inauguration of the FMI which focused on raising
awareness of costs and the need for greater efficiency. Paradoxi-
ally, as Carter notes, the implementation of decentralisation
depends on close monitoring – from a central position – of what
departments actually do. Thus, the FMI aimed to achieve 'a clear
view of objectives; and the means to assess, and wherever possible
measure, outputs or performance in relation to those objectives'
(Cmnd 9058, 1958, p. 1, quoted in Carter, 1989, p. 209)

From corporate to quasi-commercial managerialism

Two aspects of managerialism contribute to the widespread shift
from corporate to quasi-commercial managerialism: first, the
devolution of responsibilities from more senior to lower levels in
the hierarchy; second, the location of responsibility at these lower
levels. Thus, individuals tend to be blamed for failings many of
whose origins lie in the structure, organisation and operation of the
service. A plethora of courses on sickness absence, sickness absence
management, alleviating stress distress, stress management, coping

with pressure in the workplace and anger management serve to divert attention from the social, policy and organisational causes of these problems.

The bureaucratic approaches adopted by some social services departments attracted criticism. 'The hierarchical model is commonly found in social welfare organisations; it is a structural arrangement which offers some benefits. . . . however, this organisational form also has many drawbacks for while it is *administratively* efficient, as Weber saw, it better fits those systems which are meant to be undertaking routine, stable, unchanging tasks; there have always been doubts about its appropriateness for social work practice' (British Association of Social Workers, BASW, 1982, quoted in Coulshed, 1990, p. 29).

From the 1970s to the end of the 1980s, there was a shift from bureaucratic, or public sector, corporate styles of local government, concomitant with the development of quasi-markets, symbolised perhaps in the legislation introducing compulsory competitive tendering (Local Government Act 1988). This shift could be viewed from within the personal social services as an inevitable accompaniment of the paradigm shift which took place during the same period, from medico-treatment to empowerment (Adams, 1996b), although there is no automatic equivalence between the rhetoric of empowerment and the consumerism which dominate key areas, such as community care, in the personal social services. Since the 1980s, rather than taking the democratic course of empowering services users and carers by making service purchasers and providers directly accountable to them, forms of accountability through charters and contracts are undertaken (Cochrane, 1994, p. 155). Empowerment then becomes a facade behind which managerialist power is increasingly strengthened.

The personal social services since the late 1980s have increasingly displayed several trends: first, rather paradoxically, towards larger and more complex organisations managed by local and central government, and a trend towards a greater diversity – and a greater number of smaller service-providing organisations in the voluntary and private sectors; second, towards a separation of senior management in the organisation purchasing services, from the professionals who provide those services; third, towards the reduction of the size of the permanent workforce in the large local authority social work and social services departments of the 1970s, more staff being bought in on short and temporary contracts around a decreasing core of full-time, permanent officials.

It is a mistake to regard such changes as simply a feature of the personal social services, as the consequence of the creation of quasi-markets, the NHS and Community Care Act 1990, or even of changes in the functioning of local authorities since the Local Government Act 1988. The creation of internal markets in the personal social services is part of a wider pattern of changes which have affected industry and commerce as well as the human services. Undoubtedly, the last Conservative government inculcated the contract culture and, in the guise of 'enterprise' management, management styles consistent with survival in a market economy. One consequence was the widespread shift of managers and professional social workers, sometimes but not exclusively, from full time state and local authority employment into part-time and short-term contracts, often linked with self-employment.

The creation of mass, short-term contracts in the contract culture undermines workers' protections and engenders a compliant, if not exactly conformist, workforce. In the 1990s, it is hard to envisage the trade unions playing much more than an instrumental role, as the adjuncts to management policies, rather than as the idealist, essentially critical advocates of a socialist, let alone global, alternative. Essentially, unions such as Unison more usually have become providers of services for the welfare of individual members, rather than organising large-scale demonstrations and social action.

Changing culture of public sector management

From the late 1970s to the early 1990s, the public sector adopted the culture, language and practice of the management of private sector commercial organisations. Farnham and Horton (1993a, pp. 237–8) have listed these as follows: a rational approach which emphasises strategic management in the setting of objectives; the separation of policy from administration; the delegation to executive units of responsibility for service delivery, shortened hierarchies, devolving responsibilities increasingly to staff with middle managers held responsible for meeting targets; the use of performance indicators; and a human resource management style encouraging individualism and discouraging collectivism among staff. Farnham and Horton argue that the development of a 'public service orientation' towards service users as consumers, fits with the development of quasi-markets; it shifts from supply-led to demand-led services which are not dominated by professional providers but are motivated by the needs of users (1993a, p. 238). Managerialism in the public sector in Britain was furthered by central government through the inauguration of the Audit Commission and Social Services Inspectorate, as major mechanisms for policy audit and the regulation of practice.

Audit Commission

The Audit Commission was the embodiment of the shift from the attempt to identify global objectives for the corporate local authority, to monitoring and measuring the efficiency of policies in practice, where the objectives were taken as given (Cochrane, 1994, pp. 148–9). Cochrane locates this in the context of other policies converging on the goal of a sharper focus on specifying which services were delivered by local authorities. Thus, the trend towards a more direct say by consumers in the relative efficiencies of different local governments was exemplified by the move to put the consumer in the position of paying directly for local services through the community charge or poll tax. It was hoped that this would produce pressure directly from consumers for greater efficiencies and, hence, lower taxes (Cochrane, 1994, p. 149). The Audit Commission had the advantage of embodying the technical expertise of quantitative analysis and management consultancy in its central staff and the mission of externally and internally reviewing, ensuring 'that audits, standards and measures were established not only as forms of external coercion or persuasion but as the means of generating the processes of change' (Henkel, 1994, p. 21). Thus the Audit Commission, being independent of government and having the expertise in the core areas specified, had more authority in the first place than the SSI (Henkel, 1994, p. 12). Two of the four directorates of the Audit Commission at its centre – Special Studies and Management Practice – led its changes: 'the programme of Special Studies was built around the selection of critical areas for evaluating, and enhancing the performance of, local authorities services. The Management Practice Development was to improve general standards of local authority management. Both operated within an overriding purpose of embedding a managerial culture in local government' (Henkel, 1994, p. 12). Special Studies advisors and consultants from whichever areas and fields were being studied were employed to ensure that the audits achieved an appropriate focus and made appropriate approaches (Henkel, 1994, p. 13). The Audit Commission also placed emphasis on internal performance review as a means by which local government could survive in the competitive market place being created (Henkel, 1994, p. 13). As with the SSI, the local authority profiles and indicators developed by the Audit Commission were able to be used externally to compare the performance of different authorities, but could also be used internally by the authorities themselves to monitor and evaluate their performance (Henkel, 1994, p. 13). By introducing the notion of 'service effectiveness' the Audit Commission 'began to break down and, in effect, re-define what it meant by effectiveness . . . key questions for the local authorities in the 1988 Action Guide on performance review were, 'is the service getting to the right customers, in the right way, with the right services, in keeping with its stated policies?' (Audit Commission, 1988c). Within this formulation, such measures of performance as amounts and levels of service delivered, response times and numbers and categories of service users could be used.

The Audit Commission has contributed signficantly to transforming the operations of local authorities from the 1980s to the 1990s. Its role as auditor has been to ensure 'that local authorities made proper arrangements for securing economy, efficiency and effectiveness in their use of resources. By economy is meant the acquisition of the appropriate quality and quantity of resources at the lowest cost; by efficiency obtaining the maximum output for a given set of resource inputs acqured; and by effectiveness the degree to which established goals are achieved' (Kelly, 1991, p. 179). In a statement of the approach of the Audit Commission published in 1994 and with a foreword signed by its Chairman and three Conservative government ministers, its role was emphasised as promoting 'proper stewardship of public finances' (Audit Commission, 1994b, p. iv). The review of internal audits carried out in 400 local government departments in England and Wales in

1986 is an example of the sophistication of the admittedly accountancy-based approach of the Audit Commission (Chartered Institute of Public Finance and Accountancy and Audit Commission, 1986). Nevertheless, the sophistication of new managerialist thinking and practice is exemplified in its statement elsewhere that cost-saving is as an incidental outcome of careful examination of the management process rather than as an end in itself (Audit Commission, undated, p. 3). Although part of this agenda concerns saving money (Kelly, 1991, p. 180), partly the aim is 'to reorient the organizational culture of SSDs from professional to managerial themes' (Kelly, 1991, p. 181). In community care, for example, financial audit has identified the variety of authorities' practices in the mid-1990s (Audit Commission, 1996a). The Audit Commission's review of mental health services for adults focuses largely on issues of resources (Audit Commission, 1992).

Ann James makes a direct link between the methods of the Audit Commission from the 1980s, both with classical management approaches and the contract culture developed in the quasi-markets of the human services. James notes that 'the methods employed in the late 1980s and early 1990s to create a contracting culture have involved a return to the five major characteristics of the classical approach (objective setting, skill mixing, restructuring according to task, chain of command and clear accountability)' (James, 1994, p. 49).

Value for money was a focus of the performance review of the probation service carried out in the wake of the Green Paper *Punishment, Custody and the Community* and as a forerunner to the introduction of national standards for performance in probation and family court welfare work (Audit Commission, 1989). At the same time, the National Audit Office carried out a study of the control and management of the probation service by the Home Office. Service effectiveness thus merged with efficiency and management and the measurement of performance and some recognition was given to the intricate relationship between, for example, process and output. It moved further towards 'qualitative performance and process measures, in its 1990 guide (Audit Commission, 1990) but has tended to encourage continuing debate in these areas, in particular through its Quality Exchange initiative (1991), rather than itself lay down a definitive approach (Pollitt, 1992)' (Henkel, 1994, p. 13).

Ironically, the stringency of the Audit Commission in monitoring financial matters is not matched by conceptual sophistication in drawing on social scientific insights, in adopting service-user perspectives to analyse the effectiveness of services. Kelly draws attention to Knapp's criticisms of the simplistic approach of the Audit Commission to assessing service efficiency, rather than building on existing research into the impact of care (Knapp, 1984, p. 16, quoted in Kelly, 1991, p. 189). The emphasis on quality control by managers emerges in the Commission's publication describing its own approach to Quality Control Review (QCR), which is targeted at managers and local office staff (Audit Commission, 1994b), rather than regarding the organisation from the perspective of service users or networks to which staff relate. The publication by the Audit Commission of its strategy paper set out its approach and objectives (Audit Commission, 1993a). This was updated in the 1996 paper which included in its strategic goals for 1996 to 2001 the reinforcement of accountability of public bodies and focusing on users, notably through 'encouraging people to ask questions' about services (Audit Commission, 1996e, p. 17) and surveys of their views (Audit Commission, 1996e, p. 16) rather than empowering service users.

Performance review was presented by the Directorate and Management Practice of the Audit Commission as 'a top-down process that should be cascaded through the organisation. Members and then managers at each level should select critical areas and dimensions to review themselves and delegate the remaining review tasks' (Henkel, 1994, p. 14). Thus, the Audit Commission 'reinforced the government's view that the work of local authorities should increasingly be conceived within a managerial rather than a political paradigm, an approach strongly reflected in the sequence of management papers beginning with *The Competitive Council* (Audit Commission, 1988b)' (Henkel, 1994, p. 14).

A typical example of the Audit Commission approach is the Audit Commission report of 1994 into personal social services for children in need (Audit Commission, 1994a). This was a very critical 18-month study of eight social services' and eight health authorities' services for children in need, particularly children in residential care and disabled children, recommending better planning, coordination and delivery of services, strategic local plans for children's services in every local authority and, most controversially, transfer of resources from child abuse to other services.

The growth in managerialism (Raynor, Smith and Vanstone, 1994, p. 140), visible in the bureaucracy of probation and the increasing importance of regulation through administration, had begun in the probation service almost a decade before the Thatcher government came to power in 1979. Raynor, Smith and Vanstone (1994, p. 139) note 'a growth in the probation service hierarchy; a decrease in worker autonomy; the emergence of the concept of teamwork; and a widening gap between headquarters management and the staff engaged in the core tasks of the agency'.

In 1989, The Audit Commission contributed its own impetus to the thrust of Home Office policies (Audit Commission, 1989). This revolved around the principle of improving management to enforce consistency in spending per offence, improving advice to sentencers and thereby reducing variations, improving inter-agency working and targeting effort into work with offenders more at risk of custody and away from minor offenders. The Audit Commission approach meshed comfortably with the search for cheaper alternatives to custody, including community-based schemes. All this implied better management systems, thereby enhancing value for money.

Ensuring central government control of local government in managed markets The Local Government Act 1992 required the Audit Commission to set a number of key performance indicators for local authority services in England and Wales. Each authority had to measure its performance against these, publishing the results in a local newspaper. The role of the Audit Commission was to compare the levels of performance each authority achieved. The Commission went through a consultation process to determine the indicators to be used as the basis for the collection of information (Audit Commission, 1993a).

Thus, the new managerialist culture of close external evaluation, for example, through management audit, although critical of how management operates, actually bites even more deeply into the territory of the professional practitioner.

The *modus operandi* of the Audit Commission and the widespread adoption of competence approaches in the human services (see Chapter 4) are mutually reinforcing. The Audit Commission emphasises 'the specification and achievement of measurable objectives' (Kelly, 1991, p. 181) in parallel with the occupational standards' lists of criteria used to assess demonstrated competence in performance. Increasingly, in the future of local authority services, such achievements may be rewarded with performance-related bonuses. The conceptual and ethical issues about their application are set to one side and they are used as a means of inducing acquiescence in the workforce with the reshaping of the work environment. The features of this new environment include the rationing of resources around the prioritisation of tasks and an increased interweaving of professional and managerial activities: more professionals are required to take on delegated managerial tasks whose parameters are prescribed by the new stricter statements about objectives and means; through the unprecedentedly great degree and detail of job and practice specification, more direct and indirect managerial involvement is achieved in practices which hitherto were solely the preserve of professionals. The total impact of these changes is still being worked through in the mid-1990s, but is likely to increase the upward accountability of front-line professionals to management and, through their pivotal location between service users and the organisation, head off the empowerment of service users and instead make them subject, through professionals, to the same stringent standards and disciplines. Community care in the 1990s is a notable example. The NHS and Community Care Act 1990 represents an unprecedented off-loading by the State of responsibility for health and social care provision, to newly-created self-managed units for residential, day and domiciliary care. Thus, the quasi-market created by the Act retains State control of key areas such as resources, whilst it 'places SSDs in the crucial role of planning to meet need and to ration demand by need assessment. The market is not allowed to allocate resources, providers will compete, but users will not. Whether a user gets a service will be determined by regulated need assessment by a case-manager' (Kelly, 1991, p. 185). The rhetoric of care planning suggests that services are needs-led. But the reality is that 'the case-manager's budget will be determined by a more global analysis of likely demands based on both demographic and service usage data' (Kelly, 1991, p. 185), and, of course, the total supply of resources is capped by the government, so the role of first line managers and practitioners tends to be to prioritise needs and devise strategies for integrating assessment and care planning with the rationing process.

Social Services Inspectorate

The Social Services Inspectorate was not created out of a vacuum, but inherited a tradition of work through staff transferred into it, stretching back to the poswar period when the children's branch of the Home Office inspected Home Office Approved Schools. In 1970, this responsibility shifted to the newly created Social Work Service in the Department of Health and Social Security, when the 1969 Children and Young Persons Act transformed approved schools into community homes with education on the premises (see Chapter 8). The Social Services Inspectorate had the advantage of being closer to social work practice, but the consequent disadvantage of being less independent of government than the Audit Commission. Henkel notes that when the Audit Commission was set up, under the Local Government Finance Act 1982, social work and the personal social services were very much subject to criticism, 'for failure to protect vulnerable people under their care or supervision or to harness scare resources to effective use' (Henkel, 1994, p. 14). In order to establish its credibility, the SSI had to use the main vehicle of external inspection of services to demonstrate to the government that it could 'identify the sources of problems and provide clear frameworks for putting them right. There were issues of authority at stake: that of the Inspectorate itself and that of government'. (Henkel, 1994, pp. 14–15). Whereas the social work service had relied on what may be called 'connoisseurial' knowledge or practice wisdom with the values implicit and 'little or no attempt made to set clear standards or measures' (Henkel, 1994, p. 15), the SSI set about using consultants and research advice to develop key indicators for service planning performance evaluation using performance indicators, outcome specification and measures and methods of relating inputs to service outputs. Inspections became more grounded in systematic frameworks rather than the 'simple aides-memoires of the past' (Henkel, 1994, p. 15). The method of the SSI, as Herbert Laming, its chief inspector, said in a Radio Four interview on 24 May 1995, was to randomly select local authorities, inspect them and produce reports for ministers and subsequently guidance to enable other providers of services to check the standards of their own practice.

By relating surveys, interview schedules and information derived from observation and discussion with staff, service users and carers, to frameworks independent of social work for the evaluation of services, 'the SSI thus developed a range of tools that could be used for self-evaluation by authorities, in advance of the introduction of local inspectorates in the personal social services under the Children Act 1989 and the NHS and Community Care Act 1990' (Henkel, 1994, p. 15). These Acts strengthened the role of the SSI in monitoring and evaluating policy in practice. By the early 1990s, the SSI had published a series of materials under the titles of *Caring for Quality* (Department of Health, 1990), Inspecting for Quality (Department of Health, 1991) and *Committed to Quality* (Department of Health, 1992), intended for use by managers, inspectors, purchasers and providers of services, front-line workers, services users and carers. The publications included some training (Educational Broadcasting Services Trust, 1992) and consultation documents sharing principles and practice, but others were intended to form the basis for the development of standards and criteria for use by managers, inspectors and others involved in maintaining and evaluating them. (See, for instance, Social Services Inspectorate, 1993a; Social Services Inspectorate, 1993b; Social Services Inspectorate, 1993c.) The developmental approach adopted by the SSI allowed interplay between the standards and criteria being drafted by inspectors being tested and revised during their own inspections (Clough, 1994), as was acknowledged, for example, in the overview inspection report of residential child care services in 11 local authorities (SSI/DH, 1993a, p. 9).

The size of the SSI grew and its scope extended greatly, in its first decade of operation. By the mid-1990s, it employed more than one hundred inspectors; its inspectorial role had extended from sections or establishments within departments to include social services departments as a whole (Shaw, 1995, p. 132). A huge amount of resources was devoted to publications regulating the work of professionals. For example, the SSI issued many volumes of guidance on practice in specific aspects of the work of the personal social services (see, for example, Chapters 5, 8 and 9). It commissioned general guidance on quality assurance of services across the board (James, Brooks and Towell, 1992). Legislation in

1996 underpinned an ongoing review jointly by the Audit Commission and the Department of Health, of 'the economy, efficiency, effectiveness and quality of performance of local authority social services departments' (advertisement for project director, *The Guardian*, 9 March 1996). This significant initiative creates a meta-framework for the inspection of the market-based economy of health and personal social services. The purpose of the proposed programme for joint reviews of local authority social services was set out in 1996 by the Audit Commission as aiming to 'assist authorities to improve the overall quality of services in ways which provide value for money' (Audit Commission and Social Services Inspectorate, 1996, p. 3).

The limitation of the concept of efficiency lies partly in the difficulty of applying it to the operations of organisations whose primary goal is not profit and for which a substitute for money needs to be found as an equivalent to measuring output in monetary terms (Simon, 1957).

Henkel notes that 'neither the SSI nor the Audit Commission has gone so far as to embrace Total Quality Management (TQM), an approach whose roots are in private manufacturing or private service organisations. However, with the advent of competition and markets has come a message that quality, and thus management for quality, is the key to survival. TQM, in part, can be seen as a set of ideas that transcends perceptions of quality control and quality assurance by embedding a corporate system of comprehensive and continuous performance review' (Henkel, 1994, p. 16). Henkel draws a distinction between the achievements of the Audit Commission and the SSI in embedding managerialism in the culture of local delivery of personal social services as 'the power of the manager and the language of targets, measurement and outcome are well embedded' (Henkel, 1994, p. 17), and the lack of coming to grips with the total quality management approach which would require 'obtaining the commitment of all staff of a philosophy of continuous improvement and individual responsibility for quality' (Henkel, 1994, p. 16). Thus the SSI has enable local authorities to move towards achieving their own effective internal monitoring and review of performance, through its development of methods and measures of evaluation of services (Henkel, 1994, p. 18). The SSI plays a direct role in monitoring the quality of practice, but indirectly its reports feed back into education and training and provide the parameters within which the future practice is contained. SSI inspections (for example, SSI, 1994b) have tended to monitor and coordinate links between the extent to which local authorities have implemented key legislation such as the Children Act 1989, NHS and Community Care Act 1990 and Criminal Justice Act 1991. The SSI and the Audit Commission operate as 'the instrument of a more fundamental revolution, the subjection of the public sector to market forces and mechanisms . . . highly consistent with increasing reliance upon contracts rather than evaluative institutions as key external controls' (Henkel, 1994, p. 18). This distinction between managerialist approaches to quality assurance and a genuine espousal of a global approach to quality makes understandable Henkel's scepticism about 'whether this form of control will be in the name of quality as against price in the public sector' (Henkel, 1994, p. 18). It is plain that quality assurance in the human services has been as much a means of monitoring the effectiveness of quasi-markets as a global mechanism for evaluating the quality of services. In other words, the mechanism of quality assurance is accountable to the state and the employer rather than to the professional, the service user and the carer. In achieving this, the methodology of the SSI needs to be sophisticated enough to penetrate local authority practice and assemble a realistic picture of what is going on. Annual reports of the Chief Inspector of the SSI (SSI, 1992; SSI, 1993d; SSI, 1994a; SSI, 1995) give further insight into official perception of this approach, focusing on the user perspective. The SSI fulfilled its function of monitoring the quality of services by gathering two kinds of information: 'general information about what happens in the personal social services' and 'data when carrying out formal inspection duties' (SSI, 1995, p. 67). There was an increased emphasis on gathering users' and carers' views 'about the services they receive', through 'postal questionnaires, meetings with groups of users and carers during inspection, fieldwork, interviews with pre-selected individuals, general invitations to users and carers to make contact with inspectors, and many informal contacts' (SSI, 1995, p. 67).

The assumptions of managerialism derive largely from a rejection of arguments justifying public, that is state, monopolies in any significant aspect of the health, criminal justice and welfare services. This implies hostility to certain groups of employees, notably trade unionists and others regarded as potentially disruptive or disaffected, in the public sector. Public sector employment gives such workers, in what an economist such as Hayek (1960), who has contributed to New Right thinking, would term a producer group, an unacceptable degree of scope to interfere in the free market. Cutler and Waine note that this critique has been extended by the New Right to welfare professionals. According to this, they have the opportunity to intervene in the market place of health and social care, by promoting their special interest, possibly at the expense of the public interest (Cutler and Waine, 1994, p. 14). Social work practitioners and educators who have not accepted new market principles, managerialist control and competence-based training and practice (see Chapter 4), may be perceived as dissidents working to undermine quality assurance, rather than acting as its guardians, by critically scrutinising the assumptions on which prevalent methods are based.

The new managerialist agenda

The new managerialisms occupy a place contested by other, potentially conflicting, interests, such as, in some areas, increasingly vociferous service users. The term 'new managerialism' is used here in recognition of the fact that the version developed in the human services in the 1990s is adapted to the quasi-market situation, in contrast with the precursor concepts of management in industry in the earlier decades of the twentieth century. The new managerialisms express aspects of government 'promotion and support of the values of entrepreneurialism and methods of business management' (Kelly, 1991, p. 178).

The new managerialist agenda – ensuring effective control of the professionals by the managers – is based on assuring the quality of the products of the professionals' work. This is in contrast with the old-style centralised organisation, in which their work would be judged by the extent to which, for example, they had kept within budgets. Although at first sight this description does not conjure up a picture of the local authority social services department, it follows closely the discourse about the shift from so-called service-led to needs-led community care being engineered by the Social Services Inspectorate and the Department of Health in the early 1990s. 'There was, of course, in all this no suggestion that costs were unimportant or that balance sheets did not matter – on the contrary the emphasis was placed on ways of ensuring that value added through quality assurance was paid for at premium rates' (Cochrane, 1994, p. 152).

One outcome of the adoption of quasi-commercial, or new, managerialisms has been the increased tendency of the public sector to claim that it has come of age, in taking on board the experience of commerce and industry and developing the necessary expertise to become enterprising in the market economy. The signs of this – business plans, business consultants, marketing contracts, management consultancies – are in the raising of the profile given in local government to the language of the business world, the discourse of profit and added value. By these means, despite the transformation of local authority social services departments' roles from providing to enabling authorities, new managerialism enables managers to demonstrate their indispensability.

The new social work manager exemplifies the complex, multi-faceted and contradictory nature of the new managerialism: committed to regulating the financial viability of the develolved budget, yet to a needs-based response to clients; retaining control of significant decisions yet advocating empowerment of workers and service users; playing a part in the dominant managerial processes of the organisation, yet attempting to adhere to profess-ional values (see Table 3.1).

Different forms of managerialism, including new managerialism, are capable of changing continuously, to keep pace with profess-

Table 3.1   Two forms of quasi-commercial managerialism

Claimed values	Office/professional	Democratic/empowering
Goals	output directed	outcome/impact based
Working methods	managers direct	all stakeholders participate in management and practice
Relations between stakeholders	hierarchical	cooperative
How agreement achieved	imposed	negotiated

ional discourse. Thus, the coincidence of growth of corporate styles of bureaucratic managerialism from the 1970s, post Seebohm and reorganisation of local government, plus the introduction of quasi-markets, placed in a vulnerable and uncertain position those practitioners and users concerned with managing and working out together the tensions between consumerism and service user empowerment.

The features of quasi-commercial managerialism in the contract culture impact distinctively on workers at all levels: reinforcing age, gender, ethnic, divisions and inequalities, favouring staff with an open-ended commitment to work, thus relatively disadvantaging still further those needing professional and personal development time, or with family commitments (Pringle, 1996). Selling one's self, body and soul, to the agency was more and more the required norm, or taking early retirement and going private, selling services to one's former employer on a spot contract basis.

Hardline and softline new managerialist styles in monitoring and evaluating quality

Managerialism survives in a variety of settings, a context of constant change and a climate of uncertainty by being flexible and as ingenious as the creativity of its adherents can push it. A feature of managerialism in the human services is the ability to take on board to some degree the implications of criticisms and complaints and the working style of operating on the conceptual territory of opponents and critics. In a complex organisation there is room for both the 'softline' manager who has developed this to a fine art and the 'hardline' manager who will have none of it. Some situations demand both working in tandem, side by side. Others offer opportunities for one approach more than the other. This distinction between two styles of manager is simplistic in the sense that in practice many managers operate on the continuum between these extremes and often an experienced manager will switch rapidly between one working style and another.

Softline managerialism is more difficult to confront, since it often shelters behind a claimed commitment to empowering staff and democracy in the workplace. but the softline managerialist monitors every step of the practice, albeit covertly, perhaps in the guise of offering support or consultation. Or, the professional is encouraged to work as part of a team. Direct intervention by the manager at key points of decisionmaking then is more natural, since it occurs, for example, when the manager is called upon to chair case review meetings. Softline managerialism accepts the rigours of the quasi-market but presents the appearance of attempting to reconcile this with the ideals of empowering service users. In the short run, or in face-to-face interaction with practitioners and service users, the softline managerialist – such as a first line manager – is likely to impress as an honest broker whose allegiances lie with colleagues, professionals and professionals and service users rather than with senior management.

Hardline managerialism may be used directly to control and direct policy and practice in the personal social services organisation. Its presence may be cloaked by the activities of softline managers who reinforce the impression of commitment to empowerment, and maximum participation of, service users. But hardline approaches often will dictate the parameters within which softline work takes place. They set boundaries around what can be negotiated, force the pace on a particular change, or impose, for example, a policy of rationing services. One hardline version of managerialism involves the creation of a compliant network of contractors in place of the former sometimes questioning, critical and at times belligerent or intransigent workforce of social workers. Such professional autonomy as existed is held in check by strong management controls, notably the sanction of suspending or cancelling the contract if the products are not considered satisfactory. The rhetoric of consumer satisfaction feeds into this perspective rather than challenging it, in several ways: first, the consumer is not, by definition, a producer or a participant in the production process leading to the design or delivery of the service; second, the consumer represents the dispersed interest of individuals who only become identified as a collective at certain points of consumption (such as the local social services offices), and then only as defined by the service providers (for example, the foyer may have few seats, appointments may be staggered, people may enter by one door and leave by another); third, the power differential between providers and consumers and the social distance between them are sustained by the professional and bureaucratic culture of social workers and the personal social services organisations purchasing and providing services (for example, structures and working methods, so the discourse goes, are so complex that only a simplified version is presented for the information of consumers, thus minimising opportunities for detailed critical questioning of what is provided and how it is provided). Thus, the local authority may set up panels for people to give feedback on the quality of services, but this tends to be simply as consumers, rather than as empowered collaborators in the co-production and delivery of those services (Adams, 1996a, pp. 227–8).

Managerialism, consumerism and empowerment

There are tensions between the themes of managerialism, consumerism and empowerment (Adams, 1996a, pp. 19–23). Tensions between the managerialism which permeates the health and personal social services and the value base of empowering social work are left to the practitioner and first line manager to address, in their interaction with colleagues and work with service users. These tensions generate issues which are not amenable to facile, technical solutions, and actually may be unresolvable.

Mechanisms such as inspection and registration and quality assurance may be employed by senior managers to maintain standards and assure the quality of services.

A consequence of managerialism is that managerial and professional power all too often tended to be deployed at the expense of service users. Managers and professionals dominate the marketplace of the human services rather than service users, in the sense that, in the hospital or in community psychiatric care, for example, patients and carers traditionally have not paid for services, have not been used to having a voice in the standard of care they receive, and have remained relatively powerless in the face of medical professionals. Thus, in some settings managerialism could mean simply the mutually reinforcing deployment of professional and managerial power. Of course, there are professional areas which differ – pupil involvement in project work in schools, for instance – but these have tended to attract increasing criticism from traditionalists, from the late 1980s onwards. Also, whilst parent power up to a point has been encouraged, pupil power has not (Adams, 1991).

Since the late 1970s, there have been tensions in the relationship between generic practitioners and the managers of social services departments. To some extent, these tensions were embodied in the ways the new departments were organised and the transitional problems of change, at the organisational and individual levels. Etzioni's (1969) analysis of the nature of semi-professions provides a partial explanation, in that local authority social workers, for example, are in part expected to make autonomous judgements as professionals in the work for which they are responsible, yet at the same time are local government officers in line management, accountable to office managers. So, in the area of decisionmaking in complex situations, for example, social workers constantly have to reconcile their multiple accountabilities: to service users, colleagues, professional values, their employers and the State.

From the viewpoint of theoretical perspectives on the organisation of the personal social services, though, Ann James points out that the predominant pattern since the 1970s illustrates five main features which derive from Taylor's advocacy of scientific management: first, work is shaped by objectives determining the specification of tasks; second, the specification of specialised tasks is associated with workload measurement and the monitoring of quality to ensure targets are met; third, activities are grouped into functional units and certain activities such as planning are separated from task supervision; fourth formal relationships between individuals in functional units and lines of accountability are set up; fifth, as much authority as possible is delegated to the person responsible for a task (James, 1994, pp. 46–7). James attributes many of the bureaucratic and mechanistic features of the personal social services to the legacy of Taylor's ideas:

> It is difficult to over-estimate the influence of Taylorism on the construction of a post-war industrial Britain. It is even harder to imagine what the newly emerging National Health Service and Local Authority Children's Departments and later Seebohm's Social Services Departments would have looked like without this heritage. The departmental approach, the line management hierarchy, the separation of planning from supervision, the task specification according to function or user group, the specification of objectives from the top, and the delegation of authority are clearly the characteristics of health authorities and local authorities and of the large voluntary agencies who sought to imitate them. Indeed Taylorism and the classical school provided

the ultimate rational process by which the monolithic and bureaucratic organisation personified in William Morris's municipal town hall could deliver services. (James, 1994, p. 47)

Impact of new managerialisms on social work

It could be that the increasing tendency of staff in the personal social services to watch their backs rather than champion the interests of service users fearlessly and forcefully is a consequence of the contract culture rather than managerialism. Probably though, it is a sign of the indivisibility of these combined influences. Without doubt, the development of managerialism in the contract culture leads to the skewing of contractual obligations of staff towards protecting the positions of managers and employers, rather than prioritising the accountability of all membes of the organisation to the public interest in general, and specifically, individual service users. The recommendations of the Nolan Committee go some way to addressing this imbalance, but in the personal social services highlight the need to address shortcomings in existing practice and unevennesses across the public, voluntary and private sectors rather than presenting an even profile of high quality practice (see Chapter 10).

Key indicators for quality management in social work

EXAMPLE 3.2

Hattie, the team manager and David a social worker are discussing the strategy to be adopted in developing a non-managerialist approach in the work of the team. They decide they share some responsibilities and hold some separately. Among their shared responsibilities is the need to develop openness in management style and a willingness to be questioned critically about their respective actions. They decide to meet regularly with the other stakeholders they identify, and who identify themselves, to discuss these issues. They also draw up an immediate list of aspects of their commitment to quality services which managerialist practices put at risk: the need to deliver a value-based service through anti-oppressive management, the necessity for a workplace culture which cares for staff, and the need to develop an empowering organisation. They use these as the starting point for discussion between themselves, and with other colleagues, service users and carers. They recognise that tackling this list is the beginning of an open-ended task, not one with a pre-defined end.

Delivering a value-based service through anti-oppressive management

The increasing emphasis on joint working, partnership and empowerment in the personal social services should be reflected in their management style. The principle of anti-oppressive management needs to be carried into practice. Some key aspects of this have been detailed in the first book of the first module of the Health and Social Services Management programme (Salaman, Adams and O'Sullivan, 1994, pp. 6–22).

Developing a staff care culture

The implication of this for the personal social services is that without an organisation-wide, cultural change in operating practices, the impact of changes affecting contractual obligations of some staff, will be limited. A core feature of the anti-oppressive management style is that it facilitates the development of an organisational culture which nurtures staff, rather than expending, exploiting and ultimately burning them out. Some key aspects of such an approach are being developed in pioneering work by Jeff Hopkins, working in collaboration with Unison and BASW. The first publication in the series of guidelines emerging from this work is entitled *Dealing with Violence and Stress in Social Services* (BASW and Unison, undated) and other titles are in preparation, on such aspects as Staff Care and the Management of Absence from Work, Staff Care and Disciplining Staff, and Staff Care and the Management of Complaints.

Developing an empowering organisation

A senior manager said to me: 'total quality is not achieved in this department by democracy. The systemic approach is not for liberals.' We can reframe this. Democratisation in the workplace is costly, in time and other resources. The process of empowering work cannot be hurried. The manager may not have time to go through the process. The temptation to use a pre-digested package as a checklist and use it like an instruction manual on quality assurance, is to be avoided. Such mechanical techniques have the appeal of superficially democratised processes, but are inherently autocratic, or at best manipulative.

The positive impact of management on service users and carers needs maximising. The effects of new managerialisms, if unchecked, are likely to bring significant harm to service user empowerment. Kelly notes the irony that the bureaucracy of so-called models of administrative is widely citicised by professional practitioners, yet this very bureaucracy is often 'more respectful of claims to professional autonomy' (Kelly, 1991, p. 181) To give one example, the trend towards shorter, task-limited contracts within the personal social services reduces the long-term planning an individual worker can undertake and, consequently, the scope for individuals and groups of such workers to engage in service development and progressive practice.

There is a risk that the new managerialisms will lead to the supplanting of human service values and a balance-sheet approach to corporate and small unit managers alike. Like head teachers ('Heads sacked like soccer managers', *The Guardian*, 1 June 1995), social services staff immersed in the contract culture are more likely than formerly to be hired and fired like football managers, according to league tables of national and local performance.

Nevertheless, the balance-sheet is not all on the debit side. It is true that there is a need for managers to develop statements of purposes, goals, policies, find ways to motivate people, reduce alienation in the workforce, improve morale and adopt collaborative approaches to quality maximisation in specific services. However, there are examples of positive initiatives by management in these directions. Newham's total quality manager Bernadette Manning, co-author of a package of materials on quality in child protection, advocates leadership by management as essential to the development of strategies and procedures. A midlands unitary authority's Social Services Department has a quality manager who is accountable directly to the deputy director (operations). The Department has developed a quality strategy which links with the Department's values statement. The next stage is for this departmental strategy to be linked with the Authority's Children's Services Plan and Community Care Plan and for staff in each of the eight Areas of the unitary authority to develop a statement of local objectives which relates to the Department's strategy and to local needs.

Conclusions

This chapter has shown that, whilst the rhetoric of policy and practice, insofar as it concerns service users in the personal social services, increasingly focuses on participation and empowerment, managerialism operates so as to complicate this endeavour, through redefining power relations, notably between professionals and service users, but also between professionals and managers. The features of managerialism described in this chapter should not create the impression of a conspiracy by powerful managers to subvert the quality of the personal social services. The creation of internal markets in health and the personal social services is predicated on the assumption that a greater diversity of providers will not only improve choice for purchasers and service users, but also will enhance the quality of services. In practice, the greater the number of providers, the more fragmented and complex the task of assuring quality across the sector and, at the very least, ensuring a basic standard is maintained – a greater problem in social services, with a greater number of small providers, than in the area of health. A further problem faced by commissioners and purchasers of social services is the complexity and pace of the changes in the map of provision. This superimposes even more difficulties on an already difficult task (Sang, Lambley and Rush, 1993).

The next chapter considers, among other factors, the impact of different aspects of managerialisms on social work education and training.

4

Quality Education for Social Workers

Professional education for social workers is increasingly vulnerable to the kinds of erosion which threaten to undermine professional practice as a whole. So, a critical examination of key aspects of the struggle to achieve quality education for social workers also offers some indicators as to how quality professional education for social workers may be sustained.

Struggles for quality

Roger, head of a social work department for more than a decade, and Rashinda a lecturer in that department since a year ago, with ten years practice experience, have just been confronting each other in a staff meeting, over many different shortcomings in the Dip.SW. These have affected staff and students adversely over the past six months. Roger's view is that there is nothing to be done but – using his nautical imagery – to keep the department afloat by rocking the boat as little as possible, thereby avoiding discussing the issues because, basically, nothing can be done to improve anything. Rashinda clashes with him because she regards this as the counsel of despair.

This situation, or variants of it, is not uncommon. Social work education is under attack and its context and content have altered dramatically during the working life of the two people portrayed above. This chapter considers these factors and what can be done to address them positively.

Changes in social work education

The growth of provision of education and training for social workers has been stimulated significantly by deficits in practice. The establishment of the first training school for staff in Barnardo's followed a scandal when an 18-year-old girl at a home in the north east of England became pregnant. 'Students studied child care, child psychology, hygiene, first aid and home nursing, children's hobbies, games and Bible story telling' (Anon (undated), *Barnardo's Children*, pamphlet, Ilford). Eileen Younghusband's endeavours in the 1950s to advance the cause of social work training were motivated partly by a desire to level up professional standards of education and practice which were, to say the least, uneven (Adams, 1996a, p. 36).

Those engaged in education and training, whether their stake is as teachers, learners or line managers, work in a fundamentally different environment to that which existed in the 1960s or 1970s. The values of liberal education which permeated many social work and social care, not to say residential care, courses, have been largely superseded by a new discourse. Whilst this shows the influence of the paradigm shift from treatment to empowerment which has taken place since the 1980s (Adams, 1996b), it also takes due account of the significant territory acquired by competence-based approaches to education and training, at N/SVQ and qualifying levels (Kelly, Payne and Warwick, 1990), as well as in post-qualifying and advanced education, and, overlapping these, in the area of management development.

The term 'struggle' seems particularly appropriate, since it echoes the language of a period in the late 1960s and early 1970s when some of the now senior academics and senior managers in the personal social services were political activists. The contenders included the government, academics, with bodies, notably CCETSW, playing an intermediary role between the major interests with a stake in education and training in the personal social services: government, employers, professional social workers, social care staff, university and college staff, researchers, service users and carers and 'the public'. Social work education and training shows the impact of the contract culture, with programmes and educational institutions being forced to compete in the marketplace of the purchase and provision of education and training services.

The cause of managerialism in social work education and training has been advanced on the grounds of the desperate need to improve quality, in the light, for example, of successive scandals highlighting the shortcomings of practice. This aim has been furthered by a move towards competence-based education and training and the reduced status and deskilling of what traditionally might be regarded as specifically professionally qualified social work tasks – task-centred social work, for example – relative to other functions such as managing care plans.

Probation services under the pressures of financial constraints from the mid-1990s increasingly sought to contain and reduce spending by freezing staffing and filling vacancies internally, often through directing staff from one post to another. However, since such tactics did not increase the overall pool of available staff, some services resorted to filling vacancies through the competitive internal advertising, for example, of probation officer posts to other grades, such as that of professionally unqualified probation service officer (PSO). Other services began to contract out services to the voluntary and private sectors and considered allocating to administrative and PSO grades some basic functions such as holding reporting centres for individuals and groups of clients, or conducting initial interviews with clients. These methods had in common the sacrifice of quality professional services to the goal of cost-saving.

Impact of criticisms of social work on professional education

In the mid-1990s, social work was under increased attack by the government. Many shortcomings of practice which were the outcome of a complex mix of political, policy, organisational, managerial and practice factors, were laid at the door of social workers, either individually or as a profession. In 1995, the then chair of CCETSW Geoffrey Greenwood described low public confidence in social workers, with 75 per cent of residential staff and 93 per cent of home help staff remaining unqualified in the workforce of the personal social services (*The Guardian*, 22 September 1995). The most comprehensive survey to date of the experiences of CQSW and Dip.SW students up to the point of qualification, and their supervisors, identified many weaknesses in current programmes in England, Wales (Marsh and Triseliotis,

1996) and Scotland (Triseliotis and Marsh, 1996). In particular, only half of former students attributed their readiness to practise to the quality of their course; 40 per cent of practice placements were described as poor.

Quality assurance: increased control over education of social services staff

Measures set up by bodies such as the Central Council for Education and Training in Social Work (CCETSW) for the purpose of quality assurance, in effect, operate as long-arm means by which central government exercise increasing, if indirect, control over how professionals worked in practice. The delivery of quality services following the Children Act 1989 and the NHS and Community Care Act 1990 depended on improved standards of practice in social care and social work. From the mid-1980s, national standards for performance, education and training were developed, initially by the National Council for Vocational Qualifications, and subsequently by CCETSW, which effectively provided a framework – linked undisguisedly to claims for the consequent enhancement of quality – for the central enhanced regulation of social care training and qualifying and post-qualifying social work education. The Autumn edition of the Local Government Management Board publication *Towards a Quality Workforce* (Anon, 1993, p. 1) for example, contained an article on page 1 under the headline 'Achieving Quality' which asserted that 'this movement 'towards a quality workforce', affecting and involving the whole of British industry, is not just about rationalising and improving the UK's qualifications framework. It is also about establishing measures of what people should be achieving in the workplace to be effective now, and in the foreseeable future. . . Local authorities can immediately make use of the published standards for a whole range of workers.' Ironically though, the role of CCETSW in the shaping of the standards for the social work profession of the mid-1990s has amounted to that of regulator rather than liberator (Jones, 1996a; Webb, 1990–1).

Responsibility for assuring the quality of qualifying and post-qualifying education and training for social workers in the UK rests with CCETSW. Quality assurance is carried out on the basis of CCETSW's published standards (CCETSW, 1996). CCETSW's role, consistent with the general approach of the government, involves ensuring that social work programmes equip qualifying social workers to perform to a minimum 'national occupational' (CCETSW 1996, p. 4) standard of basic competence, rather than making quality statements based on the goal of striving for excellence in practice. There is a significant gap between this quality maintenance approach of CCETSW and the goal of quality maximisation outlined in Chapter 2.

There is a need to sustain quality professional and post-qualifying education for social workers in the face of policies and responses to social work and social workers which threaten this. But ambivalence is sometimes expressed by politicians and the public, and in the mass media, towards what social workers do. In suspected child abuse cases, for example, they are vilified at one time for intervening too readily to protect children, and at another for not intervening sufficiently early or strongly. This ambivalence runs alongside more hostile attitudes towards the anti-oppressive values of the social work profession expressed increasingly openly in the latter years of the last Conservative government.

The moves by government described in Chapter 3 to develop managerialist styles and competence-based educational strategies may not consciously represent a collective will to undermine the social work profession. But their negative impact is clearly discernible on the social work profession (Cannan, 1994/5). It is exemplified also in the critique by social work educators, in the face of the undermining of the social work profession by social policy and government (Jones, 1989) and the downgrading and derogation of social work education (Jones, 1996b). But social work educators had been on the defensive for a decade or more, previous to this. Social work educators had expressed alarm collectively since the mid-1980s about the hostile political and social climate perceived as threatening the integrity of professional social work as a critical presence in higher education (Harris, Barker, Reading, Richards, and Youll, 1985, p. xiii).

The shape of the workforce in the contract culture lends itself to enhanced regulation rather than the creation of a radical agenda for an empowering practice (Webb, 1996). The vast majority of community care is required by law to be delivered by providers in the independent sector. Child protection services in some areas are moving in the same direction. Increasing numbers of social workers are contracted to service providers by agencies supplying temporary and sessional staff. The re-creation of the workforce as a dispersed interest mirroring the fragmented interests of service users and carers, is the antithesis of circumstances which might further social services as a learning culture. Many former full-time staff now are re-contracted on part-time or sessional contracts. Such trends increase divisions in a workforce in the personal social services already working in conditions of great uncertainty and stress.

Social work education in crisis

Social work education and training is in crisis. This crisis partly revolves around tangible questions such as the supply of resources. Partly though, it is an issue of the nature and credibility of university and college-based professional education.

The changing nature of the workforce in the personal social services generates fresh, ever more complex demands for education and training for staff, in a resource-constrained environment where full-time, or even part-time paid, release from work to study is becoming less likely. The creation of quasi-markets in the 1990s has strengthened the positions of purchasers and providers in the personal social services relative to educational institutions, which have had little alternative but to agree to providing N/SVQ (Care Sector Consortium, 1991 and 1992) and qualifying Dip.SW programmes with broadly similar competence-based approaches. At post-qualifying and advanced levels, the development of a consortium-based framework by CCETSW has encountered sufficiently diverse reactions from established and new agency or university programme providers, to create a hiatus in developments whilst an accommodation between existing provision and new regulations is negotiated. A further complication is the tension between the often expressed wish of professional bodies such as CCETSW for a UK-wide approach to such matters. This is in the face of the reality of the diversity of the organisation and legal basis for social work, in Wales, Scotland, Northern Ireland and England.

This fact that some aspects of education and training are UK-wide, as opposed to specific to one or more of the four countries Wales, Scotland, Northern Ireland and England, makes the analysis of education and training issues more complex.

CCETSW occupied a somewhat ambiguous position (which critics from government and radical perspectives could equally have viewed as precarious) between employer and educational interests, with right-wing politicians from the 1980s onwards increasingly ready to use alleged shortcomings of social work education and training as evidence that CCETSW was not doing its job. In the face of this undermining activity, pressure from practitioners, educators and specific interests such as Black, disabled and women's groups, from the mid-1980s, contributed to CCETSW playing a positive role in advocating, and publishing, on behalf of an increasingly clearly articulated view of anti-oppressive practice. On the other hand, however, CCETSW played the key role in restructuring education and training to reflect the priorities of the government, in two key ways: it brought the statement of minimum requirements for social workers in the UK at the point of qualification into line with the occupational standards developed for care workers at N/SVQ levels 2, 3 and 4; it introduced a notion of partnership based on consortia of educational and employer interests, rather than perpetuating the traditional roles of universities and colleges as what might be termed 'lead bodies' in this area. Whilst advocates of competence-based and employer-led training supported such changes, critics alleged that their combined impact amounted to a dilution of the content of qualifying programmes and downgrading of educational standards. Finally, partly in response to strong criticism from government on the grounds of its alleged skewed value base towards some discriminated-against groups – notably Black people and women – at the expense of a generalist equality perspective, and partly because of demands that its use of funds was more tightly regulated, in 1995 CCETSW instituted a new and elaborate system of quality monitoring in social work qualifying programmes throughout the UK.

The credibility of social work education has less clearcut boundaries than some of the more material, resource-based issues, but is just as important; it revolves around a loss of confidence on the part of some employers of social workers that social work educators can deliver meaningful, relevant training within the existing frameworks. The legitimacy of social work education as a largely university-based enterprise has been questioned increasingly since the late 1970s, when CSS (Certificate in Social Services) schemes came into being. There has been a trend in higher education since the mid-1980s towards more flexible provision, including more work-based and part-time programmes, especially in the former polytechnics, now the new university sector. Since the 1980s, employers have pressed successfully for a larger stake in social work education and training. Where formerly they only achieved parity as partners with colleges, in running the Certificate in Social Services (CSS) schemes, now they take part as joint partners with universities and colleges, in all qualifying and post-qualifying programmes in the UK approved by CCETSW.

Debates about the nature and quality of education and training since the 1980s have focused on a number of related aspects: the issue of quality and standards, in the relationship between education and training: the vulnerability of the former to dilution by the latter; the question over the validity and the appropriateness in social work education and training of competence-based approaches, particularly those continuous with N/SVQs; the debates about the positive or negative impact of quasi-markets on social work; the place of anti-oppressive/discriminatory practice and equal opportunities policies and practices; the complex, and fragile, bureaucratic partnerships between service providers and educational institutions managing social work programmes; shortages of adequately resourced learning opportunities; the nature of, and links between, structures, standards and assessment in qualifying, post-qualifying and advanced programmes; and finally, the drive of the Home Office till 1997 to remove qualifying training for probation officers from higher education.

There is a question as to whether creating internal markets in health and social care, and importing other aspects of the business approach, plus the shift to employer-led N/SVQ-style training with its disaggregation of complex tasks into components, fragments the process of delivering quality services and, in effect, leads to similar alienating consequences for the workforce as does the adoption of assembly-line work in manufacturing industry.

Factors affecting social work education

Education and training is central to the goal of developing quality social work, but is often relegated to the sidelines in considerations of how to achieve quality. This paradox is more striking, given the centrality of educational institutions in both social work research and devising and operating education and training programmes in social work. Also, it is ironic that such a seemingly marginal profession in terms of its size and status, when taken alongside the healthcare professions, should attract the consistently high level of direct intervention by ministers that social work apparently warranted during the early 1990s.

The struggle for quality social work educaton takes place in the context of massive expansion in the further and higher education sector. There are increasing demands from students for more, and more advanced, education and training, and from employers for reliable, qualified staff, the widespread adoption in the personal social services, of competence-based approaches to education and training and the growth of work-based training, notably in probation work, closely tied into the NCVQ framework of practical competences – one possibility feared by Parsloe at the beginning of the decade (Parsloe, 1990, p. 209).

The move towards competence-based approaches to qualifying education reflects and reinforces the translation into policy and practice of 'the ascendancy of training over education', as employers have developed their roles in determining vocational competence (Issitt and Woodward, 1992, p. 43). It also illustrates the fact that 'at all levels the education systems itself is being reformed and the vocational and academic are being linked together' (Issitt and Woodward, 1992, p. 43). The adoption of competence-based approaches links directly with the growth of the new managerialism. Issitt and Woodward draw on the work of Davies and Durkin (1991), who point out how the needs of the employers and the market are increasingly equated with the 'national interest'. Thus, 'the notion of competence is an important ingredient in operationalising social policy solutions to current economic and political problems in which the lack of competitiveness of British industry and unemployment are two major factors' (Issitt and Woodward, 1992, p. 42). Issitt and Woodward distinguish two approaches to competence: 'one bottom-up, reflecting the needs and interests of ordinary people, the other enshrined in top-down policies that are part of the restructuring of all the state's activities in welfare. The former stresses the importance of providing alternative routes to professional competence, with the starting point being the needs of the client group or consumer. The latter prescribes, with all the power of government behind it, what is thought to be required by employers to get Britain out of its present economic morass' (p. 44). Issitt and Woodward (1992) identify three particular features of the concept of competence – its specification, teaching and assessment – as the jumping-off point for a detailed critique of its application in the human services (pp. 45–51). Central to this critique are three aspects: the need to maintain a service-use and worker-based practice, rather than simply instrumentally implementing employers' requirements (p. 53); to avoid reducing competence statements to a minimalist position 'that does not embrace the creative, intuitive and anti-oppressive nature of progressive work with people' (p. 52); and for the process of qualification to transcend the tension between being divisible into manageable units which learners and assessors find meaningful and providing a holistic, educational route to progressive practice.

Quality assurance is potentially a two-edged weapon, wielded by management either as an end in itself or as a means to the end of cutting resources. The development of occupational standards for social workers and probation officers enabled managements to reallocate to administrative staff some tasks formerly carried out by them. For example, in 1997, Unison opposed the recruitment by Liverpool social services of 18 non-professionally qualified 'resources officers' to act as duty officers in the local authority's eleven field work offices. Unison regarded the argument that this would free social workers from paperwork as a rationalisation for the provision of services on the cheap by employing unqualified staff at lower rates of pay than qualified social workers (Cooper, 1997, p. 2).

It has been easier for this approach by the NCVQ to be adopted at the lower levels than at higher levels, partly because more immediate questions can be focused on the expertise of occupations where training is obviously limited, such as in child-minding, than at the higher levels such as the work of surgeons, where there is a good deal of public faith in a higher level of expertise. In the latter case, it may be much more difficult to establish that what went wrong in a particular case had anything to do with the failures of the system of training staff. Much more commonly, questions of shortcomings in services tend to revolve around the issue, for example, as to whether an individual surgeon was incompetent, for other reasons. In contrast, the abduction on

14 August 1992 of a baby by a person claiming to be a child-minder led to increasing pressure for compulsory registration of all people who care for children as child-minders. At that time, the process of registering all child-minders by local authorities, which is required by the Children Act 1989, was still incomplete, in the sense that nannies and baby-sitters still did not have to be registered (Adams, 1994, p. 86).

Criticisms may be made of competence-based approaches to professional education and training, on the basis that they focus selectively on skills, neglect personal qualities which are difficult to measure and tend not to reflect readily the conceptual basis of critical reflection and action (Cockerill, 1989; Mangham and Silver, 1986; Sparrow and Bognano, 1993; Tichy, 1983). National Vocational Qualifications (NVQs) and Scottish Vocational Qualifications (SVQs) have led to some employers and educators being hesitant about adopting them in their programmes. Nevertheless, in the UK competence-based approaches, in the joint OLF/OU management development programme in health and social services, for instance, claim to have addressed these criticisms with significant success (Open Learning Foundation, National Health Service Training Directorate and Open University, 1994).

Social work: vulnerability to attack

For many years, the semi-professionalism, problematic knowledge base and contested areas of practice of social work have contributed to its low status relative to other areas of health and welfare services (Adams, 1996a, ch. 1). In contrast with the older, traditional professions of medicine and law, the autonomy and standards of social work as a newer, or semi-profession, are under attack, probably to a greater extent even than nursing or teaching. In contrast with other countries in Europe, in the UK, 'professional claims to autonomy are uneasily balanced against the legitimate claims of government to ensure efficiency and efficacy in service delivery and to curtail general public expenditure' (Wrigley and McKevitt, 1994, p. 82). The rationing of resources, in which social workers play a gatekeeping role, involves a reformulation of what is core public sector activity and what should be left to voluntary and private endeavour. Simultaneously with the upgrading of their gatekeeping role as rationers of public services, the supplanting of the medico-treatment paradigm with the paradigm of empowerment (Adams, 1996b) gives them even less claim than hitherto to the unique territory of knowledge, values and expertise which necessarily underpins the professional enterprise (Nokes, 1967). Hence, in the 1990s, social workers are particularly vulnerable to undermining of their status as autonomous professionals:

> Doctors, lawyers and teachers, overwhelmingly state employees, were (and still are) allowed to codify their own standards and guidelines, entry requirements and promotion criteria. It is only in the last decade that sustained state attention has been given to the curtailment or abridgement of these professionals' 'freedoms'. This process has largely been an adversarial one, reflected in the idea that a managerialist ethic is now in the ascendant, with the professionals on the defensive, ethically, socially and economically. . . Such a perspective is, of course, overblown; yet it does reveal an important point. The professional cadre of public service employees *is* on the defensive, their traditions and sapiential authority *is* being questioned, their legitimacy *is* under close and sustained scrutiny. Academic commentary on professionals is largely couched in terms of power analysis: its framework is underpinned by the notion that professionalism is, by and large, a cloak for self-interest, that its ethical base is a measure of social closure not a means for standards in service delivery. (Wrigley and McKevitt, 1994, p. 81)

Although debates over education and training issues seem marginal, the thrust of critics towards marginalising them may derive from a desire to destabilise a source of professional power, and therefore threat. One way of weakening the social work profession is to undermine it by loosening its roots in qualifying and post-qualifying education and research. An example of this was the refusal of the Conservative government in the 1980s to grant the case of social work educators and CCETSW for a three-year qualifying diploma in social work (QDSW). One consequence was that the two-year Diploma in Social Work was developed in the late 1980s to replace the existing CQSW and CSS as the UK qualification for social workers, whilst the Irish Republic moved towards most of the rest of Europe by adopting a three-year qualification.

The Conservative government, with hindsight, were unlikely to have agreed to lengthening qualifying social work programmes from two to three years, as proposed in 1987 by CCETSW. Of the two possible scenarios outline by Parsloe in 1990 – one of a growing partnership between educators and employers investing in their respective strengths; the other of 'an employer take-over with the logical result that social work education will be largely in-service and closely tied into the NCVQ framework, where employment competencies are the desired end' (Parsloe, 1990, p. 209) – the current situation approximates more to the latter.

Uncertain future of qualifying programmes for probation officers

In the probation area, in the early 1990s the Home Office indicated its intentions to impose its own training agenda on the profession and separate it from higher education, what the then Home Secretary Michael Howard viewed as the negative influence of some universities. In the resulting struggle, the civil servants in the Home Office may have been surprised at the unanimity and the strength of the opposition mobilised against the proposals, from the CVCP, ACPO, NAPO, JUC/SWEC to the MPs of all political parties who spoke against them in debates in April and December 1995 in the House of Lords, the second of which led to the government being defeated (but to a reversal in the Parliamentary Home Affairs Committee the following day). The review of probation training led to the publication of the Dews Report (Dews and Watts, 1995) and on 29 September 1995, Michael Howard announced his agreement with the recommendations of the Dews Report, his intention both to distance probation qualifying training from the Diploma in Social Work and to encourage the recruitment of personnel who had worked formerly in the police and the armed services. Opposition was fierce, notably from the National Association of Probation Officers (NAPO), the Association of Chief Probation Officers (ACPO), JUC/SWEC and probation qualifying programmes in universities. A well-orchestrated campaign began with a debate in the House of Lords on 14 April 1995, during which no less that three former Home Secretaries spoke against the proposals, coming to a crescendo in autumn of

1995, when NAPO announced it was seeking a judicial review to challenge the Home Secretary's intentions.

The Dews Report which was published in February 1995, simultaneously with the final draft of the CCETSW review of the Dip.SW, reflected the Home Office view that the future of qualifying training for probation officers lay in the workplace, cut off from the Dip.SW, although perhaps using modules supplied by the universities. Dews was consonant with the view of the then Home Secretary Michael Howard, that the probation service should become more of a correctional service than hitherto and that entry should be extended to allow former staff from the armed services to enter and qualify as probation officers, through an employment-based route. The appointment of probation service officers (PSOs) as apprentice probation officers contributed to the strategy of replacing university-based qualification programmes with work-based training.

The threat to the quality of qualifying education for probation officers which with the publication of the Dews Report (Dews and Watts, 1995) was manifest five years earlier, in relation to plans to strengthen punishment in the community, with a corresponding shift in probation officers' roles, towards control and away from treatment. Allan refutes the argument running through government plans for community service (Home Office, 1988a), the Green Paper *Punishment, Custody and the Community* (Home Office, 1988c) and the proposals for bail hostels (Home Office, 1988b) 'that the courts do not have full confidence in the alternatives to custody run by the probation services because they are insufficiently punitive' (Allan, 1990, p. 29). The corollary to this argument is a matchless example of scapegoating, as Allan implies, for 'as a result, offenders are being unnecessarily sentenced to imprisonment and the probation service is being blamed for the crisis in the prisons' (Allan, 1990, p. 29).

The arguments of the Dews Report may have been fuelled in part by the disenchantment of long-qualified staff with the CQSW courses they had undertaken. But there was a prevalent view, reflected in the Dews Report, that the areas of particular practice in probation work, of the successor to CQSW, the Dip.SW, represented a marked improvement. But that the Dews Report was driven by managerialist concerns, was illustrated in the lessons drawn in a consultant's report (Dews and Watts, 1995, F Annex) between the recruitment and training of air traffic controllers, youth workers, speech therapists and probation officers.

The widespread campaign of opposition to the Dews Report delayed the inexorable government move towards the development of a work-based professional qualification – possibly in the form of a diploma in probation studies – for probation staff. By February 1997, dissension within the Home Office-led steering group responsible for developing new NVQ-style competences ground this exercise to a halt. After Labour's victory in the General Election of May 1997 it seemed increasingly likely that some compromise would be agreed by the Home Office, with universities still playing a major role in a higher education professional qualifying programme for probation officers, but at a discrete distance from any social work programmes.

Registration of staff in the personal social services

Repeated inquiries into shortcomings of social work have highlighted the lack of control by UK-wide, national, or local authorities over the nature and quality of staff employed in the personal social services. The inquiry report on Castle Hill School (Brannan, Jones and Murch, 1992) states that Ralph Morris, the proprietor, used false qualifications to promote the school (Gulbenkian, 1993, p. 140). Following a National Institute for Social Work report in 1990, which recommended the setting up of a General Social Services Council, an action group was set up in January 1992, with a brief to 'promote and improve standards of practice, training and conduct in the personal social services . . . primarily through the registration of those working in the services, and through the regulation of conduct and practice' (Gulbenkian, 1993, p. 152). The action group notes: 'Recent inquiries, such as that of the Warner Committee, have exposed the lack of an effective, co-ordinated system for excluding from employment those found guilty of serious misconduct and criminal offences. The existence of a register should assist in preventing such cases from recurring' (General Social Services Council Action Group Final Report, 1993, quoted in Gulbenkian, 1993, p. 153).

Future directions for social work education

Three possible scenarios of the future can be envisaged. The first is that social work partners health care in new configurations and alliances which do not swamp it, but enable progressive practice, sometimes collaborative, sometimes involving meta-professional identities, e.g. in community care, to emerge. A variant on this, the second scenario is the prospect of bypassing, and transcending, the competence approach espoused by CCETSW, as programmes of education and training in the human services become more diverse. The Dip.SW would simply become less relevant as educational provision and social work practice moved beyond it. Finally, the Domesday scenario views social work as disappearing from higher education, perhaps following the review of further and higher education undertaken by Sir Ronald Dearing in the mid-1990s (National Committee of Further and Higher Education, 1997). Consequently, qualifying social work would move towards further education and post-qualifying and advanced towards that part of the university sector also involved in research. Thus, the merging of basic social work qualifications with N/SVQs would involve a competence-based approach buttressing managerialist moves to curb professional autonomy. Noel Timms's comment on the Dip.SW in 1991 foreshadows this nightmarish future:

> Social work is now to be considered as a collection of assessable competencies from which social work emerges fundamentally as a matter of management: the selves of social workers and clients are to be managed as are time, objectives, limited contacts, packages and resources. In terms of the traditionally formulated twin objectives of social work (cause and function, the expressive and the instrumental), the new Diploma represents the triumph of function and of an instrumental orientation. Above all, the Diploma represents a significant increase in the Council's (CCETSW's) control of the profession rather than in its concern that social work should flourish. (Timms, 1991, p. 213)

Dominelli argues that the introduction of such a competence-based approach to social work training, through the revised CCETSW Paper 30 (CCETSW, 1996) and the procedures for quality assuring the Dip.SW (CCETSW, 1995a, 1995b), contributes to the deprofessionalisation of social workers (Dominelli, 1996).

Towards quality social work education

Ironically, given the determination of Home Secretaries in both pre-May 1997 Conservative and post-May 1997 Labour governments to reduce the stake of higher education in the professional training of probation officers through the Diploma in Social Work, there is widespread satisfaction with the existing system among educators, employers and newly qualified practitioners. Marsh and Triseolitis refer to probation as 'the jewel in the crown' of the system of professional education in social work in the UK (Marsh and Triseliotis, 1996, p. 203), though they specify weaknesses in Scotland, such as criticisms by newly qualified staff of qualifying training, induction courses and supervision (Triseliotis and Marsh, 1996, p. 67). However, the survey by Marsh and Triseliotis suggests nine reasons why newly qualified probation staff enter practice significantly better prepared than their social services counterparts:

> the clear agency view of the need for training that appears to affect motivation; the protected, defined place that work with offenders has on social work courses; specialised class units at the earliest stages; probation staff directly involved with class teaching; two probation placements; the quality of supervision both during training and in work; the matching between training and work; relative continuity between last placement and work; induction, in-service training and workloads organised specifically and appropriately for newly qualified staff. (Marsh and Triseliotis, 1996, p. 209)

EXAMPLE 4.2

Rashinda recognises the paralysis which has gripped Roger, her head of department (see Example 4.1), and convinces that person and all other staff, together with a number of students and some staff from agency partners, to spend a full awayday off campus. Half the day is spent working in pairs and small groups facilitating each other in identifying problems. The remainder of the time is spent working out a set of agreed principles for future action. At the same time, 'staff care' (see Chapter 3) measures are taken to support any individuals and groups who can be identified as suffering from isolation, alienation or loss of morale. The following headings in italics represent the list of principles worked out. It is augmented by the extract from the research of Marsh and Triseliotis, which was just published in time for the awayday, and which a colleague brought to that meeting:

Developing a political and policy culture which endorses the value of social work

The foundation of quality social work is adequate support by policy-makers and politicians for the stakeholders in professional education and training of social workers. Ideological support is necessary, as well as financial and human resources. Rather than passively accepting dominant reality, members of the department, and their partners and other contacts, contribute actively to various local, regional and UK-wide networks and organisations concerned with promoting social work values and social work as a force for change. Not only does this energise the staff and students, but it also provides allies, when pressures within the department, or the locality, are great.

A progressive curriculum for career-long education

Educators and employers need to regard social work education as a career-long continuum, rather than as ending at the point where a social worker becomes qualified (Marsh and Triseliotis, 1996, p. 220). Members of the department, agency partners and students develop their ideas about transforming the course provision and constructive proposals emerge within a short timespan, which, ironically, because of the enormous demand in the personal social services for enhanced expertise, and the increasingly market-driven university environment, are welcomed by managers.

Recognition of the demanding nature of social work

Newly qualified social workers in the survey in the early 1990s by Marsh and Triseliotis identified a formidable list of expectations of what makes a good and/or competent social worker: 'being non-judgemental and having a sound value base; having problem-solving ability, clarity of direction and capacity to make assessments; possessing professional knowledge and know-how; understanding of law and procedures; being able to relate, [being able to] communicate and listen; [being able to]show care and respect for people; [being able to] have empathy and a sense of humour; [being able to] have life experiences and self-knowledge; being honest, patient, confident to challenge; possessing personal strengths and resilience' (Marsh and Triseliotis, 1996, p. 202).

Adequate, appropriate education for social workers

The contents of a desirable qualification programme for social workers identified by Marsh and Triseliotis (1996, pp. 219–20) include:

- 'relevant connections to previous student experience (including the role of that experience in low motivation for training);
- clear and different routes for different specialisms, with agreed generic core content;
- an agreed practice curriculum, including practice placements/supervision, with close involvement with the courses;
- a match between specialism (covering both practice and teaching) and the first job and/or the matching of last placement and work;
- practice staff directly involved in class teaching;
- enhanced quality of social work teaching, with an agreed curriculum for social work theory, and good practical examples of theory in action;
- much greater attention paid to the teaching of social work skills using concrete practice situations;
- an increased level of law teaching;
- better and more applied teaching of psychology;
- teaching on information technology and on finance;
- increased attention to the writing of reports;
- tutors with on-going social work experience and practice teachers/supervisors who are familiar with theory – possible a combined role;
- an agreed approach to the place of child protection skills and knowledge in basic and post-qualifying training.'

Professional education for social workers requires more resources and, as part of the commitment of CCETSW and employing agencies to quality maximisation, should be located in the context of the goal of 100 per cent qualification rates for staff in social services and social work departments as a whole. It should be anticipated that empowered students will become more vociferous and more litigious. This is already happening. Alison Utley reported in early 1997 a number of cases of students suing their colleges and universities for alleged shortfalls in the courses they were undertaking (Utley, 1997, p. 4). It may be argued that teachers, trainers and researchers in social work should also become more assertively critical and contribute to the transformation of social work, and social work education into activity for change. This would generate challenges to the trend towards a higher educational culture dominated by new managerialism and enterprise rather than educational values: to challenge aspects of the contract culture in which social work education is immersed and, most urgently and to confirm the essentially political nature of the operation and content of professional education for social workers.

Conclusions

This chapter has examined the main factors contributing to the very tangible problems experienced by all involved in social work education – academic staff, practice teachers, students and others. It has attempted to set out a possible strategy and an agenda which offers a way out of the alienation, isolation and loss of morale which may be experienced by individuals and groups in such circumstances.

The next chapter analyses aspects of proceduralism and standardisation in criminal justice work which illustrate the key features of quality maintenance. This is the first of the four approaches outlined in Chapter 2, which are considered in turn in the remaining chapters of this book.

5

Maintaining Quality: Standardisation and Proceduralism in Criminal Justice Work

Standards and procedures make a major contribution to the process of quality assurance. But under certain conditions the processes of standard setting and proceduralisation may become less helpful, or even counter-productive. This may happen, for example, when they become fetishised as ends in themselves, rather than used as tools in the pursuit of professional excellence. At their worst, standards may simply convey to staff the message 'never mind your thoughts about this situation, this is what you have to do'.

Standards and procedures may be portrayed either as the best way to guarantee services, or as eroding vulnerable areas of professional practice. This chapter considers the potential and limitations of standard setting and the devising of procedures. These should not be regarded as ultimate goals of quality assurance, but simply as important contributors en route.

Standard setting and proceduralism: examples and trends

EXAMPLE 5.1

Matilde is a social worker working with a couple experiencing marital problems. The husband, a schedule 1 offender (that is, with a conviction for a serious sex offence), is on supervision to a probation officer, having recently been discharged from serving more than three years of a four-year prison sentence. She has just had a phone call to say that the only daughter, aged 14, has made an allegation whilst at school, that her father has been abusing her over a period of years.

The social worker needs to follow procedures governing situations where abuse is disclosed. This situation is complicated by the existing relationship of the offender with the probation service, the need to clarify what precisely was disclosed at school, and to whom, what happens next as far as investigating and meeting the interests of family members is concerned, and communicating with police and other agencies what is happening, so that they can take any necessary action.

As far as the procedures are concerned, the social worker may have views and feelings about the requirement to work within procedures. The worker may view procedures with enthusiasm, indifference or hostility, or at times, different combinations of these. A procedurally-based approach is described by one quality manager as 'not likely to appeal to liberals' and as 'more suited to people who like to work with and within closed systems' (personal communication to the author). This highlights two features of proceduralism: its suitability for managerial control where mechanisms of self-regulation are non-existent or weak; its tendency in some circumstances to erode or override the autonomy of the professional. In complex and difficult areas of practice and straightforward areas alike, however, procedures have the merit of bringing a level of standardisation to practice, which otherwise would be difficult to attain.

Standard setting as a stage in quality assurance

Standard setting is inadequate as a final goal in quality assurance, but may be regarded as a key stage in the process. It may form part of approaches to quality maintenance or enhancement, though it commonly stops short of maximisation. Two forms of standards setting are noteworthy: in particular services and across the UK and Europe. These are closely related and may interact, of course, but are considered in turn below.

Trend towards setting standards in particular services   Since the early 1980s, there has been a significant move towards publishing standards for a wide range of services, among which criminal justice and probation services are only a small part. These have included work with children in the form of no less than ten volumes of procedures for implementing the Children Act 1989 in key areas such as fostering, adoption, guardianship and family placement (Department of Health, 1991d), work with deaf–blind people (Social Services Inspectorate, 1989b), residential care of older people, (Department of Health, 1989b; Department of Health, 1990a), residential care for people with a physical disability (Department of Health, 1990b), residential care of people with mental health problems (Department of Health, 1992e), and residential care of people with learning disabilities (Department of Health, 1992c). Significantly, perhaps, there is no legislation underpinning standards for home care and pre-school work with parents and children. Some local authorities have taken initiatives and published their own guidance on good practice (see, for instance, Humberside County Council, undated). Such standards are not always published by official bodies. They may be developed in the independent, that is, private and voluntary, sector, partly as a means of advancing the case for improved services, for example, in such areas as daycare and residential establishments for older people (Centre for Policy on Ageing, 1984), services for people with terminal illnesses (National Association of Health Authorities and Trusts, 1991) and home-based care and inspecting and registering providers of social services, for example, in nursing homes (National Association of Health Authorities and Trusts, 1985).

Standards and procedures do not in themselves assure quality. Experience in the London Borough of Newham social services department suggests that they are no necessary guarantee that practice will become more consistent and quality improve (Manning, 1996, p. 6).

Setting standards across the UK and Europe Two main sets of standards are applicable to products and services in the UK – British Standards and European Standards. These are published, and from time to time updated, by Standards Boards operating under the aegis of the British Standards Institute (BSI). This is the independent London-based body responsible for preparing British Standards.

The main standards consist of the following equivalent British and European standards: BS 4778/ISO 8402 and BS5750/ISO 9000/ISO 9001. British Standard BS 5750 was very widely referred to in the UK from 1987 to 1994 as the authoritative standard against which to judge quality systems. From 1994, BS 5750 was incorporated in the European Standard 9001 (BS EN ISO 9001: 1994), which has the status of a British Standard (BS). The other international standard of relevance is ISO 8402 (BS EN ISO 8402: 1995), which contains definitions of concepts used in quality assurance.

Using British Standards as a route to assuring quality in the personal social services in general and social work in particular, suffers from two major weaknesses: the process by which such standards are developed and their consequent character. Steve Casson observes that BS 5750 and ISO 9000 are not in themselves quality awards or definitions of quality, or even comprehensive definitions of how to assure quality, but simply provide 'a definition, agreed internationally, of the systematic elements of good management practice' (Casson and George, 1993, p. 151).

The process of developing these standards is by committees dominated by commercial organisations and bodies representating industrial and manufacturing. Thus, BS 5750 was developed by Technical Committee QMS/22 of the BSI, among the 64 members of which, mining, steel, railways, engineering aerospace, surveying and motor manufacturers were represented. The closest bodies to the personal social services were the Association of British Healthcare Industries, the British Surgical Trades Association and the Health and Safety Executive. The University of Salford was the only educational institution represented (British Standard BS EN ISO 9001: 1994, inside front cover). Unsurprisingly, given the constituent bodies involved in its formulation, the character of British Standard 5750 focuses on systems for the design, development and production, installation and subsequent servicing of goods (British Standard BS EN ISO 9001: 1994, pp. 5–9). Quality standards are intended to be applicable to any product, the term 'product' referring to either material outputs or services, such as insurance, banking or transport (BS EN ISO 8402: 1995, p. 3). But the broad scope of the standards means that the concepts informing the British Standards on quality are dominated by commercially driven language, rather than embodying the values, policies and practices of the human services in general, or the personal social services in particular. British Standard BS 4778, for example, discusses the contribution of people to quality in Section 9. This discussion is restricted to staff responsibilities in terms of what is called 'human reliability', defined in terms of a person's ability 'to perform a required function, (British Standard BS 4778: Section 3.1: 1991, 21.3.1, p. 19); there is no mention of the contribution of consumers or customers let alone service users (British Standard BS 4778: Section 3.1: 1991, p. 19); human performance is discussed in relation to industrial processes and reliability in terms of the shortcomings of people as contrasted with machines: 'A major difficulty with human reliability is its variability compared with mechanical/electrical components, even when environmental conditions remain constant' (British Standard BS 4778: Section 3.1: 1991, 21.1, p. 19); human failure is conceptualised in terms of 'the termination (or non-achievement) of a required function' (British Standard BS 4778: Section 3.1: 1991, 21.2, p. 19) and human error is defined as an action which 'has the potential to produce an unintended result' (British Standard BS 4778: Section 3.1: 1991, 21.3.4, p. 19); these conceptualisations reflect a functional view of human activity. An associated restriction on the judgement of quality in professional practice is evident when BS 4778 is considered in conjunction with the definitions in BS 8402. For example, British Standard 8402 defines quality improvement in terms of action taken 'to increase the effectiveness and efficiency of activities and processes' (British Standard BS EN ISO 8402: 1995, 3.8, p. 28). This does not enable judgements about what practitioners do to make the distinction between the nature of professional activity and intervening factors in its context. Terence O'Sullivan distinguishes intrinsically sound decisions in social work from those which are effective, by reference to a range of factors which may intervene, which are outside the control of the professional (discussion with the author). This is of great relevance in considering the many criticisms of social work which get laid at the door of social workers, rather than being apportioned throughout the organisations and networks contributing to the purchase and provision of services.

Further, the general requirements of a quality system reflect a top-down view of the responsibility and authority of management for quality in the organisation (British Standard BS EN ISO 9001: 1994, p. 4).

Two main conclusions can be drawn from this examination of European and UK quality standards. First, there is a need to locate debates about quality maximisation holistically at the level of politics, policies, organisations and managements, rather than simply scapegoating professionals. Second, it highlights the lack of a discourse concerning empowerment – of any of the stakeholders to the process of service provision – from the British Standards concerning quality.

Registration, inspection and quality assurance

There is some overlap between registration and inspection and quality assurance, but these areas remain distinct from each other and in many local authorities are located in separate departments and offices. However, since 1984, residential provision for older people in the independent sector has had to meet certain standards laid down by legislation (Registered Homes Act 1984) and the practice of inspection has had a growing importance for every area of the personal social services, to say nothing of criminal justice. Significantly, inspection and registration figure in the list which Leckie identifies as the components of a quality assurance process: 'consumer surveys; the setting, monitoring and developing of standards (input, process, output and outcome standards); information systems; staff training, development and supervision; a quality policy; quality control mechanisms, such as inspection units and complaints procedures; and user involvement' (Leckie, 1994, pp. 128–9).

Inspection procedures may contribute either to quality imposition, maintenance, enhancement or maximisation (see Chapter 2), depending on their nature and purpose. The role of inspection depends on whether it is regarded in a more restricted sense as part of the mechanism by which shortcomings in the product or service are identified and rectified, or as having a broader part to play in the management of product and service development and delivery.

Leckie points out that registration and inspection should not be confused with quality assurance, since it is primarily about control (Leckie, 1994, p. 129). In such circumstances, there is a risk that authorities will use inspection as the primary approach to quality assurance and that staff will equate quality assurance with correcting mistakes, or investigating complaints, rather than achieving excellence.

Ian Sinclair has carried out research into the quality of residential care for older people. Research by Gibbs and Sinclair (Gibbs and Sinclair, 1992) points up the difficulties of ensuring consistency of judgements, and hence the validity, of the inspection process involving independent inspectors visiting residential homes for older people and making judgements about their quality.

In 1996, a review by the SSI of about 50 per cent of the local authority social services inspection units found that almost half still fell short of the laid down standards (SSI, 1996).

In the criminal justice system, HM Inspectorate of Prisons have performed an increasingly significant role in the 1980s and 1990s, in identifying weaknesses in institutional provision. In the mental health field, the Mental Health Commission (see Chapter 6) plays a comparable role to both the prison inspectorate and the board of visitors which is attached to each penal institution.

Case study: spread of standards and procedures in criminal justice

In one sense, the criminal justice system has been governed by rules – often reflecting culture and custom, over how prisons were run and punishments should be carried out – for centuries. Since Victorian times, legislation has increasingly introduced requirements in place of informal agreements. In 1952, the Detention Centre Rules, and in 1964, the Prison Rules and the Borstal Rules formalised the running of penal institutions for adults and young offenders. Uniformed prison officers were controlled by Standing Orders and a constant stream of Home Office circulars; administrative and governing grades were regulated increasingly after the Fulton Report (1967) by rules such as those set out in the *Handbook for the New Civil Servant* (Home Office, 1967). Job appraisal became part of the management culture of the Prison Service after the Fulton Committee report, which incorporated the Prison Service into the Civil Service (Home Office, 1971).

The introduction of new measures to assure quality in criminal justice work has an ambiguous significance. Quality assurance may perform a progressive or a retrograde role, for example in probation practice (Kemshall, 1993). Traditionally, the prison system has been a classic example of a bureaucratic organisation run by the above procedures, governing almost every aspect of prison life and work. But this approach has been strengthened since the 1970s by the work of HM Inspectorate of Prisons and backed up since the early 1980s by the development of central government bodies to oversee such approaches, notably the Audit Commission and, in allied social services, the Social Services Inspectorate. The Audit Commission (1989) has promoted a standards-based view of quality, focusing on using an assessment of 'the economy, efficiency and effectiveness of the probation service' (Audit Commission, 1989a, p. 68) as the basis for the quality of the work done. The development of National Standards parallels the introduction of NVQs at levels 3 and 4 in criminal justice work and may be criticised for inappropriately importing commercial and industrial language and culture into professional practice (Hayman, 1993, p. 180). Mark Oldfield, a research officer in Kent Probation Service, views the introduction of computerised systems for monitoring work and spending in the probation service as symptomatic of the growth of managerialist management (Oldfield, 1994, pp. 186–92).

From the early 1970s, Taylorism was on the ascendant in the Prison Department.

EXAMPLE 5.2

Staff in a young offenders' institution were surprised one morning to find every clerical officer being followed around the office by a stranger with a clipboard and a stopwatch. Each action was being measured and recorded, to try to ascertain where efficiencies could be made in the performance of office tasks.

The irony of such activities is that whilst the penal system has been an excellent field for the practice of mechanistic devices based on scientific management, or its heirs (see Chapter 3), the quality of life of prisoners often has remained relatively neglected.

During the 1960s and early 1970s, the crisis over the loss of security, the trend towards increasing numbers of prisoners serving long sentences and the collapse of the ideal of rehabilitation as a goal of imprisonment (Home Office, 1973; Home Office, 1977), reinforced an existing tradition of secrecry in the public service (Franks Committee, 1972) which was to be much criticised for preventing prison staff voicing criticisms and thereby improving standards (Cohen and Taylor, 1978) and renewed a then unfashionable emphasis on control – particularly the containment of the more serious offender – at the expense of the treatment philosophy (Adams, Allard, Baldwin and Thomas, 1981).

Loss of certainty about the rationale for imprisonment and other penal sanctions

The collapse of the rehabilitationist ideal in the 1970s meant that by the 1990s the goal of quality assurance was addressed in the face of the imponderable of determining the rationale for sentencing offenders and, in any event, who were to be the main targets, or beneficiaries, of different sentencing options: offenders, victims, potential offenders who might be deterred, offenders' families and friends, or other people in the community?

EXAMPLE 5.3

The newly appointed probation officer in the prison is shocked to find that almost every request he makes to colleagues for changes to be made to some practice which seems ridiculous to him, is met by the response: 'You can't do that: Standing Orders' or 'Don't ask me. Put a request in to the Governor.'

In organisations as heavily bureaucratised as penal institutions, the weight of traditionalism and hierarchical behaviour may be taken for granted by institutionalised staff, but questioned critically by the outsider, or the newcomer.

Impact of paradoxial trends in criminal justice policy

Before the Strangeways prison riot of 1990 and the wave of riots which followed it forced the pace on the upgrading of cellular accommodation and the reduction in numbers of prisoners sharing cells, the Home Office was already actively pushed by H.M. Inspecorate of prisons to consider the treatment of vulnerable prisoners and the ending of the practice of 'slopping out' which involved prisoners, whether one, two or three in a cell, keeping chamber pots in their cells and emptying these on a daily basis (Home Office, 1989b). The aftermath of the Strangeways riot saw an intensification of informed professional debates about the future philosophy of the penal system (Home Office, 1993), but until the landslide victory of the incoming Labour government of May 1997, changes in criminal justice policy emphasised expanding the prison population through more deterrent, and longer, sentences. Under the Labour government, reformers and professionals hoped that debates about the future of parole for medium and longer term offenders (Home Office, 1990c), the meeting of the needs of particular groups of prisoners such as those with HIV/ AIDS (Home Office, 1991f), sex offenders (Home Office, 1991e), the quality of throughcare support for adults and young offenders (Home Office, 1990b), prison regimes for women prisoners (Home Office, 1991g), treatment programmes for drug users (Home Office, 1991h), the improvement of health services for prisoners in the newly created internal markets for the purchase and provision of healthcare (Home Office, 1991i) would not be swamped by considerations such as how to contain the projected continuing increase in the prison population (Home Office, 1991e), the vexed question as to whether to retain private prisons, in pursuance of policies established in the late 1980s (Home Office, 1988c) and the vital need to protect the general public from crime (Home Office, 1990a), deter potential offenders and give adequate recompense to the victims of crime (Home Office, 1991a).

During the 1980s, now that treatment and reform were generally agreed to be unattainable goals for penal institutions, the Home Office engaged in a largely fruitless search for a positive rationale for imprisonment, apart from the obvious one of keeping criminals out of the community (Home Office, 1986; Home Office, 1987; Home Office, 1988a; Home Office, 1990a). Bail hostels provided a potential, if marginalised, alternative to custody (Home Office, 1988b), but were all too often used as an additional custodial measure for remand prisoners who otherwise would have remained living at home.

In the early 1990s, whilst reformist debate exemplified in the report on the Strangeways prison riot in 1990 (Woolf and Tumin,

1991) has concerned the urgent need to introduce greater humaneness and concern for human rights into the penal system, the main areas of criminal justice policy have moved towards harsher conditions and more deterrent sentencing. The former Home Secretary, Michael Howard, also was determined to push probation officers into a more controlling role than hitherto.

Yet paradoxically, and simultaneously, there were moves towards increasing lay and consumer involvement. Inspection teams in HM Inspectorate of Probation from the summer of 1994 had included lay people in three local services. The arrangements of local area probation services for monitoring and inspection were reviewed in 1995, with a view to making them 'more responsive to the needs of customers and users' (Prime Minister and the Chancellor of the Duchy of Lancaster, 1995, p. 116). Every probation service by the Autumn of 1994 was required to publish an annual report, incorporating a statement of progress towards nationally determined key performance indicators. In Northern Ireland, the Social Service Inspectorate continued to carry out inspections of probation services. *A Code of Operating Standards* was issued in April 1994. The Scottish Prison Service was committed to publishing national standards on prison-based social work, by the autumn of 1995 (Prime Minister and the Chancellor of the Duchy of Lancaster, 1995, p. 115). National Standards for the probation service were published in March 1995, aiming to 'strengthen the supervision of offenders in the community, provide punishment and a disciplined programme for offenders and build on the skills and experience of practitioners and service managers' (Prime Minister and the Chancellor of the Duchy of Lancaster, 1995, p. 116). The ultimate managerialist ploy was the announcement in April 1996 (*The Guardian*, 11 April 1996) that the Home Secretary intended to link a performance-related pay element of the salaries of probation officers with the reconviction rates of their clients.

The publication by the Prisons Board of its Vision and Values paper specified a series of values on which prison staff should base their actions in achieving six 'principal goals'. However, these referred to the maintenance of 'order, control and discipline' without any mention of 'justice', save in describing the care of prisoners as necessitating staff treating them with 'fairness, justice and respect as individuals' (Player and Jenkins, 1994a, p. 27).

Performance indicators and performance related payments   In the
1990s, performance indicators and payment according to performance became accepted means by which central government could
overcome difficulties associated with the creation of markets to
provide services, whilst retaining central control of local practice,
from a distance. The Audit Commission played a strategic role in
advancing this function. The Audit Commission published information on the work of councils in England and Wales, during the
financial year 1994/95, compared with the previous year where
statistics were available (Audit Commission, 1996a, 1996b and
1996c, Volumes 1, 2 and 3), and using a standard set of performance indicators (Audit Commission, 1993), detailed in full in the
appendix to Volumes 1 and 2. This performance indicator approach was based on the principle that people 'have the right to see
how efficiency varies from council to council and to question why
that is so' (Audit Commission, 1996a, Volume 1, p. 5). The
statistics were designed 'to help the public and councils judge
whether the latter are performing well or not and whether they are
improving their performance or not'. They were published 'to help
you judge whether your council is doing a good job', to 'help you
to judge whether or not your council is improving its performance'
and 'to enable you to see at a glance how your council's
performance differs from that of other councils' (Audit Commission, 1996a, p. 5). Local authorities and police forces were required
to publish details of their performance in local newspapers from
1995 (Audit Commission, 1996a, p. 3). The brief commentary on
social services in Volume 1 which dealt with social services among
other items, was based on statistics relating to five selected
performance indicators in 1996: the percentage of older people
over 75 helped to live at home; the percentage of minor items of
equipment provided within three weeks to help people live at
home; the percentage of adults offered single rooms when going
into residential care; the percentage of children in the care of the
local authority who are in foster care; and the number of children
on the Child Protection Register (Audit Commission, 1996a, p. 23).

Proposals for improving performance in probation services and
the prison service under the common umbrella of a correctional
agency were under consideration by the incoming Labour Government in the summer of 1997. There was little sign that the Labour
Home Secretary, Jack Straw, would reverse the moves made by his

Conservative predecessor Michael Howard, to use the move towards competence- and employment-based approaches, to weaken the link between universities and the training of probation officers and sever links with social work training altogether.

Performance-related payments from the early 1990s complemented performance indicators for the organisation, and reinforced control of the work of professionals. When the Home Office announced proposals to include performance-related payments as part of the pay provisions for probation officers in 1996, it emerged that the performance-based measure was to be applied to the numbers of pre-sentence and other reports written for the courts and to the reconviction rates of offenders on supervision (*The Guardian*, 9 April 1996).

Performance indicators often are presented as sets of measurable and significant standards. Performance measurement based on performance indicators, draws on notions such as output and outcome of an activity, or the efficiency as opposed to the effectiveness of a service. Performance indicators have been sought for various public sector services for most of the twentieth century. Cutler and Waine note that as early as 1901 Sidney Webb proposed an annual competition between local authorities, judging their sanitation, water, housing, health and related services on a number of performance indicators (Cutler and Waine, 1994, p. 27). In 1983, the DHSS published 145 indicators for the NHS (quoted in Cutler and Waine, 1994, p. 27). The effective use of indicators to measure performance depends on the quality of the indicators themselves, who sets them and whose viewpoint they adopt – management, professional, service user or other – of what the service should be providing. In the face of this potential diversity, it is noteworthy that in the UK 'the dominant model adopted has been one where initiation, design and use have derived from government and/or government agencies' (Cutler and Waine, 1994, p. 33). There may be a gap between the aspiration of setting out performance indicators which enable the effectiveness of a service to be gauged, and the reality that the indicators may not include the necessary range of dimensions of the service. Some indicators may be in conflict with others – notably short-term versus longer-term and cost-control versus outcomes for service users.

The Home Office followed the setting of national standards for supervising offenders in the community (Home Office, 1992) with a

Three-Year Plan intended to be reviewed and revised each subsequent year, setting targets for the probation service derived from
the Citizen's Charter (Shaw, 1995, p. 135). The plan for 1994–7
introduced a set of key performance indicators against which the
performance of individual probation officers could be assessed
(Home Office, 1994).

The Green Paper *Strengthening Punishment in the Community*
(1995) incorporated proposals strengthening the accountability of
the probation service to the courts. Shaw notes that 'quality
measures here, and throughout the personal social services, have
tended to be limited to those most easily obtained and those easily
measured. Only one of the ten Home Office key performance
indicators requires a qualitative measure' (Shaw, 1995, pp. 135–6).

Again, the different sectors of the criminal justice system –
prisons, judiciary, probation, police, voluntary organisations
working with prisoners' families and with vicitims of crime – have
multiple objectives which may conflict with each other. Further, it
is very difficult to envisage making a generally agreed correlation
between some of these objectives and, say, the general aim of crime
reduction in the system as a whole.

Standards and procedures and professional practice   Whilst standard setting and procedures have a part to play in quality
assurance, they are inadequate in themselves to underwrite the
quality of professional practice. In fact, reliance on procedures in
the absence of professional expertise may put the interests of
service users at risk. The SSI used inspection (SSI, 1994b) as a
means of evaluating the progress of local authority social services
departments towards implementing key aspects of the Children Act
1989 and the Criminal Justice Act 1991 and the *National Standards
for the Supervision of Offenders in the Community* (Home Office,
Department of Health and Welsh Office, 1992).

Agency status and the contract culture

The Prison Service was turned into an Executive Agency following
a review of its managerial effectiveness by Admiral Sir Raymond
Lygo (Home Office, 1991b). Although the government stated that
Agency status would not be the prelude to privatisation and the
Prison Service would remain part of the Home Office and its staff

civil servants, the trend was towards encouraging private sector participation in funding, providing and managing both penal establishments and specific services such as education and catering (Player and Jenkins, 1994a, pp. 26–7).

The dominance of the government-led agenda – prioritising crime control and the expansion of prisons at the expense of community-based, non-punitive options – has been accompanied by a restructuring of the apparatus of both institutional and community-based responses to offending, largely around the imperatives of market-based managerialism. Because the probation service and police have for many years been directly subject to control by the Home Office, and the Prison Service was until the early 1990s a department of the Home Office – the Prison Department – these trends have had a more pronounced impact on the work of professionals – police, probation officers, prison officers, governors, psychologists, prison chaplains, psychiatrists and so on – in all sectors of the system.

From 1 April 1993, when the Prison Service took on Agency status, whilst at one level Taylorism was on the decline in favour of the new managerialism, at another level the interventions of Michael Howard, then Home Secretary, in various aspects of the running of the Service and particular prisons (notably in the wake of escapes from Whitemoor and Parkhurst prisons in 1995) demonstrated the resilience of Taylorism in the face of any such changes. These interventions are indicative of the somewhat paradoxical situation of managers of penal establishments, whose autonomy was perpetually likely to be breached as a result of a particular political exigency. The changing situation of prisons and young offender institutions for a century or more has been influenced more directly by changes in central government than have other aspects of the human services, and the social services in particular.

Prisoners: consumers or citizens?

The imposition of the market economy on the prison system leads to prisoners being acknowledged formally as customers; this gives them certain rights under the Citizen's Charter alongside the general public, despite the fact that prisoners do not have the right to vote (Player and Jenkins, 1994a, p. 27). Ironically, the Citizen's Charter empowered the purchasers and providers of penal services, as consumers in the quasi-market of criminal justice, rather than prisoners, their networks of family and friends, or the victims of crime, thus distorting processes of quality assurance.

Protests by prisoners had a significant impact on the running of the prison system in the second half of the twentieth century. The report in the wake of the Strangeways prison riot in 1990, and the wave of riots in other prisons which followed it (Woolf and Tumin, 1991), is an illustration of the impact of direct action by prisoners on debates about reforms in penal policy (Adams, 1994).

Ombudsman: an independent role?

Following the recommendations of the Woolf report on the inquiry into the Strangeways prison riot (Woolf and Tumin, 1991), it took four years before the Prisons Ombudsman, appointed in April 1994, began work in October 1994, in England and Wales; in Scotland, the Scottish Prison Complaints Commissioner was appointed in October 1994 and began casework in December 1994. In Northern Ireland, no parallel appointment was made, but it was intended that the Northern Ireland Prison Service would publish a charter in 1996 (Prime Minister, 1995, p. 115). Press commentary on the work of the Prisons Ombudsman in England and Wales indicated tensions between this role and the Home Secretary. By early 1996, there were reports of a conflict between Sir Peter Woodhead, the first ombudsman, and the Home Secretary over the scope of the role of ombudsman: namely, whether the original remit 'to investigate complaints by prisoners about the Prison Service as an agency' (Prison Service spokesperson, quoted in *The Guardian*, 26 February 1996) excluded wider considerations. An attempt was made to prevent Sir Peter from having access to files concerning complaints by prisoners which affected policy rather than operational matters, that is 'to exclude from Sir Peter's remit all grievances voiced by inmates which refer to ministerial decisions or Civil Service advice to ministers – as well as those involving life-sentence inmates. He would also be banned from demanding access to all the Civil Service paperwork in a particular case' (*The Guardian*, 26 February 1996). So, the vital role of the independent Ombudsman was put at risk, in ways which revealed the threat to some Home Office and political interests of subjecting penal practices to independent scrutiny. It is difficult to reconcile official rhetoric concerning the need for quality, with such defensiveness.

Monitoring by management: enhancing control

Enhanced control, both inside institutions and from an external vantage point, depends on a detailed and speedy flow of information about what is happening. One relevant attempt to overcome the difficulties of the slowness of gathering information about the system, and its general irrelevance for purposes of management, is the Governor's 'weekly monitoring system', which attempts to gather daily information in the prison service of use at all levels of the organisation. It includes some negative indicators: for example, 'the failure to fulfil a checklist of basic routines such as weekly bathing, the distribution of mail and access to visitors, is a good sign that trouble may be brewing' (Carter, 1989, pp. 214–15).

EXAMPLE 5.4

The probation officer on the prison wing requested that a prisoner received the additional facility of telephone calls outside the normal hours of access to a telephone, but was told by a senior prison officer that the staffing rotas made this impossible.

For decades, the uniformed grade, prison officers, and their organisation, the Prison Officers' Association, have worked to maintain what they regard as their working conditions in increasingly resource-constrained establishments. The consequence of their refusal to bend rules and operate flexibly to meet the needs of the individual are that institutional practices are preserved at the expense of the circumstances of the prisoner. Organisations such as prisons are prone to institutionalised practices such as controlling prisoners and maintaining the status quo replacing their more elusive goals such as rehabilitation (Goffman, 1967; Street, Vinter and Perrow, 1966). The requirement to generate operational objectives reinforces this tendency; for example, police forces may concentrate on improving their clear-up rates for offences (Kanter and Summers, 1994, p. 223), rather than crime prevention and reduction. An associated and perhaps more worrying tendency is the trend towards allowing the procedure for measuring performance to redefine the goal of the organisation (Kanter and Summers, 1994, p. 224). In the prison, for example, the number of inmates occupying cells, or the throughput in an average year, could become the criterion, rather than the quality of imprisonment and whether or not its negative consequences outweighed its benefits. Again, in the probation service, the number of cases dealt with in a month could become the operating standard, rather than the quality of work done with people.

Anecdotal evidence suggests that the trajectory of Home Office decisions about ushering in a new, more controlling and punitive managerial attitude towards the workforce, with the recuitment of former staff from the armed services, was parallelled at local level in some probation services. In early 1996, one probation service introduced new, tighter regulations for staff, involving them signing in on the same system as clerical and administrative staff, from 8.45 a.m. to 5.15 p.m. each working day, with penalties, including an interview with the line manager, for so-called 'offenders' (personal communication by probation officer, to the author).

Precarious welfare role of probation officers in prisons

The impact of the withering of the rehabilitative cause for judicial intervention, particularly in the form of imprisonment, has caused the probation service to reflect seriously on its role in prison welfare work. The Home Office forced the pace on this, probably pressed by the government from the late 1980s. The Green Paper *Punishment, Custody and the Community* (Home Office, 1988c) set out the government's proposals for greater use of non-custodial options, but at the same time suggested that the procedures for breaches of community service orders would be tightened. It also proposed a new supervision and restriction order which could involve compensation, reparation, community service, judicial supervision, attendance at a day centre or restriction of liberty using 'tagging' or electonic monitoring. The explicit threat in the Green Paper was that if the probation service did not move towards a more overtly controlling role, then another body would be created to carry this out.

The steadily increasing numbers of prisoners in custody are due to an upward trend in sentencing, increases in sentence length and a longer time being served in custody before parole (Bottomley, 1994, p. 191). The thrust of probation work and qualifying education and training for probation officers from the mid-1990s, was away from social work. There was a trend towards greater accountability of the probation service to the Home Office (Mair, 1996, p. 36). Nellis attracts controversy (Spencer, 1995) by arguing for the value base of probation work to consist of three purposes: anti-custodialism, restorative justice and community safety (Nellis, 1995). Restorative justice emphasises constructive responses to the harm done by the offender, rather than punitive ones which typify current policy in the UK, based largely on practices of segregation, stigmatisation and exclusion (Raynor, 1996, p. 191).

Move towards harsher criminal justice policies

The Criminal Justice Act 1991 emphasised a punitive approach to sentencing, based on principles of just deserts and proportionality. The Act embodied a New Right approach to justice, many aspects of which harked back to classical criminology. Thus, sentencing was to refer to the seriousness of the offence (Smith, 1995). In 1995, this approach was buttressed by the White Paper *Punishment in the Community* on the erroneous assumption that harsher sentences, whether in prison or in the community, are more effective.

In the wake of the trial and conviction of two young boys for the murder of the toddler James Bulger, a Criminal Justice and Public Order Bill was framed which included proposals for secure institutions for juvenile criminals. In May 1994, the Bill passed through the House of Lords. It contained provisions for a £30 million per year system of five private 'child jails', in Durham, Nottinghamshire, Warwickshire, Oxfordshire and South East England, each to contain about 40 juvenile offenders from the age of 12 (*Guardian*, 17 May 1994). The incoming Labour Government of 1997 developed the Crime and Disorder Bill on the basis of targetting persistent young offenders and strengthening community sentences, as indicated a year previously (Labour Party, 1996).

Resources and prison conditions

A more or less endless stream of problems could be listed – appalling conditions in women's prisons such as Holloway; concerns over prison discipline overlying a continuing lack of justice for prisoners subjected to it; healthcare, or rather, lack of it, in prison; the state of remand prisons and the regime for remand prisoners; lack of constructive regimes for long-term prisoners; lack of resources to treat mentally disordered prisoners; lack of treatment programmes, outside the Grendon prison regime (Adams, 1996a, pp. 178–9), for sex offenders in prison. These were all associated at a superficial level with a lack of resources, but more fundamentally with the expansionism endemic in the Home Office's strategies for the use of custody and punishment in the 1990s. The tension between resources and quality services sharpened in 1995, with the swelling numbers of prisoners – increasing at 10 a week and already 52,444 in November 1995 – and the announcement on 28 November 1995 by Kenneth Clarke, then Chancellor of the Exchequer, of a 3 per cent budget cut in the prison service. Further pressure on services within prisons was anticipated, with 17 prisons already making significant cuts in probation staff, three (Littlehey, Cambridgeshire; Winchester, Hampshire; and Winson Green, Birmingham) having dispensed altogether with probation officers, and many prisons planning cuts in education staff and industrial workshops (*The Guardian*, 28 November 1995, p. 8). The impact of these cuts on the quality of prisoners' lives was further strengthened by the increased emphasis on spending on security, following the escapes of prisoners from Littlehey and Parkhurst earlier in the year.

A further area of concern was the swelling numbers of people sent to prison for defaulting on the relatively minor penalty of non-payment of a fine. The number of people sent to prison for non-payment of fines increased between 1992 and 1993 by over one-third, to more than 22,750. It was anticipated that the number jailed in 1994 would exceed the record number of 24,492 in 1982, since when numbers fell for almost a decade. The typical fine defaulter was unemployed and offending through road traffic, TV licence evasion, prostitution, poll tax non-payment, and had gas and/or electricity debts and owed rent and instalment payments (*The Guardian*, 23 May 1994).

The proposals of the then Home Secretary Michael Howard in 1995–6, for a 'two strikes and you're out' policy of life sentences for repeat rapists and attempted murderers and mandatory sentences for persistent burglars and traffickers in hard drugs, were estimated to require an additional 16 prisons for more than 6,000 extra prisoners, over and above the six new prisons already planned at a cost of of £360m, at a further cost of £5760m. This proposal for mandatory life sentences attracted criticism from judges, notably Lord Donaldson, former Master of the Rolls, who viewed it as a 'sledgehammer to crack a nut' with application only to about 40 cases per year, and as risking intervention in the decisions of the judiciary by 'despotic government' ('Howard concedes sentence package will need more jails', *The Guardian*, 11 March 1996).

The trajectory of Conservative government policies towards tougher measures to punish adults and young offenders was not significantly altered after the General Election of May 1997, by the incoming Labour government.

Beyond standards and procedures in criminal justice work

EXAMPLE 5.5

Ms H. has been in custody for six weeks following non-payment of a fine. She is a lone mother of three children under eleven, in her seventh month of pregnancy. Ms. H has grumbled to her probation officer about being shackled to her bed whilst in hospital and about how invasively her intimate examination before a visit was carried out

Challenging policies which contravene the rights of the client

Standards, procedures, circulars, memoranda and all the paraphernalia of written instructions do not in themselves guarantee quality. The reasons for this are complex and some of them vary according to circumstances. Essentially though, standards and procedures imposed by government provide parameters which may constrain practice rather than enable it to aspire to quality beyond them. In the example quoted above, it is possible for probation officers and social workers who come into contact with Ms H. and her family to distance themselves from the complaints and to focus on their formal responsibilities. But a more assertive, anti-oppressive stance will involve the professional in challenging unjust and abusive practice. Not to challenge it risks being drawn into collusion.

For several decades, the criminal justice system in the UK has faced professionals such as probation officers working in prisons with such dilemmas. The backcloth to these is the enduring dilemma of whether the profession should remain part of the prison staff and offer a more intensive service to prisoners, from the 'inside' as it were, whilst risking colluding with oppresive management and practice, or to refuse to work in prisons and simply visit prisoners as 'outsiders'.

Standards may be used by the authorities to reform services, or to reinforce existing, or even retrograde practices. The criminal justice system, especially in the relationship between the Home Office and the Prison Service, is an example of the unhelpful imposition of standards and procedures. Many have been used to reinforce retrograde practices. Their effect has been to encourage defensiveness and hostility or resistance to radical change. The impact of National Standards and the criminal justice legislation of the 1990s in England and Wales on the role of the probation officer has been profound. The autonomy of the officer has decreased. Day-to-day work is increasingly governed by throughcare and aftercare requirements requiring home and prison visits and meetings with offenders at specified intervals.

Despite the upbeat tone of the Strangeways inquiry report (Woolf and Tumin, 1991), reformists, in and outside the workforce of criminal justice, probation and social services, increasingly expressed disillusionment and loss of morale, in the struggle against a government many perceived as unsympathetic to the preservation of a reformist agenda in youth and criminal justice services in the UK. In fact, it is undeniable that these services are in a growing state of crisis, largely over the issue of their quality. This is an issue concerning the values of the system, the political commitment and policy trajectory necessary to reassert humaneness and non-custodialism in criminal justice and diversion and restorative justice, as agendas for future development. Thus, the crisis is only superficially about what to do with people to stop them committing offences. More fundamentally, government politicians and the public are intolerant towards petty young offenders, the overwhelming majority of whom will grow out of delinquency if diverted from professional and judicial intervention, and sentencing practices demonstrate excessively punitive and custodial responses to adult offenders. Resources should be diverted from additional secure units and prisons, into supporting offenders in the community, whilst restoring the victims of crime as far as possible to their circumstances before the offence was committed.

Empowering offenders and victims

Ironically, given the heavy-handed management style of the Home Office over the years, some key areas of progress in penal provision and practice have followed protests by those not directly a party to it – prisoners. Paradoxically, this may be because of their expelled status, rather than in spite of it.

This chapter has shown the nature and impact of a particularly regulatory style of management in parts of the criminal justice system, notably impacting on prison-based work and probation work (Dominelli, Jeffers, Jones, Sibanda and Williams, 1995). It illustrates how the enforcement of this way of working, through procedures derived from law and the setting of National Standards, induces compliance rather than commitment to achieving excellence. In the process, there appears to be little space for serious consideration of contributions by those major stakeholders in the criminal justice process – the offenders themselves. Prisoners are a group particularly liable to be excluded from debates about penal practice, let alone penal reforms. Their individual complaints may be processed, but collective protests by prisoners are unlikely to be.

The next chapter illustrates approaches to quality assurance in mental health based on the contribution of a range of responses to shortcomings in services, such as complaints, inquiries and investigations.

6

Rectifying Quality: Beyond an Error-Driven Approach in Mental Health

Whistleblowing, complaints and scandals, often followed by investigations or inquiries, are the most visible features of approaches to quality based on mistakes or problems. Such responses are not advocated here as adequate strategies on their own for assuring quality, but as requiring attention, since remedial action may contribute towards the response of an organisation to demands for the standards of services to be guaranteed.

Key features of quality rectification: some examples

Complaints

From October 1991, the Children Act 1989 required social services departments to have complaints procedures to enable children and/ or their representatives to make complaints. Also, the NHS and Community Care Act 1990 required every social services department to have a complaints procedure. Guidance was issued by the government, for social services departments in general (DH/SSI, 1991f) and for staff having first contact with customers, notably receptionists and telephonists (DoH and SSI, 1991d). During the late 1980s and early 1990s, many social services departments published guidance for people on how to make complaints about services. Organisations such as the National Consumer Council published detailed guidance on the practical issues associated with setting up and running complaints procedures (National Consumer Council and National Institution for Social Work, 1988). The Patients Association also published guidance for patients on the use of NHS complaints procedures (Patients Association, undated). Despite all such efforts, Norman Warner's research for the Carers National Association revealed that 44 per cent of carers surveyed did not know how to complain about services (Warner, 1994, p. 40), a discouraging finding in view of the fact that the sample was biased in favour of better informed carers (Warner, 1994, p. 11).

Inspections in the early 1990s focused on complaints procedures as part of the policy of the SSI of monitoring the implementation of legislative requirements (DH/SSI, 1993b).

EXAMPLE 6.1

Mr Houghton's daughter is 14 years old, with learning difficulties, who committed a serious crime of violence five years ago and has been moved recently from a secure unit for people with mental health problems to a children's home. Mr Houghton complained nine months ago that his daughter was not sufficiently consulted about decisions made in relation to her welfare. When he first voiced his concerns on a visit to the hospital, he was told by a nurse that the problem was that her learning disability made it almost impossible to have a conversation with his daughter. Mr Houghton refused to accept the outcome of the informal complaints procedure and now awaits a formal investigation of his complaint.

This example illustrates the need to take clients' views into account when evaluating complaints procedures (Lawson and Coffin, 1996) and implies that the speed at which complaints are dealt with often increases in direct proportion to the informality and small-scale nature of the procedure. For example, the more independent people sit on the complaints panel, the more problems there will generally be of convening and reconvening them, in a case which requires this.

Complaints procedures

Legislation supporting complaints procedures is more rigorous under the Children Act 1989 than for adults under the NHS and Community Care Act 1990. Under the Children Act 1989, complaints procedures in social services departments involve a staged approach, from informal complaints, settled without reference to more formal procedures, through formal complaints and finally review by a complaints panel, chaired by an independent person.

At stage one, the attempt is made to resolve the complaint informally. At stage two, if the complaint is not resolved to the satisfaction of the complainant, an independent person, outside the organisational or management setting in which the complaint is directed, is appointed. This person shadows the department's officer appointed to investigate the complaint and these two people write the report at the conclusion of this investigation. At stage three, if the complainant does not accept that the complaint has been dealt with satisfactorily, a single panel meeting takes place chaired by a different independent person, and comprising the complainant, two new members from the department, the independent person from stage two and the investigating officer from stage two. The report from this process – which does not have to be an agreed position by all parties – is prepared by the complaints officer and is sent simultaneously to the complainant and the director of social services. The director has 28 days to respond to the complaint, by writing to the complainant.

The strengths of this complaints process include the independent person who is intrinsic to the process and may help to safeguard the interests of the complainant and who can insist on access to any staff still working in the department, or people's records. The weaknesses of this complaints process include the fact that the power of the independent person to contact people involved with the complaint is limited to those still employed in the department. Brian McClay makes a convincing case for good complaints procedures to provide an accessible, available and empowering framework, 'capable of enabling users to feel that their complaints will be treated seriously, will be attended to promptly and will receive a considered response' (McClay, 1994, p. 164).

Whistleblowing

EXAMPLE 6.2 ██

Barbara is a social worker who has played a leading role in discussions with colleagues about their criticisms of working practice in their team. Everyone seems agreed informally that 'something should be done' to rectify the situation. She presents a list of criticisms and grievances at a staff meeting and is concerned when nobody backs her up in public. She contacts a local newspaper after a further month has gone by, during which nothing has been done by management about her complaints.

The staff member with a grievance or complaint who is tempted to short-circuit laid-down procedures for responding is creating a situation of individual vulnerability and may not progress action on the complaint. A case described in *Professional Social Work* (*PSW*, May 1994, p. 12), fictionalised but based on true events, shows the possible precariousness of the future employment of social workers when service users complain about their practice. On the other hand, social workers who 'blow the whistle' to the mass media about shortcomings in practice may be equally vulnerable to disciplinary action by their employers. Professionals allied to social work may have an obligation to report shortcomings of professional practice: nurses have a duty to report abuses and doctors have to report professional incompetence (United Kingdom Central Council for Nursing, Midwifery and Health Visiting (UKCC, 1992). But, despite widespread acceptance of the shortcomings in complaints procedures (see, for instance the findings of Brian McClay, 1994, p. 153), the revised standards for practice by qualified social workers (CCETSW, 1996a) do not incorporate this duty. However, there is a growing awareness of the need to support the efforts of all staff to sustain a critical approach and where necessary to 'blow the whistle' on shortcomings in standards. BASW (British Association of Social Workers) has published guidance for staff who wish to take action to end abuse and exploitation of clients by alerting managers to the circumstances (BASW, 1997). The term 'whistleblower' is used often to describe such action. In order for critical activity of this kind to be sustained as an effective means of maintaining standards, rather than simply rules and procedures, the complainant needs to be working in an organisational culture which encourages and protects him or her. All too often, the managerialist culture in which social workers practise is such that the whistleblower needs protection from the employer once the complaint has been made. Some contracts to supply services, or even contracts of employment, in the health and social care sector may include confidentiality clauses which, in effect, prevent the employee from voicing to outsiders criticisms of aspects of the work being done.

Unless complaints are constructed very carefully, employers may also be able to claim that the whistleblower acted from motives of personal vindictiveness, or through a personality clash in the workplace. Potential whistleblowers may need careful advice about how to test their complaint against the criterion of having reasonable grounds, before they make the complaint. Caution also needs to be exercised over how whistleblowers choose to make their complaint. It may or may not be considered in law to be a 'just cause' of complaint or an obvious source of health and safety risks.

The process of disclosure may or may not be lawful, depending on whether the person takes the complaint through a recognised legal procedure, or, for example, writes a letter to a newspaper. The law may give some limited protection for whistleblowing, in certain areas of the human services. Unfair dismissal regulations applied by Industrial Tribunals could provide protection from unfair dismissal in some aspects, for example, concerning health and safety, though there may be restrictions on the category of employee thus protected, in terms of the temporariness or short-term nature of some contracts. For example, the Nolan Committee on Standards in Public Life refers to NHS Trusts and quangos and recommends all should have a route for whistleblowing in ethical matters (Nolan, 1995). Organisations such as Public Concern At Work continue to campaign for enhanced legal protection for employee 'whistleblowers', for example, from unfair dismissal. However, people receiving services remain vulnerable, despite the insistence of various charters on customers' rights. For example, a pupil at a Nottinghamshire school was expelled in July 1997 for reportedly offering critical statements about the teaching in a comprehensive school as part of the explanation for poor performance (*The Guardian*, 24 July 1997).

EXAMPLE 6.3

A young person in a residential setting approached me and asked if he could share a secret, on condition it was not divulged to any third party. My response was to say that I could not give an unconditional guarantee of confidentiality, since if a serious allegation was made, or if the disclosure in any other way affected another person, I might have to take action involving another person. The young person proceeded then to make an allegation against a senior male member of staff, whom he said had been sexually assaulting him and intimidating him into silence over a period of weeks. I reported the allegation immediately, to the senior manager of the establishment. Responses from other staff varied from 'I suspected something' to incredulity. Despite being suspended from duty, the person accused made one attempt to persuade me that the entire incident had been blown out of proportion by malicious people, including the accuser, and then tried to intimidate me into silence.

This incident illustrates the barriers to staff dealing openly with allegations, the complexities surrounding the issue of confidentiality in the professional role, the pressures against disclosure on the person to whom disclosure is made, but more important, on the discloser. On the whole, disclosure puts the discloser who makes a serious allegation in a vulnerable situation and much support is necessary in the subsequent process of responding to the disclosure (Anon, 1995).

De Maria and Cyrell writing in the light of the Queensland Whistleblowing study, reportedly Australia's largest research study to date into whistleblowing, show a crisis in the capacity of government to respond effectively to disclosures made in the public interest (De Maria and Cyrell, 1996). The implications of whistleblowing for the law (Westman, 1992) and for government (Senate Select Committee on Public Interest, 1994) had previously been taken up. There is a notable gap between rhetoric concerning the commitment of organisations in health and social work/social services to quality and actual working practices supported by the law (Beardshaw, 1981). 'Where employees raise concerns, they run the risk of dismissal or discipline for breach of confidence. All staff are subject to the implied term of fidelity which requires that confidence between employer and employee is maintained. In addition, many NHS trusts have taken advantage of their new powers to introduce onerous confidentiality clauses, covering almost all information at all times; some of these clauses do not include the *proviso* that information that is in the public interest is not covered' (Vickers, 1995, p. 1257).

Even the centre of gravity of the admittedly non-contractual guidance for NHS staff (National Health Service Management Executive (NHSME), June 1993) is towards making the employee hesitant about blowing the whistle. It 'emphasises the serious nature of unauthorised disclosure and states that it will always be a matter for disciplinary action, even in cases where the member of staff believes that he or she is acting in the best interests of a patient or client' (Vickers, 1995, p. 1257). Also, this lack of encouragement for whistleblowing is reflected in the 'duty of confidence' in the UKCC code of professional conduct. Further, 'the well publicised cases involving the dismissal of whistleblowers such as Helen Zeitlin and Graham Pink, send a strong message to health professionals who contemplate blowing the whistle. This continues to be the case, despite clause 12 in the UKCC code that imposes a duty on registered nurses, midwives and health visitors to "report to an appropriate person or authority any circumstances in which safe and appropriate care for patients and clients cannot be provided"' (UKCC, 1992). Vickers adds that Zeitlin and Pink made criticisms of their working situations known, the former concerning the hospital in which she worked seeking the status of NHS trust, the latter in a letter to the press after failing to secure what he regarded as an adequate response to his complaints internally in the organisation. Both successfully challenged their dismissals, yet neither continued working in the original job (Vickers, 1995, p. 1257).

BASW's guidance for social workers on whistleblowing details the priority interests of service users and carers in any considerations connected with staff who raise issues of concern in social services matters (BASW, 1997, p. 3). This publication indicates that the practice of whistleblowing remains fraught with difficulties and risks to the practitioner (preface to BASW, 1997) and that 'there can also be difficult conflicts between the employers' responsibilities towards the needs of their own services and organisations and the professional ethics and practices of their employees' (BASW, 1997, p. 3).

Case study: rectifying shortcomings in mental health

The White Paper *Health of the Nation* (1992), which set out a strategy for improving the health of people in England and Wales, specified mental health as one of the five key areas for improvement. The relative weakness both of hospital patients and social workers, and the relative power of medical practitioners provide parameters within which issues concerning quality have surfaced repeatedly over the years since the mid-1960s. The focus of concerns about quality in mental health practice (Clare, 1976) was traditionally on the mental hospital as the principal, high profile site of mental health intervention in people's lives. Since the 1960s, public inquiries into shortcomings and scandals over the treatment of patients in mental hospitals have been one means by which control has shifted from traditional to new forms of management.

Whilst criticisms of mental hospitals have been the main focus of public inquiries up to the 1990s, there has been increasing critical scrutiny of healthcare in general. For many years, critical questions have been raised by commentators and official inquires about the mental hospital system in the country, notably the situation in Broadmoor and Rampton. In the early 1960s, it was Enoch Powell who, as Minister of Health, heralded the hospital closure programme which, however, did not come about until the Thatcher government, during the 1980s. Since the mid 1960s, there have been more than a dozen major reports into conditions in mental hospitals. The mass media have played a major role in making public many of the criticisms of the special hospitals. Some notable evidence has been presented in television documentaries. The initial surfacing of public concern about mental hospitals in general and those housing large numbers of geriatric people in particular, can be pinpointed almost to the day. A group of people wrote a letter to *The Times*, published on 10 November 1965, which led to an outcry about conditions in these hospitals.

Barbara Robb later described in the subsequent book *Sans Everything: A Case to Answer* (1966), the flood of hundreds of replies received in response to this letter. Following the book, the Ministry of Health set up independent inquiries once the names of the respective hospitals were revealed by the author. However, subsequent investigations of these hospitals revealed a less clearcut set of issues. Hospitals are complex organisations. It proved

relatively easy to defend existing conditions, decisions and practices against some of the vague and inaccurate perceptions of the
complainants (Martin, 1984, p. 4).

While the allegations in *Sans Everything* were being investigated,
complaints about conditions in Ely Hospital, Cardiff, were surfacing. These were published by the *News of the World* on 20 August
1967 on the basis of a statement made by a nursing assistant. Ely
Hospital had originally been a Poor Law workhouse, which
contained about 600 patients, about two-thirds of whom had
learning disabilities (Martin, 1984, p. 5). The inquiry into these,
chaired by the Conservative politician Geoffrey Howe, QC (1969
Ely Hospital Report), was to have a greater impact on the
authorities, in view of the rigour with which it was conducted
and the indisputable nature of its evidence. The findings of the
report entirely justified the original revelations in the *News of the
World*. Its opening page confirmed:

(a) Cruel ill-treatment of four particular patients by six named
    members of the staff;
(b) generally inhumane and threatening behaviour towards pa-
    tients by one of the staff members already referred to;
(c) pilfering of food, clothing and other items belonging to the
    hospital or the patients;
(d) indifference on the part of the Chief Male Nurse to com-
    plaints that were made to him;
(e) lack of care by the Physician Superintendent and one other
    member of the medical staff.

The report drew attention not only to malpractice by individual
staff, but by the failures of management and administration which
lay behind these. Martin's detailed analysis of inquiries into mental
hospitals during this period elicits from the mass of evidence two
significant features of this: 'vindictive and determined attempts to
silence complainants, with the acquiescence or connivance of
senior members of the nursing administration . . . failure by
management, lay and professional, local and regional, to concern
itself, leave alone intervene effectively, with the quality of patient
care. The hospital as a whole had been allowed to become socially
and professionally isolated, with buildings and staff morale in a
generally run down state' (Martin, 1984, p. 9).

The investigation from 1968 into conditions in Farleigh Hospital for males with learning disabilities over 16 near Bristol, led to three nurses being sentenced to significant terms of imprisonment for cruelty to patients. The inquiry report published in 1971 'pinpointed the failure of medical leadership, its replacement by a nursing management which was responsible and conscientious but limited and ill-equipped to fill the gap; above all it pointed to the professional isolation of the nursing group and the inward-looking conservatism that had developed as a result. Old-fashioned methods persisted, and were supported by a defensive staff resenting criticism and justifiably complaining of lack of support from almost all levels of management' (Martin, 1984, p. 12).

The inquiry into Whittingham Hospital in Lancashire (NHS, 1972) only took place when an extraordinary level of defensiveness and denial by staff, including senior staff, had been broken through by a number of complainants, staff and students, since

> over a period of four years student nurses complained about the treatment of patients in some parts of the hospital. The publication of *Sans Everything* led to a meeting of student nurses who made serious allegations of ill-treatment; two days later they were threatened with legal action and obviously feared victimization. The Chief Male Nurse, the Matron and the Principal Tutor combined to suppress the minutes of the meeting, and they only came to light when found by the auditors sent in by the Department of Health. Moreover, on the very next day the Chairman of the Hospital Management Committee called a special meeting of all senior nursing staff to enquire into the possibility that the types of ill-treatment mentioned in *Sans Everything* were occurring at Whittingham. There was a total denial. (Martin, 1984, p. 14)

But eventually an unrelated conflict between the Chief Male Nurse and a psychiatrist led to the latter and the Chairman of the Hospital Management Committee writing a letter of complaint to the Secretary of State, as a result of which an inquiry was called. Variable standards of nursing left some long-stay wards with patients simply warehoused in complete idleness all day long and the promotion system of the hospital corrupted by nepotism. The inquiry drew attention to the management failings which 'had allowed maltreatment and pilfering to occur, and which had stubbornly resisted all attempts to change old styles of care and to eliminate customs which took advantage of the very helplessness which had brought patients into hospital in the first place (Martin, 1984, p. 17).

Because there seemed to be a consensus about the substantive basis for the allegations, investigation of complaints about the care of patients at Napsbury Hospital, near London, between 1970 and 1972, was carried out not by an independent inquiry but by a 'Professional Investigation' led by senior staff in the hospital (Martin, 1984, p. 17). The focus of criticism was the 'unkindness or unintentional cruelty' which on occasions had resulted from the admittedly well-intentioned but intensive and idiosyncratic treat-ment methods applied by the psychiatrists and their nursing team (Martin, 1984, pp. 17–18).

Conditions in South Ockendon Hospital for about, 1000 patients with learning disabilities were subject to an inquiry from May 1972 to May 1974, following a two-year campaign by AEGIS (Aid for the Elderly in Government Institutions), the pressure group re-sponsible for the *Sans Everything* exposé, over the death of a young man of 18 early in 1969 (Martin, 1984, p. 19). This inquiry highlighted practical matters of great importance, concerning lack of clarity over which profession was responsible for which aspects of policy, surfacing in situations such as who was responsible for deciding whether internal doors should be locked. The inquiry drew attention not only on the limits of clinical autonomy for any one discipline, but also the problem of boundaries between disciplines. Traditionally these had tended to be fudged by com-promises between professions which in long-stay institutions most often took the form of a medical *laissez faire* in which doctors visited wards occasionally but left day-to-day management to the nurses. Such tactical withdrawals, however, represent a retreat from the multi-disciplinary approach to care which official policy and the Committee of Inquiry regarded as essential for institutions where the 'treatment' involved not merely medication but the whole way of life' (Martin, 1984, pp. 25–6).

The inquiry into Warlingham Park Hospital for people who were mentally ill was set up to examine a number of suicides by patients between 1974 and 1975 (Warlingham, 1976). It was exceptional in that it largely endorsed the approach of the staff to their work; it concluded that the hospital had many positive features, but that staff shortages, particularly in nursing and high quality support from community psychiatric nurses, created problems which would not have arisen in an institution where staff were less committed to progressive change (Martin, 1984, p. 29).

The relative significance of public inquiries should be weighed against the power of the media and different professional groups. The outcomes of these inquiries have contributed to the growing impetus towards the major changes since the early 1970s in the structuring and management of the health services in which they are located. Simultaneously, and paradoxically, the influence of former patients, system survivors, ex-inmates, service users, carers, relatives and others on the receiving end of hospital treatment, has grown to the point where they have a louder voice, even though their formal power to bring about reforms is limited (Hill, 1979).

The inquiry into the deaths of four patients in mid-1975 in the psychiatric unit at Darlington hospital highlighted the aftermath of disorganisation after the reorganisation of the health service in 1974; the shortage of trained psychiatric nurses and the need for better cooperation between the professions, especially between psychiatry and nursing; the isolation of the hospital from the local community; and the holding of this inquiry following the failure of an internal inquiry (Martin, 1984, p. 31).

The Normansfield Hospital Inquiry (1978) shed light on circumstances leading to a breakdown in relations between the sole Consultant in Subnormality at the hospital and nurses, who eventually went on strike, putting at risk the treatment, and the lives, of hundreds of patients with learning disabilities. Initially begun by a committee set up by the Regional Health Authority, the inquiry became a public inquiry under Section 70 of the National Health Service Act, once it became clear that the former did not have the support of the medical professions. The long-standing nature of problems and the prominent involvement of a trade union were noteworthy features of the situation in Normansfield.

The inquiry into conditions in Winterton Hospital (1979), County Durham – at about 1,200 mentally ill in-patients one of the largest of such hospitals in England – focused on specific incidents rather than management in general. Nevertheless, there were pointers to problems: 'Seclusion was being used rather freely, the amount of alcohol authorized for patient consumption seemed to be rising steeply for no apparent reason, and nurse management left much to be desired' (Martin, 1984, p. 43).

Significance of inquiries into hospital-based mental health services

Inquiries into conditions in health services, particularly in hospitals for mentally ill people, up to the 1980s illustrate the relative weakness of social work as a professional interest. The power of the medical professionals has increased the tendency for change in the quality of different areas of medical practice to be achieved through public inquiries, rather than through administrative innovation. In Martin's view, the inquiries before the mid-1970s in particular, tend to arise 'from past inadequacies of provision, and from lack of new thinking, particularly about mental handicap'. They demonstrate 'the effects of professional isolation, the low expectations of custodial regimes, the dangers of corruption in closed societies and the extent to which staff and management could go to stifle criticism of the quality of patient care. Perhaps, above all, they exposed the weakness and superficiality of the system of lay management which had failed to exert any real influence on the quality of that care' (Martin, 1984, p. 27). The inquiries between the mid-1970s and 1980 show the growing involvement of trade unions in events, the pattern of external inquiries following the failure of internal ones and the tendency for inquiries to arise from circumstances not directly resulting from complaints about lack of patient care by staff (Martin, 1984, p. 46).

Protests by patients

In the early 1970s, the Glancy Report in 1973 examined security in psychiatric hospitals, including special hospitals (DHSS, 1974) and in 1974 produced its revised report. In the same year the interim report of the Butler Committee was published (Home Office and DHSS, 1974), and the following year, after further consultations, the final report (Home Office and DHSS, 1975). Lord Butler pointed out that the committee published this interim report namely because they were appalled by conditions in Broadmoor (Cohen, 1982, p. 98). The full report of the Butler committee was published the following year (Interim Report, Cmnd 5698: Final Report, Cmnd 6244). The Butler committee was set up in the wake of the murders committed by Graham Young and Terry Iliffe, after their release from Broadmoor.

During the collection of evidence for the Butler Report, several patients carried out a protest on the roof of Broadmoor which attracted enough attention for the formation of the Broadmoor Public Action Committee. Conditions in Broadmoor continued to arouse concern in the 1970s and there was mounting pressure for investigation to be carried out (Cohen, 1982, p. 98). In 1977, the Department of Health commissioned a plan for a new 100-bed wing from its own designers and the team studied how Broadmoor worked for several weeks, finally producing a very critical report which was never published, but is discussed in Cohen's book (Cohen, 1982). In 1980 the All-Party Parliamentary Committee on Mental Health reported on the situation in Broadmoor, following allegations of ill treatment, both by former staff and patients (Report of All-Party Mental Health Committee, *The Guardian*, *The Times*, 1 August 1980).

Influence of the media

The significance of the Boynton Report into the allegations concerning the abuse of patients at Rampton hospital lay particularly in its exposure of the frailty of quality in the special hospitals, dealing with people known as 'mentally disordered' offenders. The showing on ITV in 1979 of *The Secret Hospital*, a documentary about conditions in Rampton hospital, brought into the public arena allegations of brutality by staff against offenders with mental health problems as well as a significant proportion of people with learning disabilities, confined in the special hospitals. The documentary sparked off the inquiry led by Sir John Boynton which reported in 1980 (DHSS, 1980) and led to police investigations and the conviction of some staff for criminal offences. A feature of the criticisms of special hospitals over the years has been the entrenched custodialism attributed to nurses, the custodial aspects of whose roles was emphasised by their membership of the Prison Officers Association. But the pervasive negative influence of institutional culture extended to other staff, as was acknowledged by Dr James MacKeith (now a leading consultant forensic psychiatrist at the Maudsley hospital), after he had left Broadmoor special hospital earlier in his career. David Cohen noted in 1972: 'MacKeith says that he is proud to have worked at Broadmoor but he too, had to confront his institutionalisation. While at Broadmoor, he had read a paper written by a Maudsley professor and found it unrealistic rubbish. A few months later, having left Broadmoor, MacKeith was reading a paper that was excellent but felt vaguely familiar. He suddenly remembered. This was the unrealistic rubbish he had read at Broadmoor. "I was horrified," he said' (Cohen, 1972, p. 72).

Staff groups are not homogeneous, but comprise different interests, roles and statuses. Sometimes, junior staff risk a good deal in raising concerns with their managers and colleagues. The cost of whistleblowing to a person's career can be great, as is evidenced by the experiences of Sue Machin, a former senior social worker at Ashworth special hospital in Merseyside, who was suspended and eventually sacked after allegations that she gave a patient a catalogue listing bugging devices. Subsequently, an industrial tribunal ruled that she had been unfairly dismissed and that the hospital management had 'acted unreasonably' (Sone, 1995, p. 16).

It took years of complaints and criticisms by patients and professionals themselves as well as campaigns by organisations such as MIND, before The Special Hospital Services Authority (SHSA) was set up in October 1989 to assume responsibility for the management of the three special hospitals in England, (Ashworth, Broadmoor and Rampton), taking over from the Department of Health. Before the setting up of the SHSA, the social workers in the special hospitals and other staff employed there were managed by the then DHSS. The Principal Social Workers were accountable to the Medical Directors of the hospitals. In theory, the social workers in the special hospitals should have been working consistently with the core elements of social work as carried out in all other settings, including basic values, principles and methods of work. Also, these social workers should have been affected significantly by the implementation of the Children Act 1989 and the NHS and Community Care Act 1990. The key areas in which the impact of these factors should have been felt included the balance between security and treatment, the particular features of long-term patients' long stay in the hospitals and the distinctive issues and problems arising from planning and carrying out their discharge and re-integration into the community. (Department of Health and Social Services Inspectorate, 1993, p. 14). In the 1990s, the centre of gravity of public debate revolved around the needs of the discharged patient versus the protection of the public, by introducing rigorous measures for supervising patients with mental health problems who were considered at risk of harming themselves (Goldacre, Seagroatt, and Hawton, 1994) and/or other people. The Clunis (Ritchie, Dick and Lingham, 1994) and Newby (Davies, Lingham, Prior and Sims, 1995) inquiries in the 1990s, marked the era of the introduction of more rigorous measures for the discharge, and supervision in the community, of mentally disordered offenders, and for more effective inter-agency collaboration (Home Office and Department of Health, 1995).

Contribution of voluntary organisations

In the early 1970s, MIND, under its director Tony Smythe, took on a more politically activist role than hitherto. From the late 1970s this stance moderated in respect of collective campaigns, but continued with regard to advocacy on behalf of the rights of individual patients in mental hospitals.

The work of MIND exemplifies the tension experienced in many charities between the campaigning role – carried out by members of its London-based central staff – and service provision – the continuing traditional role of its local member groups.

Inspectorial role of the Social Services Inspectorate

In all the flurries of concern about the quality of hospitals for detained patients, relatively little attention has been paid to the work of social workers. An exception is to be found in part of a detailed inspection of the three special hospitals in the early 1990s, the methodology of which illustrates how the SSI approach to inspections has developed since the 1980s. During this inspection, the SSI interviewed a range of staff including managers, directors of personnel planning and administration, finance, nursing, medical services, rehabilitation, psychology, occupations, education, training and therapy, directors of social work, social workers, nursing staff on the wards and in various activity centres within the hospitals, and representatives of other professions closely connected with the work of the hospital including solicitors, hospital managers, probation officers, chaplains and members of voluntary organisation such as the League of Friends, MENCAP, MIND and the CAB. A number of headquarters staff were interviewed including the Chief Executive, the head of medical services, the probation development advisor and social work advisor to the patient care section of the SHSA. Also, groups of interviews with patients were carried out in two hospitals, in one case meeting with the patients counsel and in another case taking part in a patients' ward meeting. Administrative and secretarial staff attached to the social work departments in each hospital were interviewed as a group. Meetings were attended including multi-disciplinary teams, mental health review tribunals, various committees and working groups such as the Admissions Bureaux and Equal Opportunities Working Groups. Three schemes offering accommodation to patients on discharge from hospital were visited. A random sample of 12 case records was examined at each hospital and other records kept in the department. Self-completion questionnaires were sent to 150 patients and their families. The initial response rate was 59 per cent for patients and 58 per cent for families. This rose to 61 per cent and 63 per cent respectively after a reminder letter was sent. Stamped addressed envelopes were included with each original letter and questionnaire. Additionally, letters were sent to 26 Medium Secure Units asking about their links with the social work department in special hospitals.

A number of organisations including WISH (Women In Special Hospitals), MIND and MENCAP were also asked about their work in the three hospitals and their relationships with the social work departments within the special hospitals. This inspection, the objective of which was to 'inspect and evaluate the management and provision of social work to patients and their families in the three special hospitals, and report with recommendations' (Social Services Inspectorate, 1993e, p. 1), provides a model for inquiries of this nature. It indicates the range of sources from which data needs to be gathered, the depth at which information should be sought and the complexity of the context in which special hospitals work.

The results of this inspection were that although the majority of families stated that they were either satisfied or very satisfied with the social work service in the special hospitals, the inspectors did not consider that the present provision of social work in the hospitals was of an acceptable standard. The nature of their criticisms revolved around the fundamental lack of clarity about the role of social workers and social work departments in the special hospitals and the lack of consistency of practice between and within the social work departments, the managerial and organisational deficiencies and inconsistencies within the delivery of social work services and aspects such as the lack or regular supervision and attention to training and staff development of the social workers. (Social Services Inspectorate, 1993e, pp. 4–6).

New managerialism in mental health

From the early 1980s to 1990, there was a shift from Taylorist to quasi-commercial managerialism, in the light of the Griffiths report. In the early 1980s, new monitoring arrangements were put in place, and in 1983 the Griffiths report led to the introduction of general managers in the NHS. In this way, Griffiths attempted to import the managerial style of Sainsbury's, through his links with this family grocery business, into the health service, by subordinating professionals in healthcare to newly created strong line management. The Griffiths proposals encountered strong opposition, especially from medical and nursing professionals. The conflict represented tensions between two styles of management, one directed by professionals whose actions were informed by their own professional judgements, and the other led by general managers superimposed on the traditional autonomy of the professionals.

In addition to the issue of treatment in special hospitals, there were wider questions of policy and practice in health and personal social services. The relationship between hospital local management committees and the DHSS changed as the nature of managerial control changed, from the 1970s to the 1990s. The influx of maingrade managers into hospitals as key sites for the delivery of NHS services accelerated from the 1970s. The reorganisation of 1974 was accompanied by the introduction of systems for planning (DHSS, 1972). Two factors which contributed further to health service administrators becoming managers were continuing inquiries into shortcomings in hospitals and industrial disputes in the health service in the late 1970s. From the 1980s, competitive tendering contributed to demands for managers to manage.

The post-Griffiths way of evaluating quality in health services in the UK, prior to the White Paper *Working for Patients* (Department of Health, 1989c), was through the medical definition of quality, that is, using 'techniques of peer review such as medical and nursing audit' (Kitchener and Whipp, 1995, p. 198). However, during the 1980s, the government and senior managers in the NHS became increasingly concerned with introducing new approaches to quality assurance to the health service (Kitchener and Whipp, 1995, p. 198). The prioritisation of patients' needs undertaken through the universal medical audit (National Audit Office, 1988) involved gathering data on identifying and satisfying customers, hence marking the transition to a conceptual and practical association of quality with marketing (Kitchener and Whipp, 1995, p. 198). Kitchener and Whipp (1995, p. 199) note that the impact of a managerially-led quality assurance approach (see Chapter 2) can be seen in the definition of the process of assuring quality in *Working for Patients* as a 'systematic, critical analysis of the quality of medical care' (Department of Health, 1989c, p. 39).

The analysis of Kitchener and Whipp confirms the significance of the functions played by management-driven approaches to quality assurance, as part of the shift to quasi-markets in the health service. However, their evidence points up a paradox, namely, that the pervasiveness of the new managerialism in the health service is still fragile at local level, particularly in the implementation of these approaches through local health service organisations, NHS trusts and other healthcare providers. They conclude that 'both managers and professionals have attempted to use the market to sustain their notions of quality. What stands out is the indeterminate nature of the internal market of the NHS, the transitory state of the current 'negotiated order' and the multiple contradictions within the discourse of quality' (Kitchener and Whipp, 1995, p. 208). Concerns about quality in the 1990s are characteristic of the style of quasi-commercialism adopted in the light of the White Paper *Working for Patients* and the NHS and Community Care Act 1990.

The mass media focused public debate in the 1990s on shortcomings of the process of discharging patients from hospitals, including failures in assessment, decisionmaking, after-care and supervision and treatment. In particular, inquiries highlighted the disastrous consequences of discharges of some patients from hospitals to inadequate community care (see p. 138).

Even though the hospital closure programme gained added impetus by the cost-cutting public sector policies of the Conservative government from 1979, the impact of hospital closures was already evident by the late 1970s. One of the co-authors of the Blom-Cooper Report notes that the number of resident patients declined from 145,000 to 80,000 between 1950 and 1978 (Murphy, 1991, p. 9, quoted in Blom-Cooper, Hally and Murphy, 1995, p. 193).

The 1990s, however, saw many of these debates and criticisms bypassed, in the introduction of quasi-markets in healthcare and medical practice. The landmark was the publication of the White Paper *Working for Patients*. This abandoned the previous emphasis on general managers in the health service in favour of turning doctors into managers.

Since the early 1990s, these proposals have been implemented through turning general practitioners into fundholders with responsibility for their own budgets, and transforming hospitals into trusts responsible for managing their own resources. This devolution and decentralisation reflected similar trends in other parts of the human services. As far as doctors are concerned, the new managerialism represents less of a revolution than might seem, since this chapter began with illustrations of the concentration of power to make clinical judgements and, in effect, shift resources as a result of clinical decisions; quasi-markets simply formalised the control of resources by medical practitioners.

Factors contributing to shortcomings in mental health

Since the late 1980s, the shortcomings of the NHS have been the subject of much debate, in the professional literature and in the mass media. Three main causes tend to be identified, though not necessarily on the basis of any empirical evidence: first, the lack of adequate management; second, the excessive proportion of the NHS represented by management; and third, inadequate resources. Arguments about the lack of resources have been illustrated by a fairly constant stream of mass media stories concerning hospital, ward and bed closures and maladministration – people receiving the wrong treatment, surgical instruments left inside patients and non-qualified medical staff masquerading as qualified for years due to inadequate management.

The DHSS introduced compulsory competitive tendering into the NHS in 1983 and the Local Government Act 1988 introduced it to local government as a whole. The term quasi-market refers to the way a free market is introduced within the constraints of general objectives set by government and central control over the operation of the market. The Griffiths Report imported to the field of community care the ethos of private business, exemplifying several features: relatively autonomous local units responsible for day-to-day running of their own budgets but accountable to, and controlled by, a central office, a local manager of each unit ensuring that the performance of staff meets the specified targets.

The managerialism exemplified by the Griffiths Report has been criticised for being too general and abstract and not rooted in the services it concerns, not addressing the differences between the profit-motivated commercial sector and the benefit-to-people-based health and social care sector, and, in its hierarchical approach, not clarifying how the relationship between the relatively stable bureaucratic management and the relatively precarious professional management of the organisation will work in the ultimate interests of the people requiring professional services. In such circumstances, 'it is difficult to see how the multi-divisional structure can operate without attempting to subordinate and control professional practice' (Cutler and Waine, 1994, p. 5).

The NHS is not a homogeneous organisation, with features which apply universally to all categories of staff. The situation of social workers is quite different from that of managers and doctors. Their circumstances fall somewhere between nurses, health case assistants and ancillary staff. Social workers, like these other groups, experience a more Taylorist style of management than do doctors. Much of what is said about the conditions experienced by nurses applies to social workers: 'a more bureaucratic form of governance, closer supervision, greater accountability for mistakes and a clearer hierarchy of command than medicine. This occurs despite the sometimes isolated working conditions' (Walby and Greenwell, 1994, p. 62). The changes in qualifying training for social workers may have an impact on hospital social work, as the roles of an increasingly numerous workforce of health

care assistants, many holding N/SVQs, expand. Also, social workers increasingly are likely to be affected by contractual changes
(CCETSW, 1993, 1995c). The compulsory competitive tendering of
ancillary work may lead to more rigorous scrutiny of quality and
standards of service. But, insofar as the general tendency is for the
tendering process to induce lower wage levels and poorer conditions of service among staff (Walby and Greenwell, 1994, p. 65), its
practical impact is to create a contract culture which, in the non-
medical, non-core (that is, nursing and allied professional) areas is
resource-led rather than concerned with quality maximisation.
Increasingly, contracts between local authorities and health authorities involve part-time, short-term or temporary contracts being
awarded to staff. These changes may weaken the commitment of
individuals to a career in hospital social work and undermine the
collective accumulation of professional expertise.

Hospitals for people with mental health problems have been
affected by the hospital closure programme of the 1980s and the
development of community care policies in the 1990s. Hospital
social work in the 1990s, like all other activities in the hospital, has
been affected by the changing pattern of usage of different
hospitals, in the wake of the increasing emphasis on keeping costs
down in the quasi-markets for healthcare. The differential costs
associated with maintaining different hospitals, and the high costs
linked with some forms of treatment, are ingredients in the
financial statements which can either redeem or damn an entire
hospital.

> The threatened financial disaster facing London's many expen-
> sive, old, specialist hospitals in areas of declining population
> made the government draw back from the full workings of the
> market. A special commission, the Tomlinson Commission, was
> set up to plan the orderly closure of selected London hospitals.
> This led to a series of campaigns run through the media to save
> particular hospitals. For a while it seemed that paternalistic
> rationalization had replaced the use of a market mechanism, but
> by the autumn of 1993 the internal market was threatening the
> financial viability of the hospitals that Tomlinson had retained.
> Planning and politics, or perhaps, trial by the media, appear to
> be important continuing elements of the system. (Walby and
> Greenwell, 1994, p. 66)

Health Authorities, as in Wales (Welsh Office, 1991), set standards at which services they contract have to aim. Here is a hypothetical example of the criteria by which service providers judge quality:

- each patients to have an individual care plan
- effective communication between hospital, clinic, patient, relatives and the patient's GP, to enable all these parties to make more informed choices
- involving carers, the GP and any other interested party in appropriately arranging a patient's discharge
- reasonable waiting times for out-patients, explanation to be given if any patient has to wait more than 45 minutes for an appointment
- reducing numbers of people waiting for operations
- clear agreements between GPs and consultants about the time scale of admissions of patients
- patient satisfaction surveys to be undertaken by provider units in selected areas
- prompt and effective response to complaints and outcomes reported regularly to the health authority for monitoring
- comprehensive audit of quality in provider units, to identify the current situation and future plans
- quality framework, incorporating quality into the services of providers.

In one sense, the major outcome of the Reed (DH, 1992b) review of health and social services for mentally discharged offenders published in November 1992 which led to two working groups – on high security and related psychiatric provision and psychopathic disorders – was a strengthening of social control over such people rather than enhanced treatment. The Mental Health Act Commission set up under the Mental Health Act 1983 acts as a watchdog over provision and practice regarding detained patients under mental health legislation. However, despite the recorded increase in the use of the Mental Health Act 1983 to detain patients, this body points out in 1995 that it still is not informed of every detention and discharge (Mental Health Commission, 1995, p. 6). The Mental Health Commission monitors the revised Code of Practice on the conduct of the Mental Health Act 1983, the supplement of which deals with the supervised discharge of mental health patients. The Mental Health Commission also investigates complaints under the Mental Health Act 1983, Section 120(1)(b). It deals with matters concerning consent to treatment, inquests and deaths of detained patients, the detention of adolescents and young people, older people and other groups, compulsory admission, aftercare under Section 117 of the Mental Health Act 1983, and various aspects of the quality of life in hospital, such as ethnic and women's issues.

The fact that it is often a matter of chance whether an offender with serious mental health problems is processed through penal or mental health custody indicates more than a diagnostic uncertainty. It draws attention to the vague borderline between the labels of mental disorder and criminality. The likelihood that some commentators will exclude penal institutions from a consideration of the health and social services gives this attribution real significance for the offender.

Shortcomings in mental health provision, especially in the community, came to light through a number of serious incidents, some involving fatalities, which led to two particularly significant inquiry reports, one following the death of Christopher Clunis, in 1992 (Ritchie, Dick and Lingham 1994) and the other led by Sir Louis Blom-Cooper (Blom-Cooper, Hally and Murphy, 1995). The report into the treatment of Christopher Clunis uncovered a cumulative series of failures and omissions by different people and agencies – largely of inter-professional communication and collaboration, a lack of available resources and skills in diagnosing his potentially dangerous condition – from the first time he attended hospital in July 1987 until he stabbed Jonathan Zito in December 1992 (Ritchie, Dick, and Lingham, 1994, pp. 105–7).

The Blom-Cooper report (Blom-Cooper, Hally and Murphy, 1995) of the inquiry into the events leading up to and surrounding the stabbing by Andrew Robinson of an occupational therapist at the Edith Morgan Centre, Torbay, on 1 September 1993, raised serious questions about the under-use of Guardianship orders under the Mental Health Act 1983, in cases where treatment was necessary to a person's stay in the community, particularly with people with schizophrenia and related disorders and those with recurrent manic depressive disorders. Blom-Cooper's report of the public inquiry into the care and treatment of Jason Mitchell by Suffolk Health

Authority and the circumstances leading to his being convicted for triple killings in December 1994, highlights the value of improved training for the members of Mental Health Review Tribunals including an element of auditing of complex clinical cases (Blom-Cooper, Grounds, Guinan, Parker and Taylor, 1996, p. 246).

The Blom-Cooper report examined the problem of how to ensure that patients with chronic disorders, needing treatment outside the hospital, received it. The report revisited the arguments for and against a compulsory community care order made in the review of the Mental Health Act 1959 and not carried further in the Mental Health Act 1983 (DHSS, 1978). The British Association of Social Workers in 1979 had suggested existing measures needed strengthening and in 1987 the Royal College of Psychiatrists (RCP) made proposals for enforced injections of neuroleptic medication in the community backed up by little else, which found little support and were subsequently abandoned (Blom-Cooper, Hally and Murphy, 1995, p. 194).

In 1993, fresh proposals by the RCP for a community supervision order included provision for the patient's consent to the order to be obtained before discharge from the hospital and the identifying of a designated supervisor. The government's response, partly as a way of addressing the concerns of the RCP and partly in the wake of the great public, and mass media, reaction to events such as the death of Jonathan Zito, was to introduce supervised discharges, pursing the principles of the Care Programme Approach. From February 1994, all health authorities had to use supervision registers identifying people with severe mental illnesses who represented a significant risk to themselves or to other people; subsequently, the Department of Health issued further guidance (NHS Executive/Department of Health, 1994).

The Blom-Cooper report asserts that the Mental Health Act 1983 is fundamentally flawed in its link of care and treatment of people with more severe mental disorders necessarily with hospital detention, rather than with measures to ensure treatment takes place, as part of community care (Blom-Cooper, Hally and Murphy, 1995, p. 197). The report proposes the replacement of the Act, so that it 'will provide a more therapeutic framework for care, continue to control the unwarranted interventions of doctors, and yet will provide more safety and security for patients, their families and the general public' (Blom-Cooper, Hally and Murphy, 1995,

p. 198). This translates into proposals for powers for the compulsory care of mentally disordered people, wherever they live and in the context of their care plan (Blom-Cooper, Hally and Murphy, 1995, p. 199).

Evaluating the contribution of mental health commissioners

The Mental Health Act 1983 included provision for mental health commissioners to act as independent reviewers of the circumstances of detained mental health patients. Given the particular vulnerability of conditions in hospitals for detained patients to degradation, the Mental Health Act Commission was set up under the Mental Health Act of 1983 with an inspectorial brief to monitor standards of these services. Mental Health Act Commissioners make visits to hospitals and other units where detained patients are resident. Among the total of just under 100 mental health commissioners are people from different disciplines and professions associated with health and social services – nurses, psychiatrists, social workers and so on – as well as some lay members. The participation of service users of mental health services is not ruled out in principle but commissioners tend to be no less vulnerable than any other members of the community to the stresses of the role, when visits to establishments and institutions are being carried out. There are some notable strengths of the system of mental health commissioners. These include the ability to make unannounced visits – made at any hour of the day or night – to inspect all aspects of hospitals and other settings where mental health patients are detained, and to have access to all records and to all staff and patients. Such inspections produce observations which can be fed back to the institutions concerned, in the form of a critical snapshot of conditions for patients.

The work of the Mental Health Commission itself has acknowledged its limitations (Mental Health Commission, 1995), and from time to time the efficacy of the system of commissioners can be called into question. How was it, for example, that despite the requirement that members of one panel per hospital of specially appointed mental health commissioners visit each special hospital at least once a month, in early 1997 serious sexual abuse was alleged to have taken place in both Ashworth and Broadmoor? Three other weaknesses of the mental health commissioner role are noteworthy.

First, hospitals in general are large and complex organisations. As a result, staff may make improvements only gradually. The impact of attempts to improve practice by such external agents as Mental Health Act Commissioners is limited by the extent to which staff in a particular hospital are willing to take criticisms on board, rather than reacting defensively. Second, they may not investigate clinical matters, nor the circumstances of patients who are in hospital under duress but who are not detained by law, for example 'sectioned' under the Mental Health Act 1983. Third, they may only investigate the conduct of community care for previously detained patients at the invitation of the director of social services.

Beyond an error-driven approach in mental health work

The failings of mental health provision lie partly in the problematic identity of the person with mental health problems, i.e. having a medically rather than a socially defined problem, and partly – for detained patients such as mentally disordered offenders – in their ambiguous location between the criminal justice and health services. The various organisational, technical, financial and professional shortcomings of mental health policy and practice identified above are superimposed on these inherently problematic features.

EXAMPLE 6.4

Saul has called a meeting of the multi-disciplinary staff group in his psychiatric ward in the hospital, to discuss how to overcome long-standing problems of low staff morale, in the wake of several inquiries into serious allegations of shortcomings and malpractice in various aspects of the hospital services. The meeting starts very negatively, but eventually comes up with a number of positive recommendations, listed below as two sub-headings, for further work in future meetings of the staff group:

Increased participation of service users in resourcing and service development

The quality of services – such as community mental health provision – which at present remain medicalised and firmly locked into professional budgets would be enhanced by giving service users greater power over the resources to develop these services (Rogers, Pilgrim and Lacey, 1993).

Detained patients: providing resources to balance risk against needs

Current mental health policies point towards instituting greater caution over discharge and more control in post-discharge supervision. The longstanding need for more mentally disordered offenders to be diverted from prison and other mental health resources to be increased accordingly has been noted by no less an authority than the Mental Health Commission (1995, p. 73). An alternative approach involves working towards maximising the benefits to all stakeholders in the situation, by reframing the issue as one of support rather than control – providing sufficient resources to *support* the discharged offender, to minimise the risk of breakdown after discharge.

Richard Jones's authoritative manual on mental health law details guidance on the supervised discharge of mental health patients, under the Mental Health (Patients in the Community) Act 1995, supplement to the Code of Practice published in August 1993 pursuant to Section 118 of the Mental Health Act 1983 (Jones, 1996, pp. 642–56). Approved social workers are 'key players' in the successful implementation of Section 117 of the Mental Health Act 1983 and the Care Programme Approach (Mental Health Commission, 1995, p. 132).

This chapter has shown the importance of preserving and enhancing measures to respond to complaints and whistleblowing concerning services. But it has also drawn attention to features of such problem-based activities which render them inherently limited.

The next chapter illustrates child care approaches to enhancing quality, based on audits of professional practice.

7

Enhancing Quality 1: Professional Audit and Progressive Practice in Child Care

Auditing is the term used by the Audit Commission to refer to processes of checking whether public money is being spent economically, efficiently and effectively. There is a degree of tension between this finance-based concept and the professional basis for social work. Professional audit is the term used here to express the tension between professional practice and financially-led auditing procedures. The nature and meaning of professional practice is often a matter for debate and controversy. Auditing practice, on the other hand, is bound by legislation. The code published in July 1995 which governs the auditing practices of local authorities in England and Wales is a statutory requirement under Section 14 of the Local Government Finance Act 1982, as amended by Section 20 and Schedule 4, paragraph 4 of the NHS and Community Care Act 1990. This chapter examines arrangements made for assuring the quality of professional activity, to establish whether or not the standards are adhered to, with particular reference to child care in fieldwork and residential settings.

Auditing and progressive practice: some examples

EXAMPLE 7.1

'Charity covered up child abuse', was the headline over an article in *The Guardian*, concerning Scope, formerly the Spastics Society, which 'yesterday admitted to covering up 10 years of child abuse at one of its schools' (2 February 1996). Fourteen children aged 4 to 12 with profound and multiple learning disabilities, some with additional cerebral palsy and sensory impairment, were abused at Hawksworth Hall School, Guiseley near Leeds. The abuse was discovered in an investigation in 1993, when it was found that a female member of staff had acted aggressively towards the children, including slapping them across the face. The staff member was sacked, but reinstated on appeal, and left three months later. According to *The Guardian*, 'when the school's headteacher and its former education officer were questioned by a parent and school governors and social services, they both denied the incidents had taken place. They flouted both the law and Scope's own child protection procedures when they failed to report the allegations of abuse to social services' (*The Guardian*, 2 February 1996). However, the former headteacher alleged later that he had reported the incidents to Scope, whose managers failed to act ('Ex-head accuses bosses of abuse cover-up', *Yorkshire Post*, 6 February 1996, p. 1). According to *The Guardian* (2 February 1996), 'the allegations only came to light after a parent complained about another matter in 1994 and an external inquiry was launched. Policy were called in and a file passed to the Crown Prosecution Service, but parents were told last month no action would be taken.' Subsequently, the parents decided to take private legal action.

The separation of purchasers from providers and the trend towards service providers in the marketplace of the personal social services being contracted on the basis of their known profile of successful previous contracts, in terms of meeting quality standards, increases rather than decreases the temptation for staff to attempt to preserve as cosmetically 'clean' view of their organisation's facilities as possible. This contravenes the principles of openness to scrutiny and the maintenance of a culture of self-critical awareness, implicit in the first Report of the Nolan Committee (see Chapter 2).

The above example shows how pressure towards maintaining the appearance of a well-managed child care unit may conflict with the necessity to rectify serious abuses within it. A number of principles of basic child care practice are embedded in the example, notably the necessity for anti-oppressive, ethical practice based on respect for people, fulfilling legal requirements, and enabling parents and children to participate in decisions made by child care staff.

However, such incidents of abuse, given the inability of many of the victims to communicate about them, may greatly exceed those which have come to light, and may have continued for many years when they are exposed. In this case, the abuse predated by almost a decade the development of quasi-markets in health and social care. The acting director of operations for Scope said 'Children as profoundly disabled as some of these are so vulnerable that they are totally dependent on adults for their well-being. They are sitting targets' (*The Guardian*, 2 February 1996). Such shortcomings are rooted not only in defective management and the inadequacies of staff and staff training, but also in the particular vulnerability of some disabled people to abuse and the societal norms and expectations which do not encourage it to be challenged.

A management approach involving searching audits of practice could uncover the extent of any shortfall in standards, in such a situation. It is necessary to ask what kind of auditing style would ensure this. It is possible to carry out an audit by working simultaneously from different points in the organisation – that is, from management, practitioner and/or user vantage points. The following example indicates that during this process it may be difficult to achieve the goal of enabling all stakeholders, including users, to participate in the process.

EXAMPLE 7.2

A group of students were set the task of drawing a chart of the social services organisation, or their child care setting, indicating with lines where power and accountability were located. All but one omitted the service users from the chart. Even that one student had difficulty linking the service users to any other groups of staff. The two views of the organisation, from senior management and junior staff points of view, emerged from the diagrams drawn. From the top, the family tree was much flatter. From the bottom, the hierarchy tended to be presented as cliff-like. One person drew a figure at the bottom of the page bowed down by an enormous weight.

Two points emerge from this: first, there is no consensus about the nature of the organisation and the place of staff and clients in it, particularly the latter, as a relatively dispersed group lacking formal links with processes and structures for decision-making and the exercise of power; second, the image of the organisation may act as a barrier to enabling service users to achieve empowerment.

In theory, any aspect of organisational practices may be audited. Ideally, professional audit will be part of the work of the team, rather than perceived as imposed from outside.Thus, it may feed into, and be fed by, reviews and supervisory practices in a team or locality. In any case, for it to be effective, the routes between its outcomes and existing formal arrangements for professional development, operational management and so on, will need to be made explicit.

The analysis of managerialism, (Ch 3), by no means implies that the power of senior, or indeed any, managers is absolute. The growing power of bodies such as the Mental Health Commission to inspect social services from the vantage point of particular professional interests, renders local authority social services departments and their partner providers of social services increasingly prone to monitoring, and on occasions investigation, by independent bodies. The consequences of independent investigations for managers can be dramatic. The Meadowdale inquiry in Morpeth, in 1995, covering the years since the home was set up in 1972, for example, led to the resignation of the director of social services, through the widening of scope of the inquiry to all children's homes in Northumbria, and the finding of malpractices in one of them (Donegan, Lawrence, 1995, 'Catalogue of child abuse "ran for more than 10 years"', *The Guardian*, 25 October, p. 2).

Approaches to auditing

Different auditing approaches predominate: conventional, focusing on quality imposition or maintenance; and progressive, focusing on quality enhancement or maximisation.

The *conventional* approach fulfils more restricted financial goals and the managerialist requirement of controlling practice. It relies typically on a technical, tick-list approach. For example, the approval by the Association of Chief Probation Officers of a PSR *Quality Assessment Checklist* for pre-sentence reports (PSRs) clarified the criteria which should be used to judge the quality of PSRs. Key items included assessing the risk of re-offending, the risk of harm to the public, the likelihood, capacity and motivation of the offender for change and indicating how the risk could be managed or reduced. Significantly, the criteria did not prescribe the use of custody only as a last resort.

The *progressive* approach to audit attempts to engage with the complexity of professional practice – not least the difficulties of decision-making and, despite standards and checklists, the lack of a single answer to problems. This approach also takes on board possible structural features of this, rather than pathologising them. There is a need to evaluate the advantages and disadvantages of different approaches. The progressive approach is committed to user participation, but the conventional approach may not be. There is an embryonic focus on professional audit and progressive practice in many areas. Resources are often devoted to checking procedures are carried out and various error-driven activities.

The views of service users and carers may be incorporated in the audit of quality, by individuals or groups of representative samples taking part in group-based feedback on services. Questionnaires are a widely used conventional means of gaining feedback and are subject to the limitation of people's capacity and motivation to complete them. Arrangements need to be made, in any case, to ensure that the language of questionnaires corresponds with that of the people completing them and that they can be completed by a person with a visual impairment. Group-based feedback is likely to offer participants more direct opportunities for communicating their views. However, arrangements need to be made for people with sight and hearing impairments in particular to participate, and for interpreters where group members include non-English speakers. Also, group dynamics and the nature and style of group leadership will affect the feedback. It may be necessary for group leaders to be clearly stated to be appointed from an independent setting, with no formal links with the service-providing agency, for example.

Professional audit may ideally be associated with quality enhancement or maximisation approaches than those of quality rectification or maintenance. Risk analysis may be used to buttress managerialism (Example 7.3); an organisation-wide strategy may employ adult learning principles (Example 7.4) and be based on principles of staff care (Example 7.5):

EXAMPLE 7.3

In a Home Counties social services department, risk analysis is used as the basis for management to decide how the work is allocated and thereby to ration services. The main criterion by which cases are prioritised is the likelihood of current or future physical or sexual abuse of children. Case managers manage the assessment procedures, then allocate the highest risk cases to professionally qualified and experienced social workers. Protection apart, the other needs of children and their families are met by contracting out services to specialist voluntary and private agencies, such as those dealing with housing problems, educational difficulties, drug abuse and family support.

This approach has the advantage of evidence-based practice (see p. 179) that it reduces the seeming uncertainties of decisionmaking in social work: draws on such research as points towards the efficacy of specific interventions; and marginalises methods – such as long-term therapeutic work with possibly abused children – deemed less cost-effective. It suffers from four main weaknesses: it fosters the myth that a solution to every human problem encountered by social workers lies waiting to be discovered; it assumes good social work is necessarily subject to experimentally-based outcome evaluation (preferably through randomly controlled trials); it potentially deskills professionals working with people; it reinforces resource-led, managerialist practices.

EXAMPLE 7.4

In Kingston upon Hull, the process of quality assurance is divided into three aspects: staffing (including staff development), personalised care (including services to individuals and associated resources) and the environment (including how services may be facilitated). A unit may take on the task initially of carrying out the process focusing on staffing; subsequently, services to individuals may be tackled; later, the wider area of resources and the environment may be addressed. A repeat of the process at one stage may be carried out a year or two later. Thus, quality assurance is viewed as a process akin to staff development within an adult learning model. This process may be initiated by a wide range of means. Their precise nature does not matter, so long as it produces enough material for an initial analysis of results.

At the next stage, it is noteworthy that the initial perception of many staff that most of their problems are due to lack of attention to issues such as resources, by senior management, shifts as they list issues that they can tackle within the team. This process, together with the sharing of the report with other stakeholders in quality, is the crux of quality assurance at the level of the providing unit.

Subsequently, it is important that the results of the previous stages are fed into subsequent decision making concerning future targets, and into departmental management and, eventually, to the social services committee (information supplied by Mal Blackburn).

EXAMPLE 7.5

Staff from two neighbouring residential child care establishments meet and are comparing notes. In establishment A, 30 per cent of staff have been on sick leave at any one time over the past six months. In establishment B, the figure is nearer 10 per cent. The staff discuss possible explanations for this contrast, including local conditions, recruitment policies, management styles and working practices. There is a general consensus that stress at work is largely responsible for the higher absences in establishment A. The meeting concludes by deciding to press for a staff care policy to be developed and implemented in both establishments and for continued monitoring of the situation, by further joint staff meetings among other measures.

Often, such areas as staff care are implicit in codes of professional conduct. Codes of practice on professional activity fulfil a similar function to standards of service. However, guidance such as BASW's code of practice on expression of staff concerns (Anon, 1995, p. 9) and subsequent guidance for whistleblowers has a distinctive significance, since it adopts the view that responsible practice includes raising issues of concern where appropriate (BASW, 1997).

Case study: addressing concerns about quality in child protection

Beyond gut responses to scandals

Since the 1940s, a combination of factors has put quality high in professional and public concerns about public sector child care.

But these concerns are not homogeneous; nor do they reflect a consensus about values, policies and practices in child care in professional and domestic settings. These are not exclusively related to shortcomings, but emerge clearly when a particular issue reaches the public domain, often via the mass media. A great variety of stances have been taken in relation to scandals over child care. Towards one extreme, there is the 'moral panic' view. Rojek, Peacock and Collins (1988, p. 149) do not dismiss child abuse as a fiction, but nevertheless, they say: 'Moral panics in social work have occurred in respect of care of the elderly, the mentally handicapped, drug addicts, alcoholics, and the unemployed. However, nowhere have the panics been more severe, nowhere more unremitting, than in cases of child abuse.' Towards the other extreme is the 'tip of the iceberg' view. This argument is exemplified in the commentary by the former manager of a children's home in Gwynedd, who was sacked subsequent to making allegations about widespread sexual abuse of children in care in children's homes in Wales and north west England. There had been twelve previous internal reports by Clwyd council, and one by Nicola Davies Q.C. for the Welsh Office only the conclusions of which were published. After the decision by the outgoing Clwyd council not to publish the fourteenth inquiry report (Jillings, Tunstill and Smith, 1996), Taylor said in an interview by Roger Dobson of the *Independent on Sunday* 'I believe the abuse may go back 30 years. I have spoken with young men who were abused in the late 1960s. It is something which became part of the culture. In all, more than 2,000 children may have been abused. At times, homes had 100 admissions a year on average and 46 homes were investigated. The police took nearly 3,000 statements and they did not go back 30 years' (Dobson, 1996, p. 5).

It would be difficult to begin a discussion of quality child care anywhere other than with the prominence of a succession of scandals about the maltreatment of children, by parents, or adults in the parental role, and by child care staff, notably in residential child care provided by local authorities. The mass media and voluntary organisations such as Barnardo's, National Children's Homes, NSPCC and the Children's Society have played a role in publicising these. But at times, voluntary organisations, notably the RSSPCC (House of Commons, 1992–3) have themselves been under critical scrutiny for shortcomings in their own child care.

The Pindown inquiry led by Allan Levy and Barbara Kahan (1991) led to the Department of Health introducing guidelines preventing the physical restraint of children. In 1991, Frank Beck, head of a children's home in Leicestershire, was given five concurrent life sentences for the sexual and physical abuse of up to 200 children. The deputy principal of Bryn Estyn children's home in Wrexham from 1976 to 1984 was given a 10-year prison sentence for offences against children.

Implications of the accumulation of inquiry reports

Progress in practice has scarcely been helped by the sheer volume of repetitive scandals and inquiry reports in child care since the early 1970s. The trend has been for this to lead to some legitimate criticisms of the practice of child care, but also to the cumulative scapegoating of social work in general, rather than broad-based upgrading taking place in the resourcing, management and professional education of staff in child care, whether based in residential work or fieldwork. Inquiries into particular incidents of abuse of children provided an impetus for changes in policy and practice (Asquith, 1993). Parton (1985), argues that the emergence of child abuse as a problem was conceived in the 1970s as a medico-social issue which required the expertise of doctors, particularly paediatricians and social workers, to treat. In the 1980s and 1990s, the public debates about sexual abuse and parental rights suggest that social work has a role to play in reconstructing the nature of child protection practices and also in contributing to debates about the nature and form of the family itself (Parton, 1991, p. 214).

There has been a tendency for most of the influential inquiries into child care over the postwar period to have been carried out at one remove from the government, by service-providing authorities themselves (see Table 7.1 for an illustration between the years 1973 and 1985).

Moving inquiries beyond scapegoating social workers

Whilst at the technical level, histories of formal inquiries into the shortcomings of child care can be narrated as though they are consensual, in reality, the proceedings of inquiries tend to be microcosms of the contemporary debates and conflicts in which

Table 7.1   Types of inquiry: the example of child abuse, 1973–85

Inquiry and date	Initiated by
Graham Bagnall 1973	Salop CC
Wayne Brewer 1977	Somerset ARC
Lester Chapman 1979	Berks and Hants CC/HA
Lisa Godfrey 1975	Lambeth SSD and others
Neil Howlett 1976	Birmingham CiC/HA
Maria Mehmedagi 1981	Southwark BC and others
Steven Meurs 1975	Norfolk CC/HA
Shirley Woodcock 1981	Hammersmith and Fulham BC
Malcolm Page 1981	Essex CC/HA
Simon Peacock 1978	Cambs and Suffolk CC/HA
Max Piazzani 1974	Essex CC/HA
Karen Spencer 1978	Derbs CC/HA
Carly Taylor 1980	Leics CC/HA
Jason Caesar 1982	Cambs CC
Lucy Gates 1982	Bexley BC/H
Reuben Carthy 1985	Notts ARC
Jasmine Beckford 1985	Brent BC/H
Maria Colwell 1974	Secretary of State for Social Services
John Auckland 1975	Secretary of State for Social Services
Darryn Clarke 1979	Secretary of State for Social Services
Paul Brown 1980	Secretary of State for Social Services
Richard Clark 1975	Secretary of State for Scotland
Stephen Menheniott 1978	Department of Health and Social Security

Key:
ARC   Area Review Committee
CC   County Council
CiC   City Council
BC   Borough Council
H   Health Authority
HA   Area Health Authority

social work policy, theory and research are immersed. For example, whilst summary accounts of the inquiry report into the Maria Colwell tragedy tend to describe the events and list the recommendations, one of the most revealing aspects of the report is the dissenting Chapter 5 (pp. 88–115), after the conclusions, written by Olive Stevenson, which advocates a more detailed critical analysis of the context and nature of actions taken, for instance, by the social workers in East Sussex dealing with Maria Colwell and a less sweeping and judgemental approach to conclusions. Significantly, Stevenson's detailed analysis recognises the attempts of the social workers to practise within a complex and rapidly changing situation (p. 108), where staff were 'overloaded' (p. 115); it argues the need to appreciate the strengths as well as the weaknesses among the social work staff in East Sussex. Hence, she disassociates herself from the 'hierarchy of censure' (p. 115) of the report, though agreeing with some of its critical conclusions.

On the whole, the fact that inquiries into child care are carried out by employing health and social services organisations (Table 7.1) militates against independence and criticality in reports. But there are notable exceptions. For example, a report by the director of social services and housing in Bromley alleged that residential child care in the Borough of Bromley was failing to meet statutory requirements for children looked after by the local authority (*Community Care*, 9–15 June 1994, no. 1020, p. 4).

An appraisal of the impact of measures to counter shortcomings in child care needs to balance the respective parts played by different kinds of inquiries, and set against these the roles of official inquiries against the activities of statutory and voluntary agencies (such as social services departments, NSPCC, NCH, NSPCC, SSPCC, Barnardo's), the role of research and the activities of pressure groups and self-help organisations and groups, such as Child Watch and Incest Survivors. There is little doubt that the relatively minor role of judicial inquiries and the tendency for most inquiries to be at the behest of the authorities providing services themselves, has limited their authority and sometimes the impact of their findings. The abuses in Clwyd child care establishments, for example, were investigated on numerous occasions, but without the authority of the judicial inquiry set up in 1996 at the recommendation of the Jillings inquiry, could not subpoena witnesses and so had their powers curtailed from the outset (Jillings, Tunstill and Smith, 1996). As far as the influence of research is concerned, it has to be said that the report by the DHSS when publishing findings from nine research projects in 49 local authorities involving some 2,000 children, of the 'quite disturbing and depressing' situation in child care (DHSS, 1985, p. 5) was hardly contradicted by the succession of revelations over the following decade. In contrast, some pressure groups have performed an invaluable educational role (Elliott, 1993), individuals such as Beatrix Campbell have subjected child protection failures since the Butler Sloss Report in Cleveland to critical scrutiny (Campbell, 1989, pp. 224–5), and children themselves have played a significant, if underdocumented (Adams, 1991, p. 27) part in resisting aspects of their formal socialisation, notably through schooling in general and incarceration in particular in reformatories, Home Office Approved Schools and community homes.

Developing policies which counteract wider causes of child neglect and harm

Children's rights have been generally neglected, and children (and sometimes their parents) have tended to be blamed for their delinquency, rather than any wider causes such as poverty, housing, and the environment (Frost and Stein, 1992; Adams, 1996a, p. 85). At the same time, the mass media tended to blame social workers for failures of the welfare system to protect children. In fact, lapses by social workers are easier, ready-made sources of headline news than any lack of reliable statistics about the ongoing incidence of child abuse in the community at large (Franklin and Parton, 1991; Aldridge, 1994). The focus on social work practice also deflects attention from other potential culprits — the State, local authority provision in education, health (Clothier, MacDonald and Shaw, 1994) and youth provision and, of course, the household of the child as a site for abuse. Ironically also, exposure of the risks to a child being greatest from those most closely related, including family members in the same household, would have contradicted an increasingly public consensus from the 1960s about the centrality of the family as a civilising institution in society and as *the* preferred site for socialising children and young people. To say the least, social work has provided a convenient scapegoat, on which to blame the growing visibility of children's problems, in which child abuse cases assume an iconic significance. In short, structural, policy and social factors contributing to such problems tend to be set aside and responsibility either laid at the door of social work or, in a neat inversion of logic, when children commit offences, identified with the attitudes and actions of children themselves. A response to the totality of children's needs is called for. The National Bureau for Co-operation in Child Care, later the National Children's Bureau, was founded in 1958, partly impelled by campaigners for children's needs to be responded to as a totality and not through the fragmented interests of different sectors of the human services – health, education, juvenile justice or social services (Rodway and Rea Price, 1996).

Challenging the collective exploitation of children

Children's rights movements have highlighted collective exploitation of children, for instance in prostitution, child labour and paedophilia (Rodway and Rea Price, 1996, p. 4), the corollary of which is an enhanced willingness to view seriously and as a matter of high priority abuses which breach those rights. In part, this is a consequence of the increased awareness of people's rights in the wake of the horrors of the holocaust in the Second World War. A further spur to proposed legislation to strengthen children's rights has come from longstanding international campaigns (Hawes, 1991), which achieved marked progress in the adoption on 20 November 1989 by the UN General Assembly, of the United Nations Convention on the Rights of the Child. The influence of that Convention on the Children Act 1989 is reflected in the close correspondence between, for example, Article 12 and Section 22 of the Children Act, concerning the requirement for local authorities to consult children before deciding how to look after them (Buchanan *et al.*, 1993 pp. 22–3).

Research funded by the DHSS and the Economic and Social Research Council (ESRC) increasingly called into question the quality of child care practice (DHSS, 1985; DH, 1991c; DH, 1995). Inquiry reports into particular incidents of child abuse were both products of, and factors feeding into, further concerns, since they 'provided the major catalyst for venting in a very public way, major criticisms of social work in the area of child care' (Parton, 1991, p. 195). The Cleveland child abuse inquiry emphasised the need for further work to improve the consistency of joint practice between police and social workers regarding child sexual abuse. Associated problems of homelessness of young people and coordinating agency responses to children running away from home and residential care, have heightened this awareness (for example, Newman, 1989).

Working with children in the family: beyond ideology

Government-led initiatives in divorce reform, child support and social security confirmed the centrality in Conservative Party policy (1979–97) of intentions of preserving the family. However, the implementation of those aims raises many problematic issues, not least concerning the links, if any, between the ideology as opposed to the reality of improving the quality of family life through social policy.

In the field of child protection, the death of Maria Colwell was a milestone in leading to an early, much quoted inquiry report. But there is a need to examine its impact on practice, in view of the many subsequent inquiries into other situations raising similar questions about the quality of child care and protection. Twenty years later, the tendency of the government towards linking alleged increases in children's problem behaviour with declining family values and a growth in single-parent families, ironically in the aftermath of the James Bulger murder trial, led to the government declaring a commitment to tougher responses to persistent child and young offenders (Adams, 1996a, p. 199).

Addressing staffing weaknesses

In the wake of the inquiry report into the death of three-year-old Leanne White at the hands of her stepfather in 1992 in Nottinghamshire, an independent report criticised the inability of the social services department to prevent the tragedy. Simultaneously, there were two ongoing management reviews – one into high staff turnover and the recrtuitment and retention of child care staff, and the other on child protection services in the wake of Leanne White's death. Child protection teams in that county took selective strike action in support of increased funding and training, and the creation of an extra practitioner tier to encourage staff to stay in child protection practice rather than move into management (*Community Care*, no. 1016, 14 May 1994, p. 2). Three weeks later, staff were considering further industrial action. As a staff member put it: 'We did not strike for more pay. What we want to see is an improvement in the services we are meant to be providing' (*Community Care*, no. 1019, 2–8 June 1994, p. 14).

Addressing shortcomings: through empowerment rather than procedures

There is rarely scope for people – whether children or adults – to have a determining stake in the quality of care they receive (Page and Clarke, 1977). Such influence as they have had arises indirectly from their participation, for example, in inquiries, inspections and research, organised and carried out by others.

Official responses to scandals about shortcomings in child care by the state have tended to enhance officers' managerial control of professional activity, rather than empowering parents and children (Table 3.1 in Chapter 3 refers). Legal measures and increased regulation of professionals' work do not in themselves guarantee quality enhancement. The increased emphasis on child protection procedures has provided a means whereby professionals monitor children and families, and are in turn monitored and inspected by their own managements. Accountability upwards, to the employing organisation and the state, has been sharpened, rather than accountability to the child and the parents.

Developing preventive and therapeutic child care: beyond a 'fire brigade' approach

Many social services departments by the 1990s had developed a focus on protection, but as much with a view to protecting the backs of staff and the organisation, as directed towards providing a better service for children and their families. Not only did this involve acting as a fire brigade racing from crisis to crisis at the expense of preventive work, with an excessive emphasis on short-term intervention and the policing of child abuse rather than long-term therapeutic work, but also, following a prioritised work pattern all too often was governed by procedures rather than people's – and especially children's – needs.

The emphasis has been put on improving collaborative work and liaison between professionals in the immediate protection of children, rather than on strengthening the impact on children of longer-term work with them. Thus, the bulk of issues concerning quality have focused on the fire-fighting work of social workers rather than their effectiveness as therapeutic agents. This is despite research evidence pointing to the necessity for long-term work with children who are victims of abuse (Gibbons, Conroy and Bell, 1995).

The activities of social workers as therapeutic agents exist alongside, or in tension with, their responsibilities as agents of the state through their employers, for exercising legal powers and duties. There has been a shift since the 1970s towards the latter at the expense of the former (Cloke and Davies, 1995). Parton concludes that this 'involves the superimposition of legal duties and rights upon the therapeutic and preventative responsibilities, essentially for the protection of clients' (Parton, 1991, p. 194). The consequences of this, far from furthering the principle of the Children Act 1989 that the interests of the child should be paramount, include an emphasis on following procedures and rules, or what Parton refers to as legalism (Parton, 1991, p. 193). 'Within an emphasis on legalism, the rule of law as judged by the court takes priority at the expense of other considerations, including that which may be deemed, by the professionals concerned, as optimally therapeutic or "in the best interests of the child"' (Parton, 1991, p. 194).

The tendency for policies and practices concerning the protection of children and young people to predominate over those concerned with preserving their future welfare reflects the priorities of managements rather than the interests of service users. There is a need for therapeutic and empowering social work to transcend the predominance of the protection/control approach in responding to child abuse (Adams, 1996a, pp. 100–1). The second annual report of the Children Act 1989, published in May 1994, showed that some local authorities had more than 10 per cent of child protection cases unallocated, Hereford and Worcester having the highest proportion, at 20 per cent. There was a tendency for child protection work to squeeze out preventive work with children and families under Section 17 of the Children Act 1989.

Ensuring adequate mechanisms for recording information

Audits of practice are likely to have a significant impact on improving practice. They may expose, for instance, inadequate record-keeping or decision-making. For instance, the Social Services Inspectorate play an influential role in governing the implementation of the Children Act 1989. The Act was followed by 10 volumes of guidance and regulations issued by the SSI (Department of Health, 1991d). These were accompanied by the review of the Children Act by Sir William Utting, at the point of retirement from the role of Chief Inspector at the Social Services Inspectorate. A study of six local authorities' child protection services carried out by the Social Services Inspectorate (SSI) revealed that the authorities 'could do better' when drawing up children's plans and carrying out comprehensive assessments in keeping with DH guidance. Authorities were admonished for the 'totally unacceptable practice' of referring children for medical examinations without the prior knowledge or consent of parents and for the failure to allocate keyworkers in some cases. None of the inspected authorities had a policy or guidance on record-keeping and 'in all the authorities, inspectors considered recording was below standard. Case records consisted of a mix of handwritten and typed material and the content was often inadequate. Some case files had front sheets, but none contained regular summaries of the work. Decisions made in supervision sessions were not systematically recorded in the file and it was rare for records to be regularly read and signed by supervisors' (Social Services Inspectorate, 1994c).

Rather than laying responsibility at the door of government for failing to resource and make mandatory qualifying training for all staff in residential homes, scandals led to calls for improved training for individual staff. A report by the Association of Metropolitan Authorities (AMA) on services for children with disabilities argued that the risks of abuse in their families were compounded by the lack of support given to them. The report recommended more contact between child protection and disability services, such as common training and proper procedures for area child protection committees (Association of Metropolitan Authorities, 1994).

The struggle for quality in child care has involved many different interests and stakeholders, politicians, policy-makers, managers, researchers and professionals. Additionally, and somewhat at the margins of policy formation and service delivery, people as service users have striven against entrenched professional power in an institutional and societal context impelled by cost–benefit rather than benefits to children and families.

Case study: Improving quality in group care

Increasingly, since the 1970s, medical technology has enabled prospective parents to decide in the light of tests on pregnant women whether to proceed with the birth of a child expected to be physically impaired, or born with a learning disability. This practical choice has shifted the focus of debate to ethical considerations as to whether it is appropriate and right to exercise it. Arguments for going ahead with the birth and living with the child include references to people who have lived in ways which, by any standards, have been positive and rewarding. Arguments against include questions about what quality of life the child will have if the parents are no longer able to carry out the caring. Colin Wheeler, in the *Sunday Telegraph* (10 March 1996), under the headline 'I should have let my daughter die', catalogues the abuse his profoundly disabled daughter, now 32, has suffered from carers, and writes: 'had we known of the treatment our daughter would receive at the hands of "carers" and is likely to receive in the future, when we are dead, nothing would have persuaded us to allow our child to be born.' At the age of six, Andrée attended a day centre and Wheeler once was able to see that as she got onto the coach, the guide, with a cigarette in one hand 'held the hood of Andrée's duffle coat in the other, yanking it back when she thought Andrée staggered the wrong way and using her clenched fist to punch Andrée in the back of the head to propel her forward – using five or six punches to get her to her seat. I was later told the guide was an alcoholic who was given the job as a form of rehabilitation' (*Sunday Telegraph*, 10 March 1996). Later, Andrée attended a hospital for day care and Wheeler noticed bruising on her when she returned, but eventually had to leave her in full-time care at the hospital for two weeks. 'When she returned I was horrified to see extensive bruising to her backside, upper thighs and groin.' Wheeler complained and attended a meeting, consisting of social workers, hospital administrators and care staff, at which he catalogued the abuse. 'It was clear from the discussion that nobody had tried to investigate why or how this had happened until eventually one of the social workers announced she was confident that the bruising had been caused by Andrée masturbating herself. This was a ludicrous suggestion and completely inconsistent with

Andrée's bruising. Every woman there must have been aware that Andrée was being seriously abused in some way, yet not one of them felt able to utter one word of protest on her behalf' (*Sunday Telegraph*, 10 March 1996).

This extract enables a number of the issues affecting quality in residential and day care to be identified: the difficulty of carers ascertaining the quality of day and residential care actually received by a relative; the need for some people to have an advocate; and the need for improved selection and training of care staff, only 20 per cent of whom were qualified in the early 1990s (Kahan, 1991, p. 149). Wheeler identifies the low quality of care staff as the common factor in these and other allegations he makes of abuse against his daughter (*Sunday Telegraph*, 10 March 1996). But this example raises wider issues, now considered in more detail.

Transcending problems inherent in group care

Consideration of group care presents seven sorts of problem. First, as Kendrick and Fraser say of residential child care, the great variety of provision and the difficulties of marking its boundaries with other forms of provision raise the question as to 'whether it exists as a definable thing at all' (1992, p. 100). Second, the use of the term 'group care' has the advantage of including a continuum from group-based provision in the community to group-based residential provision. However, it implies, and excludes from consideration, another continuum of individualised care, including, for example, some foster-care settings. Third, there is a gradation also from voluntary to compulsory use of provision – for example, from children's homes, boarding special schools including LEA boarding schools, community homes with education (former approved schools) and young offender institutions. Fourth, the word 'care' invokes a question about whether residential provision for young offenders or punishment in the community can be included. (Thus, there was a dilemma about whether to deal with such provision in Chapter 6 of this book or in this present chapter.) Fifth, there is a problem in correlating perspectives on group care *per se* with judgements about its quality. Berridge (1985) demonstrates this, in taking children's homes as an example of the most widespread form of group care for that age group, and distinguishes these by so-called administrative criteria – according to the size of home and the leadership style. However, there is no necessary direct correlation between these criteria and the impact on, say, the needs of children and their rights. Sixth, there is the question about whether group care in general, and residential care in particular, should be regarded, and used, as a positive choice in the sense that the Wagner Report used the term (NISW, 1988b), or as a last resort; this is in the sense that all residential care involves losses but sometimes it offers the option with the least losses relative to other options (Booth, 1985; Clough, 1981, 1982).

Seventh, another aspect of the segregation of people from the community in special day or residential care provision is its age-graded character. Thus, controversy arose in 1996 over the decision of Calderdale council to send a fourteen-year-old boy on remand, to a staff flat in a home for older people because no secure unit places were available in the county. Whilst staff claimed the boy was given one-to-one continuous care, Tim Swift of Calderdale Age Concern stated that the home was totally inappropriate for the boy ('Anger over remand boy sent to home for elderly', *Yorkshire Post*, 6 February 1996, p. 1). This case raises questions concerning the potential conflict between different interests in the personal social services: the boy, residents in the home, the magistrates who remanded him, staff in social services, local groups representing the interests of children and older people, and professional social workers. Whilst these interests may overlap, ultimately some areas of conflict may be irreconcilable.

Managing group care as a positive caring environment

It is worth asking how, in the face of repeated findings of abuses by inquiry reports, many shortcomings persist. Part of the response may be that all too often – as was noted of the management of Staffordshire social services in the inquiry into the Pindown regime of Staffordshire children's homes – inspectorial visits (in Stafford-shire, by elected members of the county council) have concentrated 'more on bricks and mortar than on "the effectiveness of the home" as a form of care for children' (Levy, and Kahan, 1991, ch. 17.32, p. 155).

Despite the negative image of residential care, much of the practice-based literature (Beedell 1970; CCETSW, 1992) has continued to advance the argument that, properly managed, it offers a

positive environment for care provision. The Wagner Report
(NISW, 1988a; NISW, 1988b) argues that the caring environment
for children and adults alike needs to take account of the wishes
and rights of the individual and give meaningful, real choices of
alternative provision. Wagner offers five areas where residential
children's provision can make a positive contribution: respite care,
preparing for permanent placement, keeping siblings in care
together and in touch with other family members, therapeutic
provision for children who are emotionally and socially damaged,
and care and control of the small proportion of disturbed children
who require secure provision (NISW 1988b, pp. 96–7).

The decreased use of residential homes for children reflects a
disenchantment with children's homes traceable to the impact of
research on parental deprivation from the 1960s (Parker, 1988,
p. 112) and to research on the shortcomings of some community
home regimes (Cornish and Clarke, 1975; Walter, 1978; Petrie,
1980; Littlewood and Kelly, 1986), secure accommodation (Millham *et al.* 1978), and – in terms of their success rates in modifying
delinquent behaviour – virtually all penal institutions for young
offenders such as detention centres (Thornton *et al.* 1984), borstals
(Hood, 1965) and community homes with education (Millham *et
al.* 1975). On the whole, research demonstrates that the requirement that children be placed in secure accommodation reflects the
limitations of non-secure accommodation and community provision rather than the needs of more demanding and 'difficult'
children (Millham *et al.*, 1978; Cawson and Martell, 1979).

*Compensating for separations and losses associated with being
placed away from home*

Children placed away from home experience difficulties in keeping
contact with their families (Millham *et al.*, 1986), and, at the point
of leaving, the transition from residential home to community
living is often inadequately prepared for or followed up by
residential staff (Littlewood and Kelly, 1986, quoted in Kendrick
and Fraser, 1992, p. 106) and supported in the community (Stein
and Carey, 1986).

The implications of such research is supported by other findings
arguing for the location of residential provision within an integrated system of child care services (Baldwin, 1990). However,

some of the difficulties and challenges have been documented by Stewart, Yea and Brown (1989). Federations of children's units such as Druid's Heath, seem to be beset by structural problems which, if not throwing into question the rationale for integrated approaches to child care, do cast doubt on their practicality in the longer term.

Child care in the community is as prone to failures in quality as residential child care. The system of registration of child minders by local authorities does not compensate for a lack of formal selection and training in this area; there is a history of criminal abuse of children by childminders, with serious injuries and deaths on occasions. In July 1997, a child minder was imprisoned for the manslaughter of a child in her care, despite being registered with the local authority and impeccable responses to inquiries by the parents prior to the placement of the child (*The Guardian*, 24 July 1997, p. 3). Fostering is prone to abuse and, according to the analysis by Sheila Bray, the incidence of abuse is rising, with allegations of abuse made by children against about one-sixth of foster carers (Braye, 1994).

Providing adequate staffing

Many of the questions about whether quality care is possible return to fundamental issues such as the inadequacy of staffing levels and shortcomings in the training of staff (Millham, Bullock and Hosie, 1980; Stewart, Yea and Brown, 1989). Staffing weaknesses in residential child care include failures of management to address such issues as staffing levels, staff training, support and supervision and staff burnout, sickness rates and turnover (Beddoe, 1980). Moreover, when problems such as suspected or actual abuse of children arise, the inspectorial systems external to residential child care establishments in particular are not always strong enough to be capable of addressing the difficulties. There are questions about whether future privatisation of aspects of child care services will increase the vulnerability of the sector to shortcomings in services. The lessons from repeated scandals and complaints about failures in the quality of services point consistently to the need for staff (officers and practitioners) and members (councillors) to ensure that they know what is going on and are able to intervene to prevent, or to rectify, deficiencies in quality.

Unfortunately, children's rights, the abuse of children and the lack of appropriately qualified staff, have not been the only problems to arise in residential child care. There are also issues of longstanding weaknesses in areas such as the treatment of children whilst in residential care and managing the transition from residential care to the community.

Abolishing warehousing in residential childcare

Millham and colleagues (Millham, Bullock and Cherrett, 1975; Millham, Bullock and Hosie, 1978) carried out research into the tendency for residential child care to operate more as a warehouse than as anything more positive. Residential homes for children, far from being beneficial, may actually be injurious to children, to the extent that they are full of disaffected young people whose anger grows each time they are moved, perhaps frequently, to a fresh establishment. Aggressive children and young people may be moved each time there is an incident; the quiet ones who settle down may be moved to make way for them, and gradually themselves may become disaffected.

Upgrading the status of residential child care

The independent inquiry set up by Staffordshire County Council on 29 June 1990 into the treatment and care of young persons at any establishment where Pindown had been used, and to evaluate Pindown, led directly to further inquiries, initiated by the Secretary of State, into the situation of residential child care throughout the UK (see Chapter 3). The Utting, Skinner and Welsh Office reports in 1991 and 1992 emphasised the common need for policy and practice in residential child care to be upgraded in coherence and importance relative to other personal social services (DH/SSI, 1991b).

The Utting Report (DH/SSI, 1991b) and the Howe Report (Howe, 1992) both addressed the issue of training for residential staff. The Utting Report found that the proportion of residential child care staff possessing relevant qualifications had not increased in 10 years. The Warner Report (Committee of Inquiry . . . , 1992) recommended the design and introduction of a new diploma focusing on the group care of children and young people at an equivalent level to the Diploma in Social Work, as the main professional qualification for staff who worked in residential care with children. It also recommended that this should be modular and should minimise absence from the work place for staff involved. Following this, the residential child care initiative, sponsored by the government and administered by CCETSW, took place in eight approved centres in England and Wales. This initiative was time limited.

Warner also recommended that the new system for recognising and awarding NVQs should address the training needs of staff in residential child care as quickly as possible. By 1994, the government had underwritten the review of the Diploma in Social Work which was to be completed, for courses to implement, by the middle of 1995. This review was to be based on what was to become known as occupational standards, an attempt perhaps by the care sector consortium to back off from the much criticised label of national vocational qualifications which had become attached to the lower grade staff at care assistant level. Thus, the Warner Report drew attention to the need for enhanced training for staff in residential child care, but made the case for separate training, rather than the integrated training some felt would keep residential child care in the mainstream of social work.

The lack of trained staff in residential and day care, and the trend since the 1980s towards widespread privatisation of residen tial provision which distances it from direct quality auditing by the statutory sector, render children and adults as service users increasingly vulnerable to inadequate care and abuse, whether from other users or from staff. Resources allocated to inspection and research are only indirectly and partially able to compensate for the consequences of relatively low priority being given to resourcing adequate staff training, working conditions, support, professional supervision and remuneration for staff in group care. The factors are mutually reinforcing and include the low status both of staff and users in this sector, the lack of resources in terms of money, facilities, trained staff, the lack of service user empowerment (Barford and Warram, 1991) – resources for people themselves to apply to meet their needs – the widespread incidence of discrimination and abuse, and the historical tradition of segregation in residential and day care facilities and tokenism in treatment in them.

Improving coordination and provision of residential child care

Two years later, the Audit Commission (Audit Commission, 1994a) examined a wide range of services for children. Among these, it noted critically that up to 40 per cent of children aged 5 to 16 in children's homes in one local authority received no education, while in six others between 15 per cent and 30 per cent did not attend school. The report criticised poor inter-departmental planning and coordination. It also highlighted the following: a lack of procedures in almost half the local authorities surveyed for preparing plans for young people leaving care; ineffective information systems and quality assurance procedures; a lack of clarity about how to assess children in need under the Children Act 1989; the fact that only a quarter of local authorities surveyed had a joint strategic plan for children's work; and finally, the fact that only a quarter of parents and children with disabilities were satisfied with the present levels of coordination, and many wanted better information about services. The report recommended that education, health, housing, social services and voluntary bodies should work in partnership to assess the current needs of young people leaving care and draw up a strategy in the form of a Children's Services Plan (Audit Commission, 1994a).

Research has contributed critical insights into the desirable quality of child care in the following areas: promoting the welfare of children, in particular those needing placement and those moving from care to independence; catering for children from ethnic minority groups, particularly the need to maintain the child's own home and identification with the birth family in the light of the risks to the relationship between the child and the home when in long-term care; the importance of relationships between the child and siblings and step-siblings; the need to develop partnerships with parents and carers; and the need for improved policies, strategic and tactical planning when making decisions and placements involving children (DH, 1991c).

Developing progressive practice in child care

Audits may be used to reinforce managerialist strategies, or to develop progressive practice. In general terms, openness among staff and a lack of defensiveness are prerequisites for improving the quality of child care. These need to accompany a far more self-critical approach by policymakers, politicians and managers than has been evident hitherto, notably through the history of inquiries into the longstanding abuses of children in Clwyd children's homes. There is a need also for practitioners and children and young people to receive encouragement and support, so that complaints and shortcomings surface readily and at the time, rather than in retrospect, when many of the issues can no longer be addressed, problems rectified and further abuses prevented.

EXAMPLE 7.5

Carla and her colleagues in a group care setting are holding a staff training meeting. They have had the opportunity to put in place a quality assurance process over the past two years. This has enabled them first of all to develop statements concerning the standards of care which they aim to provide. Now, they are in the position of auditing their practice. One outcome of the morning's discussion was a number of problems which have arisen in recent weeks. The meeting was not called to deal with these, but they have made a convenient focus for part of the discussion. They have revisited now a number of issues which have surfaced before:

First, the tensions which may arise between the necessities of putting children's interests first, protecting children, empowering children and conducting investigations need, now as ever, to be managed. There is a division between approaches which buttress managerialism, mid-range approaches which facilitate enhancement and those which encompass quality maximisation.

Second, the paramount importance of maximising the quality of life of the person in group care depends on the development and maintenance of a person-centred environment – expressed in financial, physical and caring quality – which provides a place to live an ordinary life offering personal care and/or help, which empowers service users and constructively manages the tension between protecting people and maximising independence.

Third, they have re-examined their standards for care, and posed questions about practices, all of which, in one way or another, have been picked up by a quick check through the standards.

It should be noted that standards published in May 1990 by the Department of Health for residential homes for older people (SSI/DH, 1990a, *Guidance on Standards for Residential Homes for Elderly People*) form the basis for the standards for the accommodation of people with physical disabilities in residential homes (SSI/DH, 1990b, *Guidance on Standards for Residential Homes for People with a Physical Disability*). The summary of these (SSI/DH, 1990, p. 2) can be used as the basis for an audit of group care in general, and for that reason is adapted in the expanded list below, of expectations concerning beliefs and values, quality of management, quality of care, standards and quality of life in child care:

- *Beliefs and values*: importance of fundamental beliefs in
  - integrity and impartiality
  - worth, rights and responsibilities of the individual
  - the need to protect people who cannot protect themselves
  - the need to empower children and adults
  - the importance of training, support and adivce for staff and unpaid carers and the centrality of choice, rights, fulfilment, independence, privacy and dignity.
- *Quality of management*: the need for
  - values, linked to policies
  - information systems
  - service goals
  - information structures
  - operational systems
  - standards
  - monitoring systems
  - complaints procedures.
- *Quality of care*:
  - services which are accessible, cost-effective and appropriate in a multi-racial society
  - a safe, equal opportunities working environment which offerns job satisfaction to staff
  - professionally qualified staff, who should be equipped with the necessary expertise.
- *Standards*: i.e. criteria for judging quality, worth or value, which *must* be:
  - validated
  - as explicit and precise as possible

- justifiable and logically sound
- acceptable
- practicable
  and which *may* be:
- absolute or relative
- objective or based on subjective judgment
- tangible or intangible.
- *Quality of life*:
  - The first consideration in the operation of the group care setting should be to meet the wishes and expectations of each person and carer, responsible person or parent.

An example of the kinds of detailed application of general inventories of standards in group care which could be made in specific aspects is given in Table 7.2. The dangers of regarding such a list as anything more than indicative include substituting it for a rigorous process of working out what quality maximisation means in any given setting. Accordingly, the list is presented in the form of the results of a brainstorm, under the two headings: inadequate/ questionable and preferred practices. The following headings, of course, can be varied to suit the focus in particular circumstances.

This chapter has given some indications of the issues arising in relation to quality assurance in child care. It has focused on the question of auditing in particular, although the way in which questions about quality have surfaced has touched on the topics of the two previous chapters. Inevitably, there are tensions between adopting approaches based on parents', children's liberation or professionals' child protection perspectives on what is best fir children (Adler and Dearling, 1986, pp. 206–8).The key areas of child protection and group care offer diverse illustrations of quality assurance, but the issues raised do not necessarily contrast. The next chapter considers the next layer of quality assurance likely to be encountered: that of monitoring and evaluation.

Table 7.2   Components of quality group care

Inadequate or questionable	Preferred
Management	
Macho	Anti-oppressive
Colluding with unacceptable practices	Asserting desired practices
Education and training of staff	
Lack of any qualified staff in some settings	All staff receiving qualifying and/or post-qualifying education/training
Staffing	
Employment of unqualified staff	All staff qualified
Lack of direct supervision of staff in difficult and complex situations	At least two-deep staffing cover for complex and difficult situations
	Resisting down-grading, de-skilling of staff
Practice	
No consultation during assessment, care planning, implementation and review	Fullest possible participation of service users and carers in process of practice
Lack of privacy in group care	
No alternative choices available to service users	
Sanctions and punishments (for example, in group care)	
Corporal punishment	Use of non-punitive approaches reinforcing positive aspects of situations and actions.
Threat of transfer	
Limiting access to friends/relatives	
Public disapproval	
Forcing to wear unusual clothes	
Forcing to eat alone	
Forcing to eat food/special diets which are medically controlled.	

8

Enhancing Quality 2: Monitoring and Evaluating for Quality in Community Care

Each of the aspects of quality assurance considered in Chapters 5 to 7 generates requirements for monitoring and evaluation. Measures to monitor and evaluate the quality of services contribute significantly to processes of quality assurance. Monitoring and evaluation do not in themselves guarantee to affect quality at all. They need to be linked with policy, or management, or practice, or all of these, in order for the claim of quality enhancement to be possible.

Monitoring involves 'formative' (or on the way) activities associated with repeatedly checking key features of the components of the system used to prepare and deliver a product or service. Evaluation is the term used to describe 'summative' (or final) judgements about the goodness, appropriateness and quality of the product or service.

Monitoring and evaluating for quality work: three approaches and examples

The use made in this chapter of illustrations from community care brings to the fore major changes which affect responsibility for quality assurance in the personal social services. One of the most significant shifts has been towards local authorities contracting out and privatising services which were formerly part of in-house provision. Another shift concerns the move from providing services *for* people to various levels of consultation and participation involving working *with* them to plan, implement, monitor and evaluate services.

The uses of methods of monitoring and evaluation vary greatly from setting to setting. At one extreme, they may be marginalised. Monitoring may consist of *ad hoc* reviews of today's practice, with passing reference to comments from staff who happen to attend a hurriedly called meeting. What passes for evaluation may take the form of a brief report written by staff involved in an activity, which simply justifies it in terms of operating criteria which are distant from critical questions about its value. Monitoring may be carried out in virtual segregation from other organisational arrangements for quality assurance, such as those considered in Chapters 5 to 7, whilst evaluation is tacked on, almost as if it were an afterthought.

The cultures of some human services professions do not always encourage the view that monitoring and evaluation are central to practice. The view may be conveyed, almost by default, that they are somehow aside from the real business of the professional. The UKCC (1992) standards for the guidance of professionals in nursing and midwifery, for example, do not mention the role of evaluation at all.

Monitoring and evaluation are politically and value-driven activities. They may be deployed politically so as to justify continuing practices which are in need of revision. The decision to do this may be taken by staff most closely involved, who wish their practice to continue; or it may be taken by managers, on the grounds of not increasing expenditure, in the face of the views of staff and service users that resources must be increased to meet people's needs.

At the heart of monitoring and evaluation lie value judgements made by those who carry them out. They concern three crucial decisions: the choice of the criteria by which particular practices are judged, the selection of which information is gathered to assess performance against these criteria and the interpretation put on this information.

Approaches to monitoring and evaluation

EXAMPLE 8.1

Shelly provides a private home care service and has just been informed by the local authority purchasers of her service that they intend to set in place an authority-wide programme for continuously monitoring this and other related services, and for evaluating the services at regular intervals.

EXAMPLE 8.2

Jon has run a community resource centre for older people – which includes a day centre and support teams for providing other aspects of community care – for three years. He has just accepted an offer from a friend in a local university to include his centre in a large-scale project to evaluate such services, which the university has been running in several local authorities for eighteen months. One drawback is that Jon has no say in how the data is collected, but one advantage is that the researchers will be very sympathetic to the circumstances of his centre, or so he has been told by his friend.

EXAMPLE 8.3

Mary wants to gauge the effectiveness of the support provided by her home care agency, for which she has just signed quite significant contracts to provide services to the health authorities and social services departments in her area. Mary works with a large network of paid workers and volunteers. She decides to adopt a collaborative approach and starts the ball rolling by calling a series of meetings, one in each district, to which all people in her network – paid workers, volunteers, users and carers – are invited. She asks for volunteers to co-research the service and uses the goals identified by all as the basis for the research objectives subsequently specified, monitored and evaluated by this democratised group of co-researchers.

The above examples illustrate three different approaches to monitoring and evaluation. One helpful way to appreciate these is from the vantage point of social development. Social development is viewed as global and not as solely an activity carried out only in the Third World. The ideas informing social development have much in common with an empowered approach to community care, in Britain. For example, Marsden and colleagues, involved in research and practice in social development for many years, write of the need for projects to engage in capacity building, achieving self-reliance, empowerment and the ability to sustain them (Marsden, Oakley and Pratt, 1994, p. 2), building partnerships with poor people to enrich networks and alliances (ibid, p. 10). The four stages envisaged by Marsden and Oakley as involved in the evaluation of a social development project are indistinguishable from those stages set out by researchers (see, for example, Everitt and Hardiker, 1996) in the personal social services; they consist of preparation, execution, analysis and reflection (Marsden, Oakley and Pratt, 1994, p. 5).

The very useful way Marsden and colleagues have developed of distinguishing different kinds of evaluation corresponds very roughly to the circumstances referred to in the three above examples. They identify three main approaches (ibid, pp. 14–23):

Managerialist: Example 1: This perspective is one of 'control by enlightened leaders aimed at achieving targets, building organisational capacity and of extending and processing information and knowledge within the organisation' (ibid, p. 19).

Academic: Example 2: This perspective may involve the participants in critical analysis, but their role commonly is to assist the expert 'outside' researcher to come to his or her conclusions, rather than to shape the direction of the evaluation and control its outcomes (ibid, p. 18). The advocates of approaches based on this perspective tend to argue that participative approaches lead to an emphasis on the experience, action and learning of the participants at the expense of neglect of the wider 'objective' appraisal of the project.

Participative: Example 3: This perspective 'goes beyond the mere involvement of beneficiaries in some externally conceived intervention' (ibid, p. 31). It starts from the viewpoint that much development effort has failed to improve people's living standards significantly, and to enable them to overcome barriers to the more equal distribution of resources. It rejects positivist, traditional, and experimental approaches to research, as instruments of domination (ibid, p. 33). It involves the researcher and the other participants in collaborative action. In this sense, it has much in common with the principles of new paradigm research set out by Reason and Rowan (1981). Both collaborative and participative evaluation seem to share common ground. Evaluation is not viewed as an instrument of investigation wielded by outsiders, but is used as an instrument of dialogue and learning and thereby is integral to cooperation and the project itself. The shift to including in the running of the evaluation the beneficiaries of the project is based partly on the expectation that this will generate more responsibility among people who are commonly excluded, for maintaining an initiative they regard as their own (Marsden, Oakley and Pratt, 1994, p. 25). Some commentators advocate that people should be able to define and take responsibility for their own development on their own terms and be empowered to pursue it in their own chosen way. ' "Participatory evaluation" becomes not only the means by which to create the dialogue necessary for such a process to develop but an integral part of the process itself' (ibid, p. 31).

Great emphasis is placed on the language of the evaluation, focusing on the language used by the participants. 'They are seen to be the experts and their contribution to the evaluation, as those at the heart of the programme, is indispensable. They are thereby given priority in an attempt to learn about the processes involved in cultural and attitudinal change' (ibid, p. 33).

Dominant approaches to monitoring and evaluation focus on services with the highest political profile

The relative lack of research into all aspects of community care contrasts with mental health and child protection, where there is either a danger to others or political interests to be protected along with the interests of the person. This shows the relatively low status of the work with adults, and as a corollary, the people themselves. In child care, the Department of Health (1985, 1991, 1995) has played a prominent role in funding and using feedback from critical research, commissioned over the period since the Children Act 1989 came on to the Statute Book.

Barnes and Wistow (1994, p. 77) suggest that users and carers need to be involved at three levels in the care planning process: in the formal and informal structures and processes by which the components of plans are developed and refined; in the individual care planning and in the aggregation and interpretation of data from the individual level to the overall Community Care Plan (Bulmer, 1993); and in involvement in monitoring and reviewing the plan at an individual level, as well as being involved in determining what information should be collected and what indicators are generated in order to judge what constitutes a good service (Barnes and Wistow, 1994, pp. 77–8).

Beyond statistical performance audits

The limitations of 'number-crunching' as a means of auditing the performance of the personal social services include the omission from statistical measures of a qualitative dimension, particularly evaluation of the values and practices comprising services, as well as the impact of services on users and carers. Quite simply, the measure can only measure what is quantifiable, for the purposes of meeting a particular performance criterion, and does not necessarily encapsulate the quality of the work done with people. In the example quoted on p. 103, of performance payments for the probation service, probation officers could be drawn towards completing as many reports as were necessary for them to meet their targets, rather than doing the work necessary to ensure that those reported on were empowered and able to move forward constructively; further, there would be a dis-inducement to risking recommending supervision in the community, if the officer was penalised for further offences committed. Hence, committals to prison could rise. At a more general level, Carter points out that performance indicators are an imperfect way of evaluating the quality of public sector services, since 'performance measurement raises profound conceptual, technical and organizational problems' (Carter, 1989, p. 209). These include problems of: assessing settings where at least some significant areas of performance are not owned by the staff in them; specifying objectives which are both measurable *and* concern the organisation's value-based purposes; gathering information which is adequate to the complexities of assessing performance; the questionable ability of the state in some areas of work to impose a centrally standardised set of performance indicators and the difficulty administrators may have of gathering from professionals the data necessary to enable them to be managed (Carter, 1989, pp. 209–17). Whilst it is acceptable to use service outcomes as a key determinant of quality, rather than examining the process of quality assurance (Shaw, 1995, p. 147), the qualitative evaluation of the subjective experiences of service users tends to be the vulnerable component of this judgement (Kanter and Summers, 1994, p. 225); the criterion of impact on service users and carers is the ultimate test of quality services (Adams, 1996b, p. 137).

The ideological commitment to divesting public services of the trappings of state control contributed to the publication of the Ibbs Report (Jenkins, Caines and Jackson, 1988). This recommended the most radical change in the civil service since the 1850s: breaking up the civil service into a series of agencies; each agency to be responsible for meeting quasi-contractual obligations specified in a 'framework agreement'; the remaining 'core' of each department to create and monitor the framework agreements (Ling, 1994, p. 38). 'Alongside these initiatives, the National Audit Office and the Audit Commission were to conduct management audits which, amongst other things, were intended to root out alleged "loony leftism", professional self-serving and bureaucratic inertia' (Ling, 1994, p. 38).

In the 1980s the emphasis was on finding less hierarchical and bureaucratic ways of organising social services, hence the preoccupation with patch-based and neighbourhood-based teams. In the 1990s, the emphasis is on how to manage the mixed economy of care, as a purchaser, and assure the quality of services provided by many providers throughout the independent sector.

Strengths and weaknesses of monitoring and evaluation

One strength of monitoring is that it systematises the act of questioning critically what is actually happening in the development, production and delivery of the product or service. It also may induce a willingness to engage creatively in change, as a means of transcending identified current problems.

Monitoring is subject to the weakness that it may rely entirely on information collected by the worker being monitored, may not focus on the aspects of particular concern, for example to service users, in sufficient detail and so may not provide information which is sufficiently detailed and reliable to enable the service to be evaluated. More insidiously, monitoring may be linked with performance targets, and even performance-related bonuses or basic pay. This may undermine cohesion in the workgroup and may increase competition between workers, as the early history of Henry Ford's motor company at Detroit illustrates (Beynon, 1975).

The stressful nature of social work has been acknowledged by a joint PSW and University of Central Lanchashire survey as causing half the profession to consider leaving social work in the past three years (Anon, 1996, 'Parliamentary Concern About Social Work Stress', *Professional Social Work,* August, pp. 1–2).

Ian Sinclair and Ian Gibbs have built on their research into residential care for older people in carrying out research into the quality of care in children's homes, focusing on the role of homes, the experience of care, the immediate outcomes of care, the question as to whether homes can facilitate long-term change in residents and the implications of these for the principles which should govern care (Sinclair and Gibbs, 1996).

Monitoring performance   Measures such as total quality management (TQM, see Chapter 2) may be used to keep up the pressure on subordinate staff to improve their performance continually, in the guise of such general maxims as 'continual improvement'. This exerts pressure on workers by imposing on the work process the assumption that every aspect of a product or service can always be improved and budgets kept down, with savings of as much as 40 or 50 per cent in the costs of getting it right first time. Monitoring may be used legitimately to inform the judgement about whether this is being achieved. What may also be necessary – but may not take place, depending on whether or not it suits those responsible – is for the monitoring to take into account wider questions: how have any savings been made? what is the impact of any saving on the quality of services? what gains or losses in services can staff, service users and carers identify? what difference have service users' views actually made to any changed practices?

Tuckman identifies four components of TQM: statistically based methods of controlling the production process, monitoring procedures involving auditing and other methods, training in statistical process control and effecting culture change in the workplace (Tuckman, 1992, pp. 14–15). The normative tendency in TQM identified by Tuckman has been alluded to by Farnham and Horton who draw attention to the assumption of TQM that 'all work processes may be subject to variation which reduces quality and if the level of variation is managed and decreases, quality standards improve' (Farnham and Horton, 1993, p. 35). Thus, both Tuckman and Farnham and Horton highlight the insistence of TQM on uniformity. The imposition on the caring process of disciplines which control the workforce apparently is intended to ensure that workers are subordinated to systems and procedures regulating service delivery according to the standards laid down by management. Their work is judged by the performance criteria specified in the service contracts. If this description of some approaches to TQM is accurate, then these suffer from the weakness that whilst nodding in the direction of meeting the requirements of the service user as customer, they reinforce hierarchy whilst emphasising group team work at lower levels in the organisation (Tuckman, 1994a, p. 741), thus ensuring that implementation remains essentially in the hands of managers, rather than being directed by the empowered service user – who should be the central participant in the process.

The development of quality work with adults depends on the policy reforms and improvements in the management and resourcing of services, as well as on the nature of face-to-face work with people.

Evidence-based practice

The elevation of evidence-based social work to premier status in England in 1996 was symbolised by the creation of a research and practice development centre at the University of Exeter, headed by Professor Brian Sheldon, and funded by more than a dozen local authorities in association with the Department of Health. The positive feature of evidence-based approaches is that they force the question 'what works?' onto the agenda of policymakers, managers and practitioners and invite the collation of evaluative research to inform decisionmaking and practice. One risk, however, is that problematic, but nevertheless useful, aspects of practice will be excluded from consideration because they are not amenable to the kind of research – notably using the random controlled trial (RCT) – which is regarded as the prime source of data on effective outcomes. A further risk is that the emphasis on outcomes will divert attention from crucial questions about the quality of the process of the work.

Case study: seeking quality in community care

Functions of monitoring and evaluation in community care

Subsequent to the NHS and Community Care Act 1990, concerns about the quality of community care have surfaced mainly through independent research (see Lewis and Glennerster, 1996 for one of the few examples of independently funded evaluative research into the implementation of community care) and critical comment by service users, carers and practitioners. Prominent among these are criticisms of the lack of resources, problems of joint working, limitations of quasi-markets, problems of reconciling market ideology with managerialism, difficulties of ensuring the mixed economy of provision delivers choice and quality of services to meet needs, and the failure of guidance on quality to ensure quality services.

The functions served by quality assurance mechanisms in community care can be regarded equivocally. Quality may be viewed either as a means of ensuring that service users receive the community care services they need, or, like the arrangements for purchase and provision, as a mechanism for enforcing compliance with the managerialist agenda of control. The contradiction between the purpose of meeting human needs and developing market-based human services, surfaces particularly poignantly in the field of community care, where from time to time the mass media report cases of individuals who die through overstretched hospitals not being able to offer them treatment, or of people with mental health problems who are discharged from hospital with insufficient community support. Quality assurance in care management is a means, like purchase and provision, by which central government and local authorities may enforce compliance with the imperatives of the quasi-market and the managerialist agenda of controlling staff who work face to face with service users and carers and their immediate line managers.

It is worth emphasising that not every management in every locality takes a minimalist line on maintaining and upgrading standards of services. From many examples, we can instance attempts made in the independent sector, by East Sussex social services department to improve the consistency and quality of practice in the home care sector, which is not regulated by statutorily laid down standards (Royston, 1996, p. 26).

Developing needs-led rather than service-led or resources-led community care

In the publication *Caring for People* (Secretaries of State, 1989), the government expressed the view that five methods should be used to improve the necessary quality of services in care in the community: community care planning, registration and inspection, complaints by users, assessment and care management and service specification through commissioning and purchasing. However, this general statement conceals a problematic around the supply of necessary resources to underpin such a development (Audit Commission, 1986).

There is a fundamental contradiction between the espoused goal of the NHS and Community Care Act 1990, of improving community care through developing needs-led services, and driving these changes along with finance-led market practices. Consequently, at a day-to-day level, the aspiration towards replacing dependence on institutions with a range of community services chosen by the service user, sits uneasily alongside the financial constraints dictated by a chronic lack of resources.

The NHS and Community Care Act 1990 is among the most radical of the market-based approaches of the enabling local authorities, which under the Act shed most of the assets they owned and services they provided and became planners and purchasers of services. They were required to assess community care needs, develop community care plans, set local priorities and service objectives and develop local plans for delivering services collaboratively with health and housing authorities, as well as voluntary and private providers of care. A minimum proportion of services, to be specified, would have to be provided by the voluntary and private sectors. Social services departments would commission services specifying needs and establishing systems for bidding from potential service providers. Contracts would specify the costs (quantity) and standards (quality) of services. Social services departments would have to inspect services to ensure services met required standards (Elcock, 1993, p. 167).

The implementation of the NHS and Community Care Act 1990 entailed changes in the relations between the state and local authorities, and the statutory, voluntary, private and informal sectors at local level. Approaches to quality were developed in community care which were consistent both with the rhetoric of user empowerment and with the political and managerial motivation for these changes.

However, in practice, the language and culture of commercialism which informs the quasi-markets in health and social services at best sits uneasily alongside professional discourse about empowerment. The paradigm shift to empowerment in social work heightens existing tensions between managerially driven notions of consumer involvement and professionally inspired ideals of empowering staff, users, carers, groups, organisations and communities (Adams, 1996b, pp. 39–40).

Participation of the service user in monitoring and evaluating quality

The service user historically has played only a marginal, or non-existent, part in monitoring and evaluating services. The term 'participation' implies empowering citizens rather than treating people as mere consumers. Tuckman's analysis of the concepts of quality assurance, total quality and quality circles points up the distance between much of the rhetoric about these and a democratic model (Tuckman, 1994b). He highlights accountability to the service user as a key factor in the redressing of the power imbalance between professionals and service users when it comes to judging the quality of the service (Lynch and Pope, 1990; Politt, 1988). In the years since the mid-1980s, increasing recourse was had by the Conservative government to the concept of citizenship – a notion with a long history. This was linked with a consumerist approach to securing quality services.

The notion of citizenship was bounded by the responsibilities of the citizen rather than open-ended in the direction of citizen empowerment. Citizenship was not a product of the Conservative government in the late twentieth century. It is a longstanding liberal-progressive theme in British social and political thinking

(Bulmer and Rees, 1996). In the 1940s and 50s, the role of the citizen in the welfare state was seen in terms largely of claiming entitlements as a member of society, to a range of welfare services as of right, and ensuring democratic access to economic, political and social benefits which the state was obliged to provide. From the 1970s, this conception of citizenship was challenged from the political Left and from the Right. From the Left, its critics alleged that it undermined the motivation of individuals towards self-help. From the Right, it was criticised for excessive control by professionals of services provided through over-bureaucratic structures and procedures (Adams 1996a, pp. 21–2).

The association of citizenship with what was intended to be the archetypal consumer charter – the Citizen's Charter – was a way of legitimating a tighter hold by central government over service delivery, by the simple expedient of associating consumers with it, rather than enabling them to participate in its shaping. The White Paper *The Citizen's Charter: Raising the Standard*, which was issued from the Prime Minister's Office in July 1991, opened with the words: 'All public services are paid for by individual citizens, either directly or through their taxes. They are entitled to expect high quality services, responsive to their needs, provided efficiently at a reasonable cost. Where the state is engaged in regulating, taxing or administering justice, these functions too must be carried out fairly, effectively and courteously' (Prime Minister's Office, 1991, p. 4).

The Citizen's Charter emerged from a revitalised preoccupation of leading members of the Conservative Party, including the then Prime Minister John Major, with the role of citizens in the post-Thatcherite era. The growing preoccupation of politicians, policymakers and staff in the health and social care sector with quality assurance in the 1990s was fuelled undoubtedly by the promotion by John Major of the Citizen's Charter. Even before its publication, the then chairman of the Conservative Party, Chris Patten, announced to a Policy Studies Institute conference, 'I think that a proper target for 2010 or before is to raise standards in the public sector so high that no one will seriously believe that the private sector should be an automatic choice for those who have the resources to opt for it' (*The Independent*, 6 February 1991).

The Citizen's Charter did not lay down a uniform template for quality assurance for all areas of public services. It provided 'a toolkit of initiatives and ideas to raise standards in the way most appropriate to each service' (Prime Minister's Office 1991, p. 4). In the social work sector, quality was seen as being assured through a system of independent inspection, with a significant element of non-professional involvement by the public.

Citizenship in health and social care: a problematic future

It is doubtful whether in itself the Citizen's Charter will lead to improvements in the quality of social work services and, linked with this, there is uncertainty about what its implications are for the participation of service users, as citizens, in the process of assuring quality. The closing years of the twentieth century are unlikely to see a sudden consensus among leading political groups and interests about the concept of citizenship or what it means in practice. The Citizen's Charter could rebound on its post-Thatcherite conservative initiators and provide a handle for consumers of health and social care services to complain about shortcomings (Miller and Peroni, 1992, p. 259). It could empower service users in the health and social services to transcend the equation between choice, value for money and ability to pay on which the mixed economy of care rests, and claim the right to services which enhance, even maximise, their quality of life.

Viewed in the light of these critical reflections on quality assurance in the human services, the British Standard 5750 on quality (see Chapter 3) appears one-dimensional. It is unlikely to be able to encompass the complexity of the competing requirements of employer providers, professionals delivering services and service users. It addresses those responsible for managing production rather than addressing the goal of empowering service users. It 'provides guidelines which allow creativity and innovation to thrive without risk of disorganisation and inefficiency'; it 'can bring real economies in its wake: economies in production because your systems are controlled from start to finish, economies in resources and in time spent on planning or modifying designs of products or services' (Harland, 1993, p. 50).

The publication of policy standards by a social services department of itself is no guarantee that the quality of services will be enhanced (Hirst, 1995). Experience in the NHS shows that the operation of complaints procedures is often 'complex, slow and frustrating' (Patients Association, undated, p. 1). None of the agencies surveyed by Marsh and Triseolitis in the early 1990s had yet developed any formal system for seeking users' views about the quality of service they had received from either established or newly qualified staff. 'The general approach was that users were satisfied unless they complained. One agency had a general complaints book in which users could enter their comments and two other agencies had complaints procedures, but it was not clear how well known these were to the users. Seniors saw this as being a negative form of feedback, because users were expected only to write when they had something to complain about and not when things went well' (Marsh and Triseolitis, 1996, p. 129).

A quality-enhancing role for service purchasers and providers
Quality enhancement requires that purchasers and providers of services use feedback from monitoring and evaluation as the basis for action to address areas needing attention.

Dramatic changes which have occurred since 1990 in the organisation and delivery of education, health, penal, social care and social work services, are indicators of shifts in the relationship between service providers and issues concerning the quality of services. In part, these changes reflect the direction given by the last Conservative government towards creating internal markets in the human services, necessitating a declining role for public sector providers and an enhanced contribution from the voluntary, private and informal sectors. In part also, the perspective of that government on how quality services should be maintained had become more proactive than its predecessors. It may be in large measure due to the adoption of the consumerist model of market provision of health and social care, for example, that standards for services purchased have to be built into contracts issued and must be evaluated in services delivered, according to agreed and stated performance criteria.

Before the 1990s, the issue of the quality of community care was rooted in debates about institutional versus community provision and the categories of people most likely to benefit from maintaining in the community rather than in residential care. Consequently, other groups of people were marginalised.

Humane idealism or cost-consciousness in hospital closure programmes

Concerns about the nature, and primarily the cost, of hospital care fuelled proposals for a large-scale programme of hospital closures – particularly in the mental health and learning disability sectors – in the early 1960s, primarily in the wake of the Mental Health Act 1959. Community care policy and practice tended before the 1980s to be regarded as having a reality only in relation to the use of residential – including hospital-based – services. Among many explanations for this, radical (Scull, 1977) and liberal accounts (Jones, 1975) are prominent. Subsequently, during the 1960s and 1970s, this initiative did not develop a significant momentum. It was the 1980s before the cost-conscious Thatcher government made high priority the question of patients being decarcerated from mental hospitals, through the hospital closure programme. During this period, managerialism was growing in momentum, though formally given expression in the Griffiths Report (1983) (see Chapter 7).

Need to focus on all, and not just less dependent, older people

The Audit Commission report of 1986 argued the need to strengthen support services in the community for all older people, especially those services enabling the more frail older people to stay in their own homes (Audit Commission, 1996d). During the 1980s, research at the Personal Social Services Research Unit (PSSRU), at the University of Kent, on the quality of case management in various aspects of work with older people, including frail people in social care and primary health care and in geriatric care, found that case managers with devolved budgets were able to improve very significantly the effectiveness of social care for very frail older people at no significant extra cost (Challis and Davies, 1980, 1985, 1986; Davies and Challis, 1986). Cost was a contributory factor in encouraging the development of a debate about the nature of community care, but the quality dimension was often pushed on to this agenda by those outside the government and managerial arenas, notably voluntary agencies and pressure groups, researchers, and self-advocates among users and carers. Government motivation to establish community care programmes was linked closely to aspirations to establish a market-based structure for delivering care services to consumers. The PSSRU approach tended to focus on older people who were on the brink of admission to residential care. This bias contributed to government assumptions that community care could be implemented at no extra cost and with the result that significant numbers of older people could be diverted from residential to community care (Lewis and Glennerster, 1996, p. 122). Beyond this, there remained significant tensions between consumerism and empowerment, as espoused by many service users and professionals in social work.

Increasingly, community care became an aspect of the health and personal social services which required not only their separate and distinctive provision, but also a high degree of collaboration between agencies and professionals, in the commissioning, purchasing and provision of services. This helped to refine the ideas about new ways of structuring and delivering services expressed in precursor reports (DHSS, 1988; DH, 1989a) to the NHS and Community Care Act 1990.

Ensuring people with impairments and disabilities are not marginalised and stigmatised

On the one hand, some groups of people – such as some people with impairments and disabilities – resent being picked out and their needs highlighted, as though they, as individuals or as a category, represent a problem. On the other hand, one consequence of the widespread association between community care and work with older people is the relative ease with which the needs of other groups of people become marginalised. People with impairments and disabilities are often in this situation. In particular, children with impairments tend to be marginalised even more than children in general, as the example of Beverley Lewis illustrates.

EXAMPLE 8.4

Beverley Lewis, from her birth in 1966 suffered physical, learning, hearing and visual impairments. She lived with her mother in Gloucestershire. When she died in 1989, isolated and neglected, the Social Services Inspectorate carried out an investigation of her situation and published a report of its findings (Social Services Inspectorate, 1991,

Hear Me: See Me, Department of Health, London). A wider follow-up inspection was subsequently carried out, in pursuance of 'a Ministerial requirement for the lessons of the Beverley Lewis tragedy to be studied and disseminated' (letter from Herbert Laming, Chief Inspector SSI, to Directors of Social Services, 19 May 1993). The report of this inspection was published in 1993 (Social Services Inspectorate, 1993f).

Curbing managerialism and reinforcing professional activity

The introduction into community care of market principles and methods of operation increased the numbers and range of voluntary and private providers, but this mixed economy of care did not necessarily result in the availability of a better quality service for users and their carers. The operations of purchasers and providers were framed to fulfil the primacy of short-term goals of meeting performance targets and the specified objectives of contracts. This impacted on managers and professionals at local level. Managers increasingly were responsible for the budgets devolved to them through local cost centres. However, through the medium of reducing bureaucracy, the trend of local authorities in the mid-1990s was towards introducing performance-related pay and more short-term contracts for middle managers. In effect, this reduced their commitment to the longer term and focused them on the delivery of the items specified in their current contract. A message familiar to employees across the human services in the 1990s was that 'social services departments should accommodate themselves to the contemporary "ideal" organizational model – fitter and flatter (or leaner and meaner), stressing flexibility and adaptiveness to its business environment' (Langan and Clarke, 1994, p. 80).

Transcending limitations of quasi-markets

The New Right influence on the policy and practice of community care reflected both a pilot attempt to follow Hayek's (1960) free market assumptions and create a free market for the supply of, and demand for, community care services, and also a compromise with the wish of former Conservative Party leaders to retain government control. Thus, the much-used term 'mixed economy of care' refers to a quasi-market (Le Grand and Bartlett, 1993); in this, central government determines the level of the global supply of resources, and the device of separating purchasers from providers does not give service users as purchasers a free choice, but refers to lead agencies as purchasers, in effect managing the market by deciding to which providers to allocate resources. As Cutler and Waine put it, 'the quasi-market is *par excellence* the managed market' (Cutler and Waine, 1994, p. 20).

There is cause to doubt the extent to which quasi-markets in community care are capable of delivering satisfaction to all stakeholders: policymakers, managers, professionals and other workers, service users and carers. The quasi-market creates tensions between different areas and contradictions within each. Market processes are at odds with the political objectives of commitment to equity, access and accountability for the use of resources; consumer choice with budgetary constraints; efficiency with increased costs of administering and carrying out transactions; competition with new forms of regulation; and finally, enhanced performance through increased throughput and keeping costs down (Cutler and Waine, 1994, p. 74).

Reconciling market ideology with managerialism

There is a confusion, if not an outright contradiction, in community care between New Right market ideology and managerialist methods, where the so-called free market should operate to give the user – the consumer of services – a free choice and access to the means of meeting individual needs. This is not adequately explained away simply by referring to the role the government plays in the quasi-market. The theory of non-interference in the free market of community care conflicts with the intervention of lead bodies – the local authority social services departments – at every stage of the development of community care plans across their area and, at the micro level, the process of care management by which the needs of individuals are met in the context of the supply of scarce resources.

Addressing contradictory values

Community care services cover home care, carers' services counselling, day hospitals, day centres, residential and nursing home care and some primary health and community services over the boundary from health and social care. One implication of the community care changes is the introduction of more participative care arrangements than before 1990. Partnership between users and carers became as much part of the language of community care as empowerment, though, as noted elsewhere (Adams, 1996b, p. 37), the two concepts overlap and in some places conflict, rather than being synonymous.

At the level of values, there is a conflict throughout the process of care management, but notably during the assessment and care planning stages and at the point of service delivery, between the principles of consumer choice and service user empowerment. Assessment and care planning are the stages where, if the participation of the service user is at all meaningful, this has to be built in. Langan and Clarke, however, note the gap between the intention and the reality:

> A combination of needs-led assessment and targeted resources is claimed to offer greater scope for flexible and innovative domiciliary services. It is also supposed to put new power in the hands of the user of social services – now less of a troublesome client and more of a valued customer. In practice, the customers' new-found power is of a second-hand variety, exercised through the proxy of the care manager who purchases care on their behalf. This change rests on the assumption that such managerial assessments would produce more 'transparent' representations of the user's needs than the much criticized forms of professional assessments. (Langan and Clarke, 1994, p. 81)

Ensuring the mixed economy of provision delivers choice and quality of services to meet needs

The basic problem of the proliferation of a great number of providers in place of the former health and local authorities, whose size varies from very large to, especially in the personal social services, very small, is that of managing it to ensure that individuals' needs are met as and when they arise. This is straightforward when mass needs require a large contract which can be constructed so that a block of services, say through a hospital, is offered on an ongoing basis. It is not so easy when it involves stimulating service providers to provide in minority areas of need. The reorientation of service provision in local government since the mid-1980s has led to local authorities becoming what have been called 'enabling local authorities'. Although enabling local authorities have adopted market-based and collectivist approaches, the fact that the Conservatives were in power for so long after 1979 meant that market-based approaches, such as compulsory competitive tendering, have predominated (Elcock, 1993, pp. 164–5).

In 1994, local authorities were required to ensure that a minimum of 85 per cent of community care services were provided by the voluntary and private sectors. The 85 per cent rule, for instance, could be argued to increase consumer choice by ensuring the replacement of the virtual monopoly of local authority provision by the mixed economy of statutory, voluntary and private services. But in Humberside, where the County Council proposed to close nine homes for older people in 1994, critics alleged that residents and their relatives wanted to stay where they were and their needs and choices were not being considered; there was enough money in the community care budget to run these homes; all these homes met registration requirements; and private care cost less because staff were paid less and less was invested in staff training than in the local authority (stated in a letter to all council employees from John Ellis the former chairperson of Humberside social services committee) (*Community Care*, 9–15 June 1994, no. 1020, p. 12).

Another implication of the NHS and Community Care Act 1990 was the need for health and local authorities to define how they would meet people's continuing care needs. The implementation of NHS responsibilities for meeting continuing health care needs involved a timetable anticipating that policies and eligibility criteria would be agreed and put into effect by 1 April 1996. However, some authorities used statements of eligibility criteria as a way of limiting their liability to provide continuing care.

In one week of 1994, 2.2 million contact hours of home help or home care were purchased or provided by local authorities, an increase of 24 per cent over 1993 (SSI, 1995, p. 87). Whilst over 80 per cent of these contact hours were provided directly by the local authority, the quantity provided by the independent sector increased by nearly five times between 1993 and 1994 (SSI, 1995, p. 88).

A total of over 794,000 meals were delivered to people's homes or served at luncheon clubs during 1994, 2 per cent more than in 1992, and 80 per cent directly delivered to people's homes (SSI, 1995, p. 88). The voluntary sector accounted for over 40 per cent of meals to people's homes and almost 60 per cent of meals in luncheon clubs (SSI, 1995, p. 89). Inspections of the community care information of social services departments in four local authorities indicated that in some areas 'information was not optimised because of inadequate arrangements for collecting, updating and sharing information about services and those receiving them, thus adversely affecting operational and management decisions' (SSI, 1995, p. 69). The Community Care Published Information Initiative, launched in 1993, was intended to encourage social services departments 'to make the information they publish as helpful and readable as possible' (Prime Minister, 1995, p. 50). It was announced that local authority social services departments would implement a government-promoted framework for local community care charters published in November 1994 and in Northern Ireland in July 1995, by consulting and drawing up their own local charters by April 1996 in England and by April 1997 in Wales, in consultation with health and housing authorities (Prime Minister, 1995, p. 95). Inspection units (see Chapter 1) were increasingly scrutinised by government, through the SSI, to extend principles of openness and fairness in the functioning of local authority inspection units. Thus, in Wales, 'following consultation, the Social Services Inspectorate for Wales issued policy and practice guidance in 1994 on the adoption of Charter principles by local social services authorities in their inspection work. By the end of 1994, all authorities had open reporting arrangements in place and had begun to include lay assessors in inspections. In 1995, independent assessors will consider the even-handedness and independence of each authority's inspection unit' (Prime Minister, 1995, p. 50). Similar moves were made in Northern Ireland, following the publication of *The Charter for Patients and Clients* in 1992, which, given the common responsibilities of the four regional Health and Social Services boards, covered the entire health and social care sector. Thus, 'a new Community Services charter standard statement, published in July 1995, (which) set standards for the delivery of care in the community. Services include nursing, midwifery and health visiting, social services, child protection and child care, family doctors, dentists and pharmacists, physiotherapy, occupational therapy and chiropody' (Prime Minister, 1995, p. 56). The standards in the charter imposed more rigorous expectations on social services than hitherto, including 'notification within five days of assessment of the social services to be provided, or immediate notification if the person is at risk. Short-term breaks for carers of people being looked after at home will be agreed within three weeks of application. In an emergency, short-term care will generally be provided within 24 hours' (Prime Minister, 1995, pp. 56–7).

Ensuring guidance on quality guarantees delivery of quality services

Official (Social Services Inspectorate) guidance on the NHS and Community Care Act 1990 stresses the centrality of procedures for assuring the quality of services. Quality Assurance procedures in community care are located within the broader context of initiatives by the last Conservative government, with the aim of giving consumers a better service. The origin of this is the Citizens Charter (Prime Minister, 1991). As Brace (1994, p. 63) points out, although it was believed that the Citizens Charter gave more power to the individual citizen, it 'does not in itself offer people basic, enforceable entitlement to services, nor the right in law to fair treatment of their needs'. Nor is there a charter for social services or community care. Service users have to refer to the NHS and Community Care Act 1990 and the Disabled Persons (Services and Representation) Act 1986 for definitions of minimum standards for these services (Brace, 1994, p. 53).

Overcoming lack of resources

Service delivery involves the question of resources. At one extreme, the service user may have minimal opportunity to participate, and thus cannot exercise a meaningful influence over the range of available, but rationed, services, offering no real choices; at the other extreme, there is the situation where the service user can, in effect, negotiate services on the basis of individual needs.

Lack of resources is a repeated source of criticism. Users should be central to service planning, coordination and delivery and there should be more alternatives available to ensure that people's choices are real, based on alternative theoretical frameworks and alternative methods, such as talking therapy or non-medical crisis provision (Beeforth *et al.*, 1990, p. 30). Ironically, as Tom Ling notes, the imposition on local community care practice of tight financial controls results in a weakening of the implementation of community care policies (Ling, 1994, p. 33). The introduction of direct payments for services changed very significantly the relationship between service providers and users, as well as the process of delivering community care.

Beyond problems of joint working

One of the aspirations of official guidance on community care was to achieve seamless service, through a high level of collaboration between agencies and professionals. Lewis and Glennerster (1996, p. 193) identify three main factors which make this difficult: first, a widespread reliance on formal organisational mechanisms for joint working has revisited the working style of the 1970s rather than building appropriate arrangements for the 1990s and beyond; second, whilst arrangements for joint commissioning address the more practical problems, differences remain between organisational and professional 'work cultures, patterns of accountability, imperatives and timescales'; third, the fundamental ethos of the internal markets in health and social services undermine, or even contradict, the goal of collaboration.

Liaison and joint working between health and local authorities, in the wake of the NHS and Community Care Act 1990, is less than adequate; in many cases, joint arrangements are variable, depending on the concerns of individual staff (Audit Commission, 1996d, p. 23). The dividing line of responsibility between health and social services is sometimes difficult to determine. For example, the responsibilities of an occupational therapy service purchased by the social services department are likely to encompass healthcare. On the other hand, Lewis and Glennerster quote the example of the health manager who leaves the negotiation of this boundary to front-line workers: '"For example, you give a chap insulin and that's probably the only visitor he gets. He needs perhaps toast and tea. This is not a health task, but of course on an individual level she [the nurse] has to weigh up her own priorities and come to a decision . . . I don't want to take away my nurses' discretion to make decisions like this" ' (Lewis and Glennerster, 1996, p. 188).

An empowering approach to monitoring and evaluation in community care

Monitoring performance may be presented as part of the rational process of management (see, for instance, the account by the senior members of the Social Services Inspectorate, Mitchell and Tolan, 1994). Alternatively, it may be acknowledged to be more problematic and uncertain.

Progressive practice: a sectoral or a holistic perspective?

One way forward for progressive practice is by means of a fully theorised, social, holistic, transcendent politics of ablement, practised by workers, service users and carers (see Oliver, 1990; and see Chapter 9 of this book), in other words, a holistic, democratised and empowered approach to maximising quality. In this regard, Marsden offers a very helpful view of perspectives on the services. Two main perspectives may be encountered, according to Marsden (1990, p. 8): sectoral (specialist) and holistic (generalist). The sectoral approach distinguishes different spheres of activity for diverse professional treatment, through health, housing, social services and so on. The sectoral approach is based on questionable assumptions, according to Marsden (1990, p. 8): that a distinction can be made between the public and private domains; that different criteria should be used in their evaluation; that different areas of human activity can be isolated for different treatment. Within the sectoral approach, there is a debate between residualists and substantivists about the amount of government intervention which should be maintained to underpin activity. The substantivists argue that more intervention plays a redistributive role and lessens inequalities.

According to the holistic approach, the planner, policy maker and the change agent are all viewed as part of the analysis (Marsden, 1990, p. 8). Holistic evaluation may well take place above the level of direct action and thus will probably be perceived as less capable of achieving instrumental goals. In contrast, the sectoral approach to evaluation is likely to fail to appreciate the interconnectedness of phenomena and to achieve desired aims.

Overcoming barriers to empowering evaluation

One barrier is the tendency to focus on the evaluation project in any particular aspect of community care, rather than on the goal of empowerment itself. The project should remain merely one means by which partnerships between organisations develop and solidarity is strengthened (Marsden, Oakley and Pratt, 1994, p. 11).

Another major impediment, despite the rhetoric of empowerment, includes what Marsden and colleagues refer to as 'the chains which bind us to ways of thinking and acting, thereby inhibiting effective elaboration of successful methodologies' (Marsden, Oakley and Pratt, 1994, p. 12). This is a very helpful metaphor which focuses attention on the way traditional managerialist or academic evaluation approaches may insidiously extinguish the participative and empowering activity (Marsden, Oakley and Pratt, 1994, pp. 14–19).

EXAMPLE 8.5

Petra has been working with groups of service users and their carers to assemble data on their evaluation of the service they have received. She has found it helpful to negotiate with the users and carers the kinds of criteria she employs to evaluate the services with them. She has found some work done by Brace (1994) extremely useful in this respect, more as a check of the work already done with her groups than as a checklist used 'from the start' as it were.

Brace (1994, pp. 68–74) offers criteria against which service users may judge the quality of services. These have been paraphrased in Table 8.1, and in a few parts further developed, under the headings of information giving, first contacts, assessment, care planning, implementation of care plans, monitoring care plans and reviewing.

Table 8.1   Criteria by which service users and carers may judge the quality of
services

Information giving: People should judge information by the extent to which:
- it is accessible, ie. readily available and understood
- it gives people what they really want and need to know
- it is available in different formats, such as on audio cassette or in braille
- it has been translated into appropriate languages in use in the locality.

First contacts: The quality of the first contacts between service users, carers and
the agency may be judged by the extent to which:
- the duty officer and colleagues work as a team
- the office reception area and interview rooms have an inviting and positive
  appearance or are dull and uninviting
- how long it takes the telephonist and duty officer to answer the telephone
- how long the wait is before speaking to someone who can advise
- staff take time and trouble to understand fully what the service user is saying
- the attitude of staff is positive
- the staff member has the knowledge to respond to the contact
- staff respond straight away to any immediate crisis or need
- the criteria for being eligible for the service are made clear
- the criteria for the prioritisation of the service are made clear
- the criteria for assessment of needs are made clear
- any other professionals involved work harmoniously together
- work done by other professionals is carried out acceptably and speedily.

Assessment: Criteria used to judge quality assessment include whether:
- all staff demonstrate shared professional values acceptable to the service user
- all staff respond speedily to the request for assessment
- all staff interact appropriately with the service user, using a translator or an
  advocate where appropriate
- assessment is carried out with rather than on the service user
- carers and other significant people are appropriately involved in the assessment process
- assessment is carried out confidentially
- a clearly and fully recorded copy of the assessment is supplied to the user
- the user is provided with an effective and fair complaints procedure.

Care planning: Criteria to judge the quality of care planning include whether:
- the service user and carer view the care plan as adequately specifying their
  needs
- carers can offer the support specified in the care plan
- the service user and carer can afford the care package
- services are available as specified in the care plan
- the local authority will be able to provide or procure services to fulfil its
  statutory duty to meet essential needs.

$\longrightarrow$

$\longrightarrow$

Implementation of care plans: The criteria for appraising the implementation of the care plan include whether:
- the service user and carer accept the suitability of the care manager and key worker
- the care manager and key worker have the expertise and credibility with the service user, carer, and with other professionals, to fulfil the care plan
- all different professionals contributing to the care plan - such as home care staff, health visitor, doctor, social worker, occupational therapist, pharmacist – work as a team
- the plan meets the needs perceived by the service user and carer
- the service user and carer are empowered to control the care plan
- the cost of fulfilling the care plan is acceptable.

Monitoring implementation of care plans: The criteria for monitoring the implementation of care plans include whether:
- participating agencies and professionals work within the care plan and accept the coordinating roles of the care manager and key worker
- the service user and carer participate maximally in the monitoring process
- an advocate participates where appropriate
- the relationship with, and access to, the care manager are optimised
- necessary changes to the care plan are made promptly and readily by involved professionals and agencies
- the local authority facilitates adjustments to the care plan and budget for those acting as their own care managers.

Reviewing: Criteria for judging the quality of the process of reviewing the care plan include whether:
- the review is timely
- the style of the review makes participation by service users and carers easy
- all stakeholders in the care plan contribute to the review
- the views of all stakeholders in the care plan are taken on board in the review
- challenges to the conclusions of the review by any stakeholder – particularly the service user or carer - can be addressed in the review process.

Next steps: Criteria for judging the next steps taken include whether:
- the implications of necessary changes for all stakeholders and for future practice are specified
- further assessments are built into future planning as appropriate
- further work with the service user and carer is carried out as appropriate
- further work by the care manager and key worker is carried out as appropriate
- the implications for other professionals are acted upon
- any implications for other people are dealt with, beyond the implementation of the care plan
- evaluation is carried out as part of the total process of work with the service user and carer.

Source: Adapted from Brace, 1994, pp. 68–74.

The lists could form the basis for discussion between professionals and services users and carers when goals for evaluation are being developed. There is always a risk of such checklists simply being adopted rather than used at an appropriate point in ongoing discussion. This is one of those issues which needs acknowledging and working with, and to which there is no simple response which will eliminate it as a cause for concern.

This chapter has examined the appropriateness of different strategies for monitoring and evaluating the quality of social work. In the process, we have identified some strengths and weaknesses of a range of approaches to the monitoring and evaluation of services. It has focused in particular on features which are most useful in the task of quality maximisation. The final approach considered is quality maximisation, in Chapter 9. This points to the need for all stakeholders to be maximally involved in the design and implementation of whatever measures are taken for monitoring and evaluation.

9

Maximising Quality in Social Work

This book has examined the application of measures to assure quality in several aspects of social work practice. It has developed the argument used by Marsden, Oakley and Pratt in the field of social development, that the pursuit of quality cannot be realised by using a packages of quality assurance materials like a cookery book with universal recipes which never vary from standard ingredients, no matter what the local setting (Marsden, Oakley and Pratt, 1994, p. 23). In the process, it has surveyed the wide-spread adoption of quality in the personal social services. Chapters 1 and 2 have established a conceptual basis on which to regard the application of quality assurance in social work. Chapters 3 and 4 have discussed two particular prerequisites for quality social work. Chapters 5 to 8 have critically illustrated from areas of practice four particular aspects of quality assurance. This final chapter pulls together the main conclusions emerging from the preceding chapters; it uses them as the basis for quality maximisation in social work. General pointers for practice are based on the quality maximisation approach outlined in Chapter 2. On many occasions, policies, managers and professional practitioners in the personal social services have presented obstacles to the attainment of quality, rather than facilitating it. In contrast, much of the progress actually achieved has been at the instigation of service users themselves, sometimes helped, directly or indirectly, by the mass media.

At a fundamental level, the applications of quality assurance have deserted theory, just as critics of social work have disowned its authentic place in the problematic of the social. For these reasons, if for no other, the framework for assuring quality in social work needs reframing. This is not novelty for its own sake. As social workers know only too well, reframing is a technique used to achieve a sea change; in the case of quality social work, a cultural revolution is needed. The insecurities, uncertainties and fears expressed by many workers and service users about their circumstances will not be addressed from within the discourse of the old quality. An authentic reflective practice needs to seek transcendent frameworks which can take anti-oppressive practice, empowerment and reflective practice, towards a 'new quality' in social work.

Changing concerns about quality in social work

The notable parallels between the periodic nature of the changes occurring before the 1970s, during the 1970s and 1980s, and after 1990 in different aspects of the personal social services are unsurprising. These indicate policy changes; the wider context of social and economic changes in the postwar period; the changing nature of managerialism; and changes in the dominant paradigms of social work, notably the tensions between the shift from medico-treatment to empowerment, in the professional arena, and the consumerism which has propelled government policy and legislation in the health and social services into the 1990s.

The managerialist drive for assuring quality is positive in the sense that it enables standards of services to be scrutinised more closely than hitherto. Nevertheless, it puts the authentic professional role of social work at risk in different ways in different sectors of the personal social services, by creating the illusion of consumer choice at the expense of real user empowerment (Adams, 1996b). It also reduces the scope for value-based as opposed to bureaucratically-directed decision-making by professional social workers. The vulnerability of professional social work is increased by the use of quality assurance procedures by government, *through* and *by* managements themselves, as mechanisms to bring about change in the marketplace for health and social care services. A critical appreciation of the significance of the application of quality assurance in the personal social services in general, and social work in particular, cannot be segregated from its three major functions: depersonalising, deprofessionalising and rationing services. Depersonalisation occurs by subjecting the unique application of professional expertises to the variety of human problems and needs to standard procedures. Deprofessionalising occurs when autonomous professional practices are subjected to the discipline of bureaucratic rules, checklists and procedures. Rationing occurs where such procedures contribute to gatekeeping and other resource-monitoring mechanisms as a means of restricting activity to available resources, rather than supplying services according to need.

A recurring theme in Chapters 5 to 8 is the tension between approaches to aspects of quality assurance which are managerially led – top down, as it were – and those which are informed by the intention to increase the participation of users and carers as stakeholders in social work. This final chapter accepts the limitations of such top-down and bottom-up approaches and examines the kinds of cultural changes necessary to bring about a transcendent approach to quality assurance.

Shortcomings in social work

The following is a working definition of quality social work: *Excellent social work is social work which guarantees people access to high quality services which ensure their needs are met.* Foregoing chapters have identified many ways in which social work has fallen short of such excellence. This section summarises the observations to be made in the light of these chapters. We begin, however, with the key observations on the nature and impact of managerialism arising from Chapter 3.

Managerialism

Chapter 3 examined factors emanating from government policy and managerialism in central and local government, which have slowly but consistently undermined and degraded the practice of social work since the 1970s, and probation work since the early 1990s. Just as, at the interface with other people, social workers may witness disclosures of abuse, so politicians and managers – and CCETSW when simply acting as their agent, promoting competence-based work in the personal social services over traditional practice of social workers, and in the process downgrading much of what social workers formerly did, to N/SVQ levels 4, or even 3 and 2 – are acting out an abusive form of managerialism. Generalisation, of course, is invidious, since exceptions to the rule may be easy to find. Also, since the 1980s the dominance of managerialism in the health and social care field in Britain has not been totally negative. In some ways, managerialism has created a climate within which a sharper focus on goals and means is helpful. But, at a more fundamental level, it is hard to find evidence that managerialism has contributed significantly to the prospects for bringing about the maximisation of the quality of social work. All too often, pressure in the 1980s and early 1990s towards progressive practice encountered resistance from government, as expressed in the defensive responses of senior managers.

The importation of commercial practices into the personal social services is having an adverse effect on many aspects of social work. The commodification of social work undermines its core values. The rationing of services which underlies the management of child care and adult services contradicts the basic principles of meeting people's needs. Marketisation, notably through quasi-markets and managerialism, interpenetrates practice in different aspects of the personal social services in a way which reinforces quasi-commercial rather than social work values.

The impact of social policy under the last Conservative government has been rather mixed. On one hand, the thrust of consumer charters at a very general and superficial level has strengthened the voice of service users. But, more fundamentally, it has not significantly increased the power or resources on which service users and carers draw, when attempting to ensure their needs are met.

Repeated inquiries and exposés of the weaknesses of social work over the years have not led to marked improvements. The reasons for this are complex and cannot be ascribed to a single factor. But shortages of resources and inadequate education and training of professionals plus ancillary and supporting care staff – particularly in residential and day care – rank high on this list of factors.

One consequence of these factors is the insecurity and low morale of many service users and staff about the present, exacerbated by fears about what will happen in the future. An interpretation of what is happening is offered here, in the expectation that the rapid changes taking place will render its detail anachronistic within two or three years, let alone over a longer time span.

Discontinuity in values and practices

The overriding vulnerability of the quality of social work practice to the various problems besetting it, identified in preceding chapters, revolves around differences between the dominant values of the personal social services in the 1990s and the value base of social work. It is true that managers may despair of the failure of attempts to introduce greater consistency and quality into their services, for example, by publishing procedures and standards. Whilst attempts may be made to resolve shortcomings in the quality of social work at the practical or technical levels, these rarely can be properly addressed without an adequately resourced strategy which is rooted in the concepts and values embodied in them. Legalism in child care, commercialism in community care, managerialism in the personal social services and personalism in social work are exemplars of the warring themes which unavoidably complicate the question of how to achieve quality in social work and they exert a cumulative and potentially harmful effect on practice. Whereas in the early 1970s the Seebohm reorganisation accompanying local government reorganisation represented a long-standing consensus since the ending of the Second World War about the need for state provision in the personal social services, by the 1990s this no longer existed. Among the many factors undermining this consensus were scandals about the failings of child care and hospital care for people with mental health problems and learning disabilities during the 1970s and 1980s and, in the early 1990s, growing public concerns about community care – particularly in relation to the aftercare of mentally disordered offenders discharged to the community and the care of older people.

Just as the growing emphasis on legalism and proceduralism in social work and the bureaucratisation of services were features of the 1970s and 1980s (see, for example, Parton on child care, 1991, p. 195), so the implementation of quasi-markets in the 1990s is an indicator of the increasing predominance of the focus of *the personal* social services on the individual at the expense of *the social*. But the changes reflect also the quite different styles of management and practice embodied in social work in community care in the light of the NHS and Community Care Act 1990 and social work with children and families after the Children Act 1989. As Alaszewski and Manthorpe correctly anticipated, the former draw more or the traditions of the former welfare departments and emphasise the role of the social worker in administering services and rationing limited resources; the latter emphasise the tradition of professional child care and highlight the participation of the social worker in legal proceedings, in the role of protecting, and acting as advocate for, children (Alaszewski and Manthorpe, 1990, p. 426).

Precariousness of equality perspective in staff selection policies and practices

Herbert Laming the then Chief Social Services Inspector, interviewed on 24 May 1995 on Radio Four, the morning of the publication of the critical report on child care in Islington, located the major responsibility for ensuring the delivery of quality social work services as lying with officers and with members in the local authorities. He pointed out that in Islington, managers had allowed themselves to become diverted from the central issues concerned with managing quality, and had not ensured that they maintained a detailed knowledge of what was happening in child care. He pointed out also that local authorities as well as other providing agencies have a duty to ensure that the selection, management and supervision of staff is carried out effectively.

The report into abuses of children by paedophiles in Islington social services department locates malpractices associated with a lack of investigation of people's backgrounds, on the grounds that this could prejudice the employability of black, women and gay people. In so doing, as Herman Ouseley, chair of the Commission for Racial Equality notes, it blights the operation of good equal opportunities, by enabling opponents to infer that its principles are in error. On the contrary, in Islington there appears to have been a failure to integrate equal opportunities policies, programmes and practices into the management infrastructure of local services, so that 'such organisations "own" those answers to problems that are designed to achieve equality outcomes, and have a workforce that understands it . . . (and) that equality practices are synonymous with good management practice and result in enhanced performance all round.' Ouseley points out that political correctness should not be confused with political corruption and weak management and argues that genuine political correctness in any case is predicated on a morally correct position (Ouseley, 'Present incorrect', *The Guardian*, 1 June 1995).

But the need for firmness should not be confused with a *macho*, and perhaps cavalier, style of management. The contract culture may lead to the application of a crude equation between performance indicators in the short term and the dispensability of managers. Thus, managerialism may lead to the supplanting of human service values by a balance-sheet approach to corporate and small unit management alike. This may bring the operational dictates of the soccer clubs closer to that of the school governors, in the way soccer managers and head teachers are hired and fired according to evaluation of their performance, as David Hart, general secretary of the National Association of Head Teachers puts it, against the league tables of national results (Hart, 'Heads sacked like soccer managers', *The Guardian*, 1 June 1995).

For the reasons outlined in Chapters 1 and 2, the case for importing quality assurance procedures into social work has been made on the basis of diverse, not to say ambiguous, arguments. Some justifications, as we have seen illustrated above in the Griffiths Report on community care, have involved mimicking the moves towards quality assurance in the commercial sector; other reasons have been linked with the need for managers to take control of a sector which is reacting to criticisms from specific inquiry reports as well as generalised assaults in the mass media and experiencing the uncertainties of change, including questions raised by some commentators about whether social work can survive (Brewer and Lait, 1980). It is undeniable that total quality management (TQM), for example, can be introduced to the workforce through a devolutionary approach which maximises the extent to which employees themselves self-regulate, monitor and evaluate performance. This highlights a feature of some quality assurance processes, namely their ability to enhance the appearance of employee participation in an organisation which espouses a human relations, team-based style of working, whilst also achieving management's aim of increasing control.

Thus, there is a case for quality management, but as part of a culture change motivated by *all* stakeholders to services, and not impelled top-down by managers. If left to themselves, the different parties to social work are likely to use different arguments to support its implementation. The manager may seek control, the practitioner may look for enhanced professionalism including a better service whilst the client of the agency may hope for genuine participation in shaping and delivering services which will meet personal needs. Does this really matter, when all parties share the common goal? The range of meanings attached to different approaches to quality assurance makes it necessary to answer 'yes'. For example, if total quality management is introduced by embedding it within the practice of the worker, individually accountable to a manager for a contract, rather than through the rigorous reflective practice of co-, non-managerial supervision by other members of the professional team, then standards are maintained through managerialism rather than through professionalism.

Tokenistic involvement of clients in service delivery

Olive Stevenson expressed surprised that the concept of empowerment is described in government guidance on community care as aiming at empowering users and carers (Stevenson, 1994). Whilst the participation of service users is often presented as some kind of goal, the lack of service user participation is a symptom of the broader disempowerment of the individual rather than its cause. It relates to the consumerist approach to delivering personal social services adopted by the last Conservative government. It is a matter of human rights and the need to challenge the exclusion of some groups of people, notably those who are poor, from discourse and debates about significant participation (Beresford and Croft, 1995).

Ingredients of quality maximisation in social work

The foregoing discussion suggests a central question to be addressed in this final section: quality for whom? It is appropriate at this point to shift the balance of the discussion from *des*cription to *pre*scription, from attempting an interpretation to asking questions about how the current situation may be addressed.

It has to be acknowledged at the outset that the accumulation of the forces referred to may be ultimately and irreversibly damaging, not just to individuals on the receiving end of the personal social services, but to the nature of social work activity itself. That is, even the change of government in May 1997 may not alter the current trajectory of policy and practice. But if we are serious about quality in social work, then resources need to follow the commitment to maximise quality practice – in education and training and in agency practice.

Chapter 2 indicated that in different approaches to quality assurance, the prime stakeholder's interest tended to be defined and met differently, whether as expert, manager, professional, or as service user and worker. Subsequent chapters illustrated how particular versions of managerialism described in Chapter 3 have surfaced in aspects of the personal social services and impacted on social workers. Inevitably, this has meant that quality maintenance and enhancement approaches have been predominant, rather than quality maximisation. Nevertheless, there are strong arguments for the pursuit of quality maximisation.

The language and imagery of managerially or professionally dominated quality assurance reflect the striving of staff priority over 'clients', 'service users', 'carers', members of the general public or any other people, in their journey towards excellence of services. Unfortunately, unless quality maximisation involves the development of a holistic view, and the accomplishment of empowerment for all stakeholders in these services, then the goal of assuring quality becomes subverted, colonised and ultimately swamped by managerial and professional aspirations. The term 'quality maximisation' invites a fundamental break with that which is oppressive, divisive and non-transcendent in the sense that the personal social services engage with people's quality of life yet, unless reframed, do not offer either workers or users quality maximisation. 'Quality maximisation' is used in recognition of the risk that a quality standard, rather than being a minimum to which everyone can aspire, becomes an unattainable optimum which nobody can reach, so that people become disillusioned and cynical (James, 1992, p. 53).

Developing social work as an agent of social change

There is an abiding question as to why the mass media and public reaction to scandals in child care has been so strong and, arguably, so influential. First, the very nature of *the social* beyond individuals is a recognition of 'both the limits of family jurisdiction to deal with personal problems and the responsibility of the state to fill the breach. Precisely because the social is part of the public domain it is subject to the scrutiny of society. If Foucault and Donzelot are right, the ultimate *raison d'être* of the social is to prevent the irruption of "abnormal" or "unhealthy" acts. It follows that the social reaction against social workers is most intense when such acts occur' (Rojek, Peacock and Collins, 1988, p. 149). This raises the question as to what it is about social workers rather than the perpetrators of these acts which should attract such negative reactions? The authors refer to Foucault's point that discourse analysis is 'an instrument for those who fight, those who resist and refuse what is. Its use should be in processes of conflict and confrontation, essays in refusal. It doesn't have to lay down the law. It isn't a stage in programming. It is a challenge directed to what is' (Foucault, 1981, p. 13). So, the role of the social worker is 'to oppose . . . the view that power is centred on a subject, that fixed meanings exist, that symptoms can be traced to their original causes, that problems can be definitely and conclusively solved, and that abnormality is absolute' (Rojek, Peacock and Collins, 1988, p. 145). Consequently, 'legislative power is unpeeled, tested, and sometimes shredded. Above all, social work is social criticism' (Rojek, Peacock and Collins, 1988, p. 145). This puts the social worker on a level with the social scientist, working towards similar goals as the social critic. Clearly, this perspective on social work is highly charged with potential tensions between the social worker and the status quo, and even the exercise of legal duties and powers, where these are judged questionable. Second, there have been changes in the rate of recognition of child abuse and in its explanation. After the 1940s, the medical model concerning its explanation prevailed. Doctors dominated with theories about the battered baby syndrome, which compared child abuse to a disease which could be treated (Kempe, 1962). Bentovim and colleagues (1988) reinforced approaches based on the treatment paradigm by theorising about the dysfunctional family producing child abuse (Adams, 1996a, pp. 74–6). But there were inadequacies in the treatment paradigm, since no research has identified individual or family causative factors (Directors of Social Work in Scotland, 1992, p. 3). There is a need to locate explanations within their social and environmental context, taking into account the impact of social class, gender and ethnicity (ibid).

*Providing a legal framework to underpin openness and public
accountability*

There is a need to take seriously the implications of findings from
many inquiries and investigations, concerning the difficulty
many individuals and groups of workers and service users experience even in questioning, let alone challenging and criticising,
existing policies and practices. Organisational cultures need developing which welcome critical self-appraisal in the organisation.
Personal social services organisations need to develop cultures
which permit staff to work openly for quality maximisation,
whether this involves user participation or spotlighting shortcomings in the organisation. Yet, it is not realistic to expect any
dismantling before 2000, if then, of the market-based structures for
delivering key aspects of the personal social services, such as
community care.

On 7 August 1995, Stephen Dorrell, Secretary of State for
Health, announced that doctors' contracts would in future specify
a duty to report on colleagues' performance. But Lucy Vickers
notes that 'unless far reaching changes are made to employment
law, and the culture of the NHS, the new contractual obligation
will not answer the real concerns of staff in the NHS' (Vickers,
1995, p. 1257).

The massive growth in the contribution of the voluntary and
private sectors since the mid-1980s suggests that the principles of
public accountability and standards need to be applied with
immediate effect to these sectors. The Nolan Report specifically
targets local authorities alongside NHS bodies and executive
quangos, in its recommendation that 'a review should be undertaken by the Government with a view to producing a more
consistent legal framework governing propriety and accountability
in public bodies' (Nolan, first report, 1995, p. 65). Nolan notes the
concern of staff who wished to complain but, fearing the response
of their employers, had first recourse to the media. Nolan concurs
with Robert Sheldon MP, chairman of the Public Accounts Committee, that 'public money must never be allowed to have silence
clauses'. 'On the other hand, we would not wish to encourage
vexatious or irresponsible complaints which undermine public
confidence in institutions without due cause. We believe the best

way to achieve this balance is to develop sound internal procedures backed by an external review' (Nolan, first report, 1995, para 114, p. 92).

Finally, Nolan recommends that new board members – people recruited from outside the public sector to run public bodies – 'should on appointment make a commitment to undertake induction training which should include awareness of public sector values, and standards of probity and accountability' (Nolan, first report, 1995, para 125, p. 96). In dealing with the recruitment of new board members, the report emphasises the need for them to have an understanding of 'public sector practices' and of the proper procedures when dealing with public money.' It extends this principle to the external audit of the running of the organisation as a whole and not just its financial affairs. Nolan's one-page 'Standard of Best Practice for Openness in Executive NDPBs and NHS Bodies' implies this, focusing much attention on the need for openness of proceedings, particularly at Board level, presumably with the aim thereby of increasing public accountability (Nolan, first report, 1995, 19, p. 95).

Components of a quality assurance system include criteria for assessing and measuring quality services, the setting of strategic goals, priorities, objectives, standards, indicators and methods of monitoring and evaluating. In some circumstances, assuring quality will be a one-off situation or task-based activity. On other occasions it is an ongoing process. In each case, the principle of stakeholder participation is fundamental to quality maximisation.

Much user-oriented prescription on quality – particularly in the TQM area – actually dilutes the concept of empowerment by making a general soup of ingredients, as though, mixed thoroughly, all stakeholders somehow will emerge with a quality result. Similarly, user participation cannot be maximised simply by tacking a questionnaire on to service delivery, or even by developing customer panels (see Chapter 3), desirable though these may be. Taking up quality maximisation as a goal (see Chapter 2), involves accepting the full implications of empowering the major stakeholders in social work (see Adams, 1996b).

There is a need to acknowledge that stakeholders include not only users and carers, but the State, organisations purchasing and providing services, professionals, other workers and volunteers, in statutory, voluntary, private and informal sectors. There is a need, also, to avoid the glib statement that the goal of empowerment has been taken up universally and applied.

Recognition of the distinctiveness of social work

The field of quality assurance is replete with illustrations from commerce and, all too often, it is assumed by commentators from the commercial sector that the human services should be able to align themselves with principles and practice in that area, without undue difficulty. The reality is that the human services in general, and social work in particular, differ from the world of commerce in ways which impact significantly on quality assurance.

Displacing managerialism

We have noted the problematic nature of such components of quality assurance as performance measurement through key in-dicators, output measurement and so on (see Chapter 2). It was clear from this discussion that the situation cannot be rectified simply by adding on components. Thus, for example, adding outcome evaluation would not solve the problems of lack of crystallisation of how to evaluate the key purposes of a service and inherent limitations and ambiguities of existing performance criteria.

Integral quality maximisation

Reframing the components of quality assurance depends on the displacement of the ideology of managerialism before proceeding with the agenda of ensuring the maximisation of quality in social work. Just as other aspects of quality assurance cannot be bolted on, as it were, to a managerialist approach in order to boost its effectiveness, the bolted-on involvement of clients in the process will not ensure that the quality of service improves significantly. In fact, as Cutler and Waine point out, 'there is a symmetry between managerialism and consumerism. In both cases there is an *a priori* commitment to performance measurement which glosses over the real difficulties involved. Thus, while it is valid to argue that existing indicator sets lack effectiveness measures which would, in principle, be of value to consumers, the argument loses much of its force if such measures are questionable and ambiguous' (Cutler and Waine, 1994, p. 46). The views of service users may be sought in different ways. They may be invited to submit them, as outsiders in a relatively closed process managed totally by staff. At the other extreme, they may participate equally with staff in daily meetings at which all the business of running a therapeutic community is raised and dealt with. The Henderson hospital (Jones, 1968) is the archetypal example of this approach. Yet, even in such a situation, differences in status and power between staff and patients remain. In a visit to a therapeutic community, the author was told that all differences between staff and residents had been abolished, since the former were called workers and the latter co-workers. But, during the guided tour the senior staff member demonstrated by the way he ordered residents to do things that the power differentials remained relatively unchanged by this nominal difference in people's formal titles.

In one locality, two key features of quality assurance are the views of clients which contribute to 'standard-setting exercises, based on individual interviews to find out the preferences of users which contribute to the development of standards, and the joint development of quality measures with the local health authority, thus addressing the thorny problem of different standards being set or accepted by local health and social services agencies' (Leckie, 1994, p. 132). There are three further problems. First, it is one thing to consult the service user as a consumer, but quite another to empower the service user by participation in the entire process of designing, planning, implementing and evaluating the service. The latter is the only credible course consistent with an anti-oppressive, empowering practice (Adams, 1996b). Second, the inclusion of service users as participants raises the need to reconcile their perspective with that of other stakeholders. This raises the question about who are legitimate stakeholders: policymakers, managers, the professionals, carers, or others? It also poses the question as to the identity of the consumer: the service user, the purchaser, service provider, or the carer as the provider of informal care? Whatever one's response, Cutler and Waine add the caution that 'the project of encompassing all dimensions and all interests threatens to degenerate into an indeterminate series of measures which literally don't add up' (Cutler and Waine, 1994, p. 47). Third, the views of potential users of services who are currently excluded from receiving a given service, should be sought and incorporated in the quality assurance process. Only in this way can the issues of access to services, oppression and disadvantage be tackled adequately.

Defining, assessing, reviewing changes in, standards

Three particular points can be made here. First, ways need to be found of improving recruitment, training of staff, supervision, management, advocacy and self-advocacy by service users, access to non-recriminatory complaints procedures with rights to employment protected for staff, and a supportive culture for complaints by both clients and workers. Second, systems of independent visitors to all facilities, including homes and day centres, should be set up, in which service users and carers play an active part, alongside, supported by, but in addition to, and independent of, the current arrangements for inspection and registration of facilities. Third, the involvement of clients and carers should be supported with resources, giving them access to compensation for release from other responsibilities (such as the availability of respite facilities and grants to enable them to claim expenses) but also giving training and support to enable them to fulfil the role and help them meet up with others in similar circumstances.

Establishing and confirming the organisational commitment to quality

The contrast between Deming's view of TQM and the notions of quality control and quality assurance referred to in Chapter 2 suggest the need to establish a culture of quality in the organisation which emanates from the work group and gives staff control, rather than quality being fed in by experts and overseen by managers.

The adoption of a definition of quality which follows the consumerist model, of fitness for purpose and value for money, may fulfil the agency's accountability to financial goals. This is different from, and falls short of, the goal of accountability to the wishes and needs of colleagues, service users and carers, which is a priority of the democratic approach.

Employing qualified staff

The overwhelming conclusion of successive inquiry reports confirms the negative consequences of it not being compulsory for all social work and social services departments' staff working with children and adults to possess professional qualifications. In the 1990s, the low status and low pay of the work accompany the fact that only about 20 per cent of residential and daycare staff in childcare possess relevant qualifications (Kahan, 1991, p. 149). In fieldwork, in the inquiry into the Carly Taylor case (Leicestershire County Council and Health Authority, 1980), 45 per cent of basic grade social workers in the social services department lacked qualification and in the particular team only one out of 7 had a qualification; only one of 17 social workers dealing with the Paul Brown case (Secretary of State for Social Services, 1980) was qualified; the worker dealing with the Auckland case (Secretary of State for Social Services, 1975) at the time of Susan's birth was unqualified and newly appointed (Peyer *et al.*, 1982, p. 55).

Ensuring staff are appropriately experienced

Across the health and personal social services, there is evidence of the adverse consequences of the lack of appropriately experienced professionals in specific areas where inadequacies arise. For example, study of 18 inquiry reports into child abuse reveals that health visitors (in two cases), probation officers (in two other cases), social workers (in nine cases), general practitioners (in four cases), a consultant psychiatrist (in one case), the clinical medical officer (in one case) and the police (in one case), were inexperienced in dealing with child care and child abuse work (Peyer *et al.*, 1982, p. 56). Training was also felt to be necessary for clerical staff dealing with messages (including doctors' receptionists) for magistrates, and in settings where there is a high staff turnover or where sessional or temporary staff are commonly employed, such as hospital outpatients' and casualty departments (Peyer *et al.*, 1982, p. 57).

Providing adequate line management and professional supervision of staff

A distinction needs to be drawn between line management supervision of staff which, in the strict meaning of the term is bureaucratic, and fulfils the requirements of the organisation, and that which supports the work of professionals – such as social workers and health visitors – in face-to-face interaction with people who use the personal social services. Successive inquiry reports draw attention to defects on both counts. This is ironic, given the repeated waves of reorganisation which have swept through health and local authorities since the early 1970s.

Enhancing professionalism

Good management should not leave basic grade staff complaining of demotivation, disempowerment and burnout. In part, as Chapter 3 showed, the trend of employers in the personal social services has been towards managerialist styles which undermine and encroach on the professionalism of social workers instead of enhancing it. Rather than managerialism creating a climate where professional autonomy is weakened and social workers complain of feeling deskilled, quality social work necessitates the management function of organisations in the personal social services encouraging progressive professional practice.

Empowering the service user

The development in the health and personal social services of a version of the culture of commercial management has had a major impact since the early 1990s on the way services are planned, organised and delivered. But because many of the concepts informing this culture have significance to different stakeholders in this sector – managers, professionals in the workplace, educators, service users and carers – discourse concerning, say, empowerment is not owned by managers alone simply because official guidance colonises it: it also has attained prominence in the professional literature and occupies a vital place in user-led and self-help movements, organisations and groups (Adams, 1996b, p. 2). From a critical vantage point, Shaw comments on the inroads made by

commercialism into the personal social services: 'The languages of
cost-effectiveness, service user satisfaction, empowerment, commercial models of quality management, monitoring and evaluation,
service contracts, partnerships, staff supervision, financial decen-
tralization and outcome assessments have permeated the planning,
management and delivery of British social services' (Shaw, 1995,
p. 129). Nevertheless, one way forward is to build on that element
of user participation which is common both to government
rhetoric on empowerment and radical espousement of its substantive implications; the next stage is to acknowledge how vital to the
evaluation process is the existence of many different stakeholders
in the personal social services. Such organisations, with their
extensive and fragmented networks linking purchasers and providers of services, represent 'shifting coalitions of sub-groups, both
inside and outside, with differing views of what the organization
should produce' (Kanter and Summers, 1994, p. 229).

In the face of this complex, ever-changing reality, Shaw admits
to reaching a somewhat pessimistic conclusion: 'politicians are
primarily interested in quality as cost-effectiveness, managers aim
for organizational and staff performance controls, and welfare
professionals welcome quality as a mechanism that will guarantee
professional survival in an uncertain world' (Shaw, 1995, p. 130).
This forecloses on the contribution to be made by people receiving
services themselves, for example through protests (see Chapters 5
and 6) and through amplifying the influence of empowerment in
practice (see Chapters 7 and 8).

Some local authorities have set up consultative groups of service
users across a range of services, to gather their views. Thus, a
group may cover leisure, employment and adult education needs.
In other authorities, meetings are convened by specific service
areas, such as joint health and social services commissioning teams.
The strength of such initiatives lies in the attempt to gather users'
views directly. Criticisms of such groups include their occasional
nature – some are held only annually – the way they are run –
professionals may control agendas, chair meetings and steer discussion – and their composition – they may include selected, or
self-selected, users rather than a representative range of users. For
example, the learning disability register may not be a comprehensive source for all people experiencing learning disabilities. Finally,
there are critical questions also about whether a formal relation-

ship exists between such meetings and the decision-making process on the future nature of service provision in the locality and how far users' views can influence the nature of such services. There are dilemmas between using professional power to override the expressed views of the user and through empowering practice which recognises personal rights, offering the user the opportunity to maximise choice. An example is Mrs C., who wants her bedridden husband, who has just received stabilising pain-killing treatment for his terminal cancer in the high-dependency ward of the local hospital, to die at home rather than in hospital. But the hospital staff have reacted against this request from herself and her husband, because for them the 'normal' route is via hospice care. Mrs C's husband refuses to admit formally that his condition is terminal and will not countenance moving to a hospice. This case highlights the tension between the principle that the patient and carer have the right to choose the place of death, and the accepted practice in a particular setting. The quality of care depends on taking the wishes of the service user seriously.

Nolan identifies several features of the organisation as needing attention: the need of openness to public criticism: 'public scrutiny of what people do is probably the most powerful pressure towards probity of conduct' (written evidence by the Audit Commission to the Nolan Committee, Nolan, first report, 1995, p. 93); lessening secrecy in the operation of quangos and reducing people's feelings of alienation and powerlessness to influence the decision-making of quangos (Nolan, first report, 1995, p. 93); responding to members of the public as 'not only consumers of, but shareholders in public services' (Anne Caldwell, correspondent, quoted in Nolan, first report, 1995, p. 93)

The inquiry report (Cambridgeshire County Council, 1997) into the death of Ricky Neave in 1995 contains criticisms of social workers which are all too familiar: lack of follow-up by social workers of opportunities to investigate, and lack of adequate record-keeping. The question is whether carrying out the process of achieving BS 5750 will prevent the recurrence of such tragedies, or whether significant change depends on more resources. Again, it could be said that such shortcomings need tackling through *practice* rather than *procedures*. This final chapter does not arrive at a simple formula or checklist, designed to abolish all shortcomings. It acknowledges the complexity of the issues and the inescapable dilemmas inherent in social work. For example, social workers in child protection may be damned if they do intervene and damned if they do not. Also, many agencies face shortages of resources which lead practitioners to apply *ad hoc* rationing of what they do and how they prioritise it, at the interface with their work, at their desks and face to face with service users. But quality maximisation rests on the principle of empowering social work, which *genuinely* makes the client – in this case the child and the family – the central focus of work. Just as changing procedures will not of itself improve quality, nor will substituting the term 'service user' for 'client' – or vice versa – achieve the empowerment of people.

Total quality may not be maximisation at all, if it simply devolves responsibility for specifying policies and procedures to the level of the unit of resource and leaves it there, without management coming up with the necessary resources to underpin excellence. The consequence is that staff experience the pressure and management hold staff responsible for shortcomings, which derive in part from their loss of morale, alienation and consequent failure to carry out procedures.

The acid test: checklist of process of quality assurance

The test of the viability of the points made above is whether the basic activities associated with assuring quality can be carried out in keeping with the aspiration of quality maximization. These are as follows:

- planning, implementing, monitoring and evaluating a programme for quality maximisation
- devising a plan for introducing and developing quality maximisation
- working out a realistic schedule based on estimates of how long each stage will take
- implementing the plan
- monitoring the implementation
- evaluating the implementation.

Five elements contribute to preparing a quality assurance system:

1. Developing a statement of standards
2. Analysing the relevant activities and mapping the procedures to be described
3. Writing the procedures
4. Revising the procedures in the light of stakeholders' views, published BS and ISO statements and statements of standards
5. Carrying out an audit of each area for which procedures have been written.

A statement of standards should not be based on the minimum achievable standard; it should be an outcome of an ongoing process of debate and negotiation. This involves raising consciousness of values and incorporating them into a list of standards. Each of these is accompanied by a statement specifying the means by which it can be achieved. The process by which this statement is achieved necessitates a principled sequence of actions, as in Table 9.1.

Developing a policy statement which maximises quality

A policy statement involves specifying the purposes of the activity and/or setting. A purpose is an aim embodying one or more values. An excellent policy statement will clarify these values as well as the

Table 9.1   Developing a statement of standards of service

Principle	Action/s
Collaborative planning	Invite all stakeholders to participate
Variety of events	Informal discussion and formal meetings
Awareness-raising of issues	Up-front declarations of politics of quality assurance – costs as well as benefits; possible unintended and intended outcomes, notion of quality as process rather than simply one-off outcome
Developing value base	Educating each other and promoting view of quality services based on shared values in the setting

aims. The statement will proceed from the clarification of values and aims, to specifying how these aims will be met.

Specifying procedures

This involves clarifying and writing down what staff involved in a particular activity actually do. A good deal of work goes into writing a statement of a procedure. Quality maximisation requires that all stakeholders are involved in the process and have the opportunity to contribute to an evaluation of whether the purposes of the procedure are being achieved. In the event that stakeholders identify shortcomings, these will need addressing before the statement is finalised. The criterion for judging an *excellent* statement of a procedure is that it actually maximises quality as it is implemented. There are likely to be three components of the final statement:

1. *Field*: This details the extent of the duties.
2. *Values*: This specifies the value base of the activities.
3. *Content*: This is a step-by-step list of tasks.

The following checklist of questions can be used to assess the extent to which a particular statement of a procedure meets the goal of quality maximisation:

- Does the procedure define the field over which the task extends?
- Does the procedure state clearly what actually happens?
- Does the values statement clarify and distinguish the different purposes of the task?
- Does the procedure follow the sequence of processes involved in the task?
- Does the procedure clarify which staff are responsible for which aspects of the task?

The process of writing, revising and auditing and evaluating the procedures, and actions carried out in the wake of them, should follow the principles of participatory evaluation, set out in Chapter 8.

Conclusions

The purpose of this book has not been to evaluate social work practice as a whole. Nevertheless, this final chapter has an evaluative dimension. The conclusion could be encapsulated in the questioning title of Brewer and Lait's book, *Can Social Work Survive?* (1980), reframed as a statement. The operative phrase then should not be 'can social work survive?' or 'can social work improve?', but 'social work must maximise its quality'. The task then is to transcend the managerialist agenda and the problematic aspects of assuring quality and aspire towards this imperative.

It is not easy to be prescriptive in the detail of how to bring quality maximisation about in social work. It is evident that approaches to quality assurance consonant with the forms of managerialism which, in effect, have ushered in the massive changes in the personal social services since the late 1980s, have imposed controls on professionals rather than empowering them or service users. It is premature to attempt to guess whether the impact of these changes by the end of the 1990s will on the whole democratise or simply curtail empowerment in the personal social services (Adams, 1996a, p. 226). It is not wise either to dismiss the new arrangements cynically or to welcome them as heralding the end of the problems of the welfare state (Clarke, Cochrane and McLaughlin, 1994a, p. 11). Chapters 2 and 3 showed how managerialist styles have encroached on the concept of empowerment, rendering it vulnerable to colonisation by the consumerism which is rampant in the marketplace of the personal social services. The contract culture of quasi-markets is vulnerable also to short-termism and pervasive values of individualism and self-interested commercialism, rather than the humane, collective as well as person-based, anti-oppressiveness of *real* social work. Beyond the false promise of consumerism or technical fixes lies empowerment, in different domains, towards the ideal of fulfilment of practice. Inherent in empowerment-in-practice (Adams, 1996b, pp. 39–40) lies the opportunity of. a practice theory produced through praxis. Quality maximisation is a product of, and produces, a fully theorised progressive practice. Users' stakes in practice are threaded through the process of quality maximisation.

Social work practice in the new age entails taking on board the fragmentation of working and living environments and 'surfing the net' of global human experience beyond the limitations of Western, hierarchically and male-dominated, managerialist, product-based, ego-driven practices. The reframing of discourse around quality requires the incorporation of the transcendent discourse of maximisation, valuing philosophies (see Adams, 1975, p. 400, for a partial mapping of the territory of this dichotomy) rooted in *being* – that is, action – rather than merely *behaviour*, based upon empowered rather than empowering practice, and which is beyond managerialism. This enables empowerment-in-practice to be fulfilled at the outset. It is the starting point rather than the goal. Transformational activity embodied in non-Western practice may enable the discourse about quality to reach beyond the struggle for empowerment to the state of being empowered. Beyond empower-*ment* and anti-oppressive practice lie states of *being* empowered and non-oppressive, which are the working out of reflective practice in a holist, global sense. Paradoxically, the attainment of the state of being empowered makes the struggle for empowerment no less vital and challenging. Once the struggle to empower and act anti-oppressively is reframed in 'the new quality' as a state of being, in practice, the journey *towards* becomes *the state of*, and quality maximisation becomes lived practice rather than techniques used 'out there', away from one's self, or a theoretical abstraction.

Appendix: Inquiry and Inspection Reports

Selection of major investigations, inquiries and reports into aspects of the quality of social work

1945 *Report of Sir Walter (later Viscount) Monckton on the circumstances which led to the boarding out of Dennis and Terence O'Neill at Bank Farm, Misterely, and the steps taken to supervise their welfare*, Cmd. 6636, HMSO, London.

1946 *Report of the Committee on the Care of Children* (Curtis Report) Cmnd 6922, HMSO, London.

1947 *Report of the Committee of Enquiry into the Conduct of Standen Farm Approved School*, HMSO, London.

1954 Home Office, *The Organisation of the Prison Medical Service* (Gwynne Report), HMSO, London.

1959 *Disturbances at the Carlton Approved School*, Cmnd 937, HMSO, London.

1966 Home Office *Report of the Inquiry into Prison Escapes and Security* (Mountbatten Report), Cmnd. 3175, HMSO, London.

1969 National Health Service, *Report of the Committee of Inquiry into Allegations of Ill-treatment of Patients and other Irregularities at the Ely Hospital, Cardiff*, Cmnd 3975, HMSO, London.

1971 National Health Service *Report of the Farleigh Hospital Committee of Inquiry* Cmnd. 4557, HMSO, London.

1972 National Health Service *Report of the Committee of Inquiry into Whittingham Hospital* Cmnd 4861, HMSO, London.

1973 Department of Health and Social Security *Report of the Professional Investigation into Medical and Nursing Practices on Certain Wards at Napsbury Hospital, nr. St. Albans*, HMSO, London.

Home Office and DHSS *Report of the Review and Proceedings for the Discharged and Supervision of Psychiatric Patients Subject to Special Restrictions* (Aarvold Commission) Cmnd 5191, HMSO, London.

Salop County Council, *Inquiry into the Circumstances Surrounding the Death of Graham Bagnall and the Role of the County Council's Social Services*, Report of Working Party of Social Services Committee, Salop County Council, Shrewsbury.

Shrewsbury Group Hospital Management Committee *Report of the Committee of Enquiry of the Hospital Management Committee into the Circumstances Leading up to the Death of Graham Bagnall insofar as the Hospital Authority were Concerned*, Shrewsbury Group Hospital Management Committee, Shrewsbury.

Staffordshire Area Health Authority, *Report of the Committee of Enquiry set up to Enquire into the Circumstances Surrounding the Admission, Treatment and Discharge of baby David Lee Naseby, Deceased at Burton-on-Trent General Hospital from February to May 1973*, Staffordshire Area Health Authority, Stafford.

1974   Secretary of State for Social Services, *Report of the Committee of Inquiry into the Care and Supervision Provided in Relation to Maria Colwell*, HMSO, London.
        Essex County Council and Area Health Authority, *Report of the Joint Committee set up to Consider Co-ordination of Services Concerned with Non-accidental Injury to Children*, (Case of Max Piazzani), Social Services Department, Essex County Council, Chelmsford.
        South Ockendon Hospital Inquiry, *Report of the Committee of Inquiry into South Ockendon Hospital*, H.C.124, HMSO, London.
1975   Merton, Sutton and Wandsworth Area Health Authority, *St. Ebba's Hospital Inquiry Report*, Merton, Sutton and Wandsworth Area Health Authority.
        Secretary of State for Scotland, Scottish Education Department, Social Work Services Group, *Report of the Committee of Inquiry into the Consideration Given and Steps Taken Towards Securing the Welfare of Richard Clark by Perth Town and Other Bodies or Persons Concerned*, HMSO, Edinburgh.
        Secretary of State for Social Services, *Report of the Committee of Inquiry into the Provision and Co-ordination of Services to the Family of John George Auckland*, HMSO, London.
        Lambeth, Southwark and Lewisham Health Authority (Teaching), Inner London Probation and After-Care Committee, *Report of the Joint Committee of Enquiry into Non-accidental Injury to children with particular reference to Lisa Godfrey*, London Borough of Lambeth.
        Norfolk County Council and Area Health Authority, *Report of the Review Body Appointed to Enquire into the Death of Stephen Meurs*, Norfolk County Council, Norwich.
        East Sussex County Council, *Children at Risk: A Study into the Problems Revealed by the Report of the Inquiry into the Case of Maria Colwell*, East Sussex County Council, Lewes.
        Home Office, *Report of the Working Party on Adjudication Procedures in Prisons*, (Weiler Report), HMSO, London.
        Home Office, *The Report of the Committee on Mentally Abnormal Offenders*, (Butler Report), Cmnd. 6244, HMSO, London.
1976   East Sussex County Council, *Children and Risk: Joint report of the County Secretary and Director of Social Services*, Lewes, East Sussex County Council.
        City of Birmingham District Council and Birmingham Area Health Authority, *Joint Enquiry Arising from the Death of Neil Howlett*, Birmingham Social Services Department, Birmingham.
        St. Augustine's Hospital Enquiry, *Report of a Committee of Enquiry St. Augustine's Hospital, Chatham, Canterbury*, South East Thames Regional Health Authority, Croydon.
        Warlingham Park Hospital Inquiry, *Report of the Committee of Inquiry*, Croydon Area Health Authority, Croydon.
        Darlington Memorial Hospital Inquiry, *Report of the Committee of Inquiry*, Newcastle, Northern Regional Health Authority.
1977   Kent Area Health Authority, *St. Augustine's Hospital Committee of Inquiry: Report of Emergency Panel*, Kent Area Health Authority, Maidstone.
        Mary Dendy Hospital Inquiry, *Report of a Committee of Inquiry*, Mersey Regional Health Authority, Liverpool.
        'H' Family: *Report of an Investigation by the Director of Social Services and the Deputy Town Clerk*, Surrey County Council, Guildford.
        Somerset Area Review Committee, *Wayne Brewer: Report of the Review Panel*, Somerset County Council, Taunton.

Report of the Review Panel Appointed by Somerset Area Review Committee to Consider the Case of Wayne Brewer, Somerset Area Review Committee, Taunton.

1978 *Report of an Inquiry held at Wallasy: Paul Brown and L. Brown,* Wirral Borough Council and Wirral Area Health Authority, Birkenhead.

DHSS, *Report of the Social Work Service of DHSS into Certain Aspects of the Management of the Case of Stephen Menheniott,* HMSO, London.

Derbyshire County Council and Area Health Authority, *Karen Spencer: Report by Professor J D McClean, Professor of Law in the University of Sheffield,* Derbyshire Social Services Department, County Offices, Matlock.

Cambridgeshire and Suffolk County Councils and Area Health Authorities, *Report of Committee of Enquiry Concerning Simon Peacock,* Cambridgeshire County Council, Shire Hall, Cambridge.

Sherrard, Michael, 1978 *Report of the Committee of Inquiry into Normansfield Hospital,* Cmnd. 7357, HMSO, London.

1979 Home Office, *Committee of Inquiry into the U.K. Prison Services. Report,* (May Report), Cmnd. 7673, HMSO, London.

Winterton Hospital Inquiry, *Report to Durham Area Health Authority,* Durham Area Health Authority, Durham.

Brookwood Hospital Industrial Relations Inquiry, *Report of the Committee of Inquiry into Industrial Relations,* (Chairman D. Montague), Surrey Area Health Authority, Guildford.

St Mary's Hospital, *Report of the Inquiry Relating to St Mary's Hospital,* (Stannington Inquiry), Gateshead Area Health Authority, Gateshead.

Church Hill House Hospital Inquiry, *Inquiry into Allegations made in respect of Church Hill House Hospital, Bracknell,* Berkshire Area Health Authority, Reading.

Berkshire and Hampshire County Councils and Area Health Authorities, *Lester Chapman Inquiry Report,* Berkshire County Council, Reading.

Secretary of State for Social Services *Report of the Committee of Inquiry into the Actions of the Authorities and Agencies Relating to Darryn James* Clarke, HMSO, London.

1980 City of Birmingham Social Services Department, *Report of the Director of Social Services to the Social Services Committee, Clare Haddon born 9.12.78.,* City of Birmingham Social Services Department, Birmingham.

Secretary of State for Social Services (DHSS), *The Report of the Committee of Inquiry into the Case of Paul Steven Brown,* Cmnd 8107, HMSO, London.

Leicestershire County Council and Area Health Authority (Teaching), *Carly Taylor: Report of an Independent Inquiry,* Leicestershire County Council, Leicester.

Surrey Area Health Authority, *Report of the Committee of Inquiry into Standards of Patient Care at Brookwood Hospital,* (Chairman C, Beaumont), West Surrey/North East Hampshire Health District, Woking.

Costhill Hospital Inquiry, *Report of the Committee of Inquiry into Mental Handicap Services,* Oxfordshire Area Health Authority, (Teaching), Oxford.

Department of Health and Social Security *Report of the Review of Rampton Hospital,* (Chairman Sir John Boynton), Cmnd. 8073, HMSO, London.

Newchurch Hospital Inquiry, *Report of Members' Enquiry,* Cheshire Area Health Authority, Chester.

1981 Sandhill Park Hospital Inquiry, *Member Enquiry into Sandhill Park Hospital, Interim and Final Reports,* Somerset Area Health Authority, Taunton.

Child Abuse Sub-Committee, *Child Abuse Enquiry Sub-committee Report Concerning Christopher Pinder/Daniel Frankland (born 19.12.79, died 8.7.80), Bradford Area Review Committee, Bradford.*

London Borough of Southwark, Lambeth, Southwark and Lewisham Area Health Authority (Teaching), Inner London Probation and After-Care Service, *Maria Mehmedagi - Report of an Independent Inquiry*, Public Relations Department, Town Hall, Peckham Road, London SE5

Review Panel, *Report of the Review Panel . . . into the Death of Heidi Koseda*, London Borough of Hillingdon, Hillingdon.

Essex County Council and Area Health Authority *Malcolm Page: Report by the Panel Appointed by the Essex Area Review Committee*, Essex County Council, Chelmsford.

Bradford Area Review Committee, *Child Abuse Enquiry Sub-committee Report Concerning Christopher Pinder/Daniel Frankland (born 19.12.79, died 8.7.80), Bradford Area Review Committee, Bradford.*

1982 Cambridge County Council, *Report . . . on the Involvement of the Social Services Department in the Events Preceding the Death of Jason Caesar*, Cambridge County Council, Cambridge.

Lucy Gates Enquiry Panel, *Report of the Panel Enquiry into the Death of Lucy Gates, Chairman's Report, Vol.1. Report of other Panel Members, Vol. 2.* London Borough of Bexley and Bexley Health Authority, Bexley.

Inquiry Panel, *Report of an Inquiry Panel into the Examination of the Implications of the Death of a Child to Cheshire Central Review Committee for Child Abuse*, Cheshire Central Review Committee, Chester.

1983 DHSS, *The NHS Management Inquiry* (Griffiths Report), HMSO, London.

1984 Home Office, *Tougher Regimes in Detention Centres: Report of an Evaluation by the Young Offender Psychology Unit*, HMSO, London.

London Borough of Hammersmith and/Fulham, *Report of the death of Shirley Woodcock*, London Borough of Hammersmith and Fulham.

Home Office *Managing the Long-Term Prison System: The Report of the Control Review Committee*, HMSO, London.

1985 Blom Cooper, L., *A Child in Trust: the Report of the Panel of Inquiry into the Circumstances Surrounding the Death of Jasmine Beckford*, London Borough of Brent.

Standing Inquiry Panel, *Report of the Standing Inquiry Panel into the Case of Reuben Carthy*, Nottinghamshire County Council, Nottingham.

Independent Inquiry, *Report of an Independent Inquiry into the Provision and Co-ordination of Services to the Family of Carly Taylor by the Relevant Local Authorities and Health Services and by the Persons or Agencies to Leicestershire County Council and Leicester Area Health Authority Teaching*, Leicester County Council, Leicester.

Home Office, *Report of Her Majesty's Chief Inspection of Prisons 1984*, HMSO, London.

Home Office, *Report of the Committee on the Prison Disciplinary System*, (Prior Report), Cmnd. 9641, HMSO, London.

1986 Review Panel, *Report of the Review Panel . . . into the Death of Heidi Koseda*, London Borough of Hillingdon.

Audit Commission, *Making a Reality of Community Care*, HMSO, London.

Social Services Inspectorate *Inspection of the Implementation of the Registered Homes Act 1984 Stage 1: the Impact on Registration Authorities*, Department of Health and Social Security, London.

Social Services Inspectorate, *Social Services Inspectorate Project on Drug Misuse*, Department of Health and Social Security, London.

1987   Commission of Inquiry, *A Child in Mind: Protection of Children in a Responsible Society. The Report of the Commission of Inquiry into the Circumstances Surrounding the Death of Kimberley Carlile*, London Borough of Greenwich and Greenwich Health Authority.

Inquiry Panel, *Whose Child? The Report of the Panel Appointed to Inquire into the Death of Tyra Henry*, London Borough of Lambeth.

Social Services Inspectorate, *From Home Help to Home Care: an Analysis of Policy, Resourcing and Service Management*, HMSO, London.

Home Office, *Report of an Inquiry by Her Majesty's Chief Inspector of Prisons for England and Wales into the Disturbances in Prison Service Establishments in England between 29 April and 2 May 1986*, HMSO, London.

Her Majesty's Inspectorate of Probation: Home Office and SSI: DHSS, *Report on the Practice of Supervision of Juvenile Offenders,* Home Office and DHSS, London.

Home Office, *A Review of Prisoners' Complaints*, A Report by HM Chief Inspector of Prisons, HMSO, London.

Home Office, *Report of the Inter-Departmental Working Group of Home Office and DHSS Officials on Mentally Disturbed Offenders in the Prison System in England and Wales*, Home Office, London.

1988   Butler-Sloss, E., *Report of the Inquiry into Child Abuse in Cleveland*, Cm 412, London, HMSO.

Audit Commission, *Performance Review in Local Government: a Handbook for Auditors and Local Authorities: Action Guide*, HMSO, London.

Home Office, *Punishment, Custody and the Community*, Cm 424, HMSO, London.

Home Office, *Report by Her Majesty's Chief Inspector of Prisons on H.M. Remand Centre Risley*, Home Office, London.

Home Office, *Report by Her Majesty 's Chief Inspection of Prisons on H.M. Prison Parkhurst*, Home Office, London.

Home Office, *The Parole System in England and Wales, Report of the Review Committee*, (Carlisle Report), Cm. 532, HMSO, London.

Department of Health/Social Services Inspectorate, *Towards a Climate of Confidence: Report of a National Inspection of Management Arrangements for Public Sector Residential Care for Elderly People*, HMSO, London.

Social Services Inspectorate, *Managing Policy Change in Home Help Services,* HMSO, London.

Social Services Inspectorate, *Social Services in a Multi-Racial Society,* Department of Health, London.

Social Services Inspectorate, *Family Centres: A Change of Name or a Change of Practice*, Department of Health, London.

Social Services Inspectorate, *Health in Homes: A Review of Arrangements for Health Care in Local Authority Homes for Elderly People,* Department of Health, London.

Social Services Inspectorate, *A Wider Vision: the Management and Organisation of Services for People who are Blind or Visually Handicapped*, Department of Health and Social Security, London.

1989   Department of Health, *Homes are for Living In*, HMSO, London.

Social Services Inspectorate, *Managing Home Care in Metropolitan Districts,* HMSO, London.

Social Services Inspectorate, *Doing it Better Together: a Report of Developments in Four Locations to Establish Local Procedures for Multidisciplinary Assessment of the Needs of Elderly People*, Department of Health, London.

Social Services Inspectorate, *Inspection of Social Work with Afro Caribbean and Asian Families in Avon,* Department of Health, London.

Social Services Inspectorate, *Sign Posts: Leading to Better Social Services for Deaf-blind People,* Department of Health, London.

Home Office, *Report of Her Majesty's Chief Inspector of Prisons 1988,* HMSO, London.

Home Office, *Report by Her Majesty's Chief Inspector of Prisons H.M. Prison Cookham Wood,* Home Office, London.

Home Office, *Report by Her Majesty's Chief Inspector of Prisons on H.M. Prison Styal,* Home Office, London.

Home Office, *Report by Her Majesty's Chief Inspector of Prisons on H.M. Prison East Sutton Park,* Home Office, London.

1990 Audit Commission, *Performance Review Supplement,* Audit Commission, London.

Department of Health, *Caring for Quality: Guidance on Standards for Residential Homes for Elderly People,* HMSO, London.

Department of Health/Social Services Inspectorate, *Caring for People: Mental Illness Specific Grant Monitoring Arrangements,* Department of Health, London.

Department of Health, *Caring for Quality: Guidance on Standards for Residential Homes for People with a Physical Disability,* HMSO, London.

Social Services Inspectorate, *Inspecting Home Care Services: a guide to the SSI method,* HMSO, London.

Social Services Inspectorate, *All Change: from Hospital to Community: Inspection of Community Services for Former Long Stay Hospital Patients,* Department of Health, London.

Social Services Inspectorate, *Developing Services for Young People with Disabilities: Report on the Progress of Six Local Authorities Towards Implementing Sections 5 and 6 of the Disabled Persons (Services, Consultation and Representation) Act 1986,* Department of Health London.

Social Services Inspectorate, *Inspection of Child Protection Services in Rochdale,* Department of Health, London.

Home Office, *Report by Her Majesty's Chief Inspector of Prisons on H.M. Prison Brixton,* Home Office, London.

Home Office, *Report by Her Majesty's Chief Inspector of Prisons on H.M. Prison Leeds,* Home Office, London.

Home Office, *Report on an Efficiency Scrutiny of the Prison Medical Service,* (Efficiency Scrutiny Report), Home Office, London.

Home Office, *Report of Her Majesty's Chief Inspector of Prisons 1989,* London, HMSO.

1991 National Association of Health Authorities and Trusts, *Care of People with a Terminal Illness,* National Association of Health Authorities and Trusts, London

Levy, Allan and Kahan, Barabara, *The Pindown Experience and the Protection of Children: the Report of the Staffordshire Child Care Inquiry 1990,* Staffordshire County Council, Stafford.

Audit Commission, *The Quality Exchange: finance services, summary report,* Audit Commission, London.

Department of Health/Social Services Inspectorate, *Women in Social Services: A Neglected Resource,* HMSO, London.

Department of Health/Social Services Inspectorate, *Inspecting for Quality: Guidance on Practice for Inspection Units in Social Services Departments and other Agenices: Principles, Issues and Recommentations* HMSO, London.

Department of Health/Social Services Inspectorate, *Complaints About the Social Services Department: ideas for a Practice Booklet for Clerks, Receptionists and Telephonists,* HMSO, London.

Department of Health/Social Services Inspectorate, *The Right to Complain: Practice Guidance on Complaints Procedures in Social Services Departments,* HMSO, London.

Department of Health/Social Services Inspectorate, *Children in the Public Care: a Review of Residential Child Care,* (The Utting Report) HMSO, London.

HM Treasury, *Competing for Quality; buying better public services,* White Paper CM1730, HMSO, London.

Department of Health, *Welfare of Children and Young People in Hospital,* HMSO, London.

Social Services Inspectorate, *Adoption: in the child's best interests?: Adoption Services in Three London Local Authorities,* Department of Health, London.

Home Office, *Management of the Prison Service: Report by Admiral Sir Raymond Lygo KCB,* London, Home Office.

Home Office, *Report by Her Majesty's Chief Inspector of Prisons on H.M. Prison Coldingley,* Home Office, London.

Woolf, Rt. Hon. Lord Justice and Tumim, His Hon. Judge S. *Prison Disturbances April 1990: Report of an Inquiry,* Cm 1456, HMSO, London.

1992   Committee of Inquiry, *Report of the Committee of Inquiry into Complaints About Ashworth Hospital,* HMSO, London.

House of Commons, *Report of the Inquiry into the Removal of Children from Orkney in February 1991,* House of Commons ([HC]); 195, 1992–93), London.

National Children's Home, *The Report of the Committee of Enquiry into Children and Young People who Sexually Abuse Other Children,* National Children's Home, London.

Department of Health, *Review of Health and Social Services for Mentally Disordered Offenders and Others Requiring Similar Services,* (chairman Dr John Reed), Final Summary Report, Cm 2088, HMSO, London.

SSI, *Concern for Quality: The First Annual Report of the Chief Inspector,* Social Services Inspectorate 1991/92, HMSO, London.

Department of Health, *Committed to Quality: Quality Assurance in Social Services Departments,* London, HMSO.

Department of Health/Social Services Inspectorate, *Promoting Women: management development and training for women in social services departments,* HMSO, London.

Williams, Gareth and McCreadie, John, *Ty Mawr Community Home Inquiry,* Gwent County Council, Newport.

Social Services Inspectorate, *Managing Services in Partnership: a joint project of the National Health Service Training Directorate and the Social Services Inspectorate,* NHSTD, London.

Howe, E. *The Quality of Care. Report of the Residential Staff's Inquiry, chaired by Lady Howe,* (The Howe Report), Local Government Management Board, Luton.

Department of Health, *Guidance on Standards for the Residential Care Needs of People with Learning Disabilities/Mental Handicap,* HMSO, London.

Department of Health, *Guidance on Standards for the Residential Care Needs of People with Specific Mental Health Needs,* HMSO, London.

Home Office, *Report of Her Majesty's Chief Inspector of Prisons, April 1991– March 1992,* London.

Home Office *Report of an Unannounced Short Inspection by Her Majesty's Chief Inspector of Prisons, H.M. Prison Manchester,* Home Office, London.

Brannan, C., Jones, J.R., Murch, J.D., *Castle Hill Report: Practice Guide*, Shropshire County Council, Shrewsbury.

1993 Kirkwood, Andrew QC., *The Leicestershire Inquiry 1992. The Report of an Inquiry into Aspects of the Management of Children's Homes in Leicestershire Between 1973 and 1986*, Leicestershire County Council, Leicester.

Department of Health/Social Services Inspectorate, *Social Services for Hospital Patients: Users' and Carers' Perspectives*, HMSO, London.

Department of Health/Social Services Inspectorate, *The Inspection of the Complaints Procedures in Local Authority Social Services Departments*, HMSO, London.

Department of Health/Social Services Inspectorate, *Planning for Permanence? An Inspection of Adoption Services in Three Northern Local Authorities*, Department of Health, London.

Department of Health/Social Services Inspectorate, *Occupational Therapy – the Community Contribution: Report on Local Authority Occupational Therapy Services*, Department of Health, London.

Department of Health/Social Services Inspectorate, *Raising the Standard: the Second Annual Report of the Chief Inspector*, Social Services Inspectorate 1992/93, HMSO, London.

Department of Health/Social Services Inspectorate, *Inspecting for Quality: Standards for the Residential Care of Elderly People with Mental Disorders*, HMSO, London.

Department of Health/Social Services Inspectorate, *Corporate Parents: Inspection of Residential Child Care Services in 11 Local Authorities, November 1992 to March 1993*, Department of Health, London.

Department of Health/Social Services Inspectorate, *Inspecting for Quality: Evaluating Performance in Child Protection: A Framework for the Inspection of Local Authority Social Services Practice and Systems*, HMSO, London.

Department of Health, *Training for the Future: Training and Development Guidance to Support the Implementation of the NHS and Community Care Act 1990 and the Full Range of Community Care Reforms*, London, HMSO.

Department of Health/Social Services Inspectorate, *Inspection of Assessment and Care Management Arrangements in Social Services Departments: Interim Overview Report*, Department of Health, London.

Social Services Inspectorate, *Report of an Inspection of Management and Provision of Social Work in the Three Special Hospitals, July – September 1993*, Department of Health, London.

Social Services Inspectorate, *Standards for the Residential Care of People with Mental Disorders*, HMSO, London.

Social Services Inspectorate, *No Longer Afraid – the Safeguard of Older People in Domestic Settings*, HMSO, London.

Social Services Inspectorate, *Developing Quality Standards for Home Support Services*, HMSO, London.

Social Services Inspectorate, *Social Services Department Inspection Units: the First Eighteen Months: Report of an Inspection Conducted by SSI of the Work of Inspection Units in Ten Local Authority Social Services Departments between November 1992 and January 1993*, HMSO, London.

Social Services Inspectorate, *Progress on the Right to Complain: Monitoring Social Services Complaints Procedures 1992/93*, Department of Health, London.

Social Services Inspectorate, *Whose Life is it, Anyway? A Report of an Inspection of Services for People with Multiple Impairments*, Department of Health, London.

1994 Social Services Inspectorate, *Putting People First: The Third Annual Report of the Chief Inspector Social Services Inspectorate*, 1993/94, HMSO, London.

Social Services Inspectorate, *Responding to Youth Crime: Findings from Inspections of Youth Justice Services in Five Local Authority Social Services Departments*, HMSO, London.

Ritchie, Jean H., Dick, Dr Donald and Lingham, Richard, *The Report of the Inquiry into the Care and Treatment of Christopher Clunis*, HMSO, London.

Audit Commission, *Seen But Not Heard: Co-ordinating Community Child Health and Social Services for Children in Need*, London, HMSO.

La Fontaine, Jean, *The Extent and Nature of Organised Ritual Abuse*, HMSO, London.

Department of Health/Social Services Inspectorate, *Social Services Department Inspection Units: Report of an Inspection of the Work of Inspection Units in Twenty Seven Local Authorities*, Department of Health, London.

1995 Kilgallon, W., *Report of the Independent Review into Allegations of Abuse at Meadowdale Children's Home and Related Matters*, Northumberland County Council, Morpeth.

Home Office, *Report of Her Majesty' Chief Inspector of Prisons, April 1994–March 1995*, HMSO, London.

Home Office, *Review of Prison Service Security in England and Wales and the Escape from Parkhurst Prison on Tuesday 3rd January 1995. A Report by General Sir John Learmont*, Cm 3020, HMSO, London.

Social Services Inspectorate, *Partners in Caring: The Fourth Annual Report of the Chief Inspector Social Services Inspectorate*, 1994/95, HMSO, London.

1996 Audit Commission, *Misspent Youth: Young People and Crime*, Audit Commission, London.

Jillings, John, Tunstill, Jane and Smith, Gerrilyn, *Report on Abuse in Children's Homes in Clwyd* (unpublished report).

Audit Commission, *The Probation Service: Promoting Value for Money*, HMSO, London.

Bibliography

Adams, R. (1975) 'Truth and Love in Intermediate Treatment', *British Journal of Social Work*, 15, pp. 391–401.

Adams, R. (1991) *Protests by Pupils: Empowerment, Schooling and the State*, Falmer Press, London.

Adams, R. (1994a) *Skilled Work with People*, Collins Educational, London.

Adams, R. (1994b) *Prison Riots in Britain and the USA*, Macmillan, London.

Adams, R. (1996a) *The Personal Social Services: Clients, Consumers or Citizens?*, Longman, London.

Adams, R. (1996b) *Social Work and Empowerment*, Macmillan, London.

Adams, R. (1997) *The Abuses of Punishment*, Macmillan, London.

Adams, R., Allard, S. Baldwin, J. and Thomas, J. (eds) (1981) *A Measure of Diversion? Case Studies in I.T.*, National Youth Bureau, Leicester.

Adler, Ruth and Dearling, Alan (1986) 'Children's Rights: A Scottish Perspective', in Bob Franklin (ed.), *The Rights of Children*, Blackwell, London, pp. 205–29.

Alaszewski, A. and Manthorpe, J. (1990) 'Literature Review: The New Right', *British Journal of Social Work*, vol. 20, no. 3, pp. 237–51.

Aldridge, Meryl (1994) *Making Social Work News*, Routledge, London.

Allan, M., Bhavnani Reena and French, Kate (1992) *Promoting Women: Management Development and Training for Women in Social Services Departments*, HMSO, London.

Allan, Ruth (1990) 'Punishment in the Community', in Pam Carter, Tony Jeffs and Mark K. Smith (eds), *Social Work and Social Welfare Yearbook 2 1990*, Open University Press, Milton Keynes, pp. 29–41.

Allen, Peter *et al.* (1992) *Learning Together: Shaping New Services for People with Disabilities*, CCETSW, London.

Andrews, C. (1974) in *Social Work Today*, vol. 4, no. 12, 1974, p. 637, in Mawby, Fisher, and Hale, 'The Press and Karen Spencer', *Social Work Today*, vol. 10, no. 22, 30 January 1979, pp. 13–16.

Anon (1995) 'Guidance for Social Services on Free Expression of Staff Concerns', *Professional Social Work*, April, p. 9.

Anon (undated) *Barnardo's Children*, pamphlet, Ilford.

Apple, M. W. (1982) 'Reproduction and Contradiction in Education: An Introduction', in M. W. Apple (ed.), *Cultural and Economic Reproduction in Education: Essays on Class, Ideology and the State*, Routledge & Kegan Paul, London.

Asquith, Stewart (ed.) (1993) *Protecting Children: Cleveland to Orkney: More Lessons to Learn*, HMSO, Edinburgh.

Association of Metropolitan Authorities (AMA) (1994) *Special Child: Special Needs*, AMA, London.

Audit Commission (1986) *Making a Reality of Community Care*, HMSO, London.

Audit Commission (1988a) *Performance Review in Local Government: A Handbook for Auditors and Local Authorities: Action Guide*, HMSO, London.

Audit Commission (1988b) *The Competitive Council*, Audit Commission, London.

Audit Commission (1988c) *The Competitive Council, Management Paper No. 1*, HMSO, London.

Audit Commission (1989) _The Probation Service: Promoting Value for Money_, HMSO, London.
Audit Commission (1990) _Performance Review Supplement_, Audit Commission, London.
Audit Commission (1992) _Finding a Place: A Review of Mental Health Services for Adults_, Audit Commission, London.
Audit Commission (1993a) _Adding Value_, Audit Commission, London.
Audit Commission (1993b) _The Publication of Information (Standards of Performance) Direction_, HMSO, London.
Audit Commission (1994a) _Seen But Not Heard: Co-ordinating Community Child Health and Social Services for Children in Need_, London: HMSO.
Audit Commission (1994b) _Accounting For Independent Audit: A Joint Statement of Responsibility and Accountability_, Audit Commission, London.
Audit Commission (1994c) _An Inspector Calls: Quality Control Review Programme for Auditors_, Audit Commission, London.
Audit Commission (1995) _Code of Audit Practice for Local Authorities and the National Health Service in England and Wales_, Audit Commission, London.
Audit Commission (1996a) _Local Authority Performance Indicators 1994/95_, Volume 1. Education, Social Services, Libraries and Expenditure, HMSO, London.
Audit Commission (1996b) _Local Authority Performance Indicators 1994/95_, Volume 2. Council Housing, Recycling, Planning, Benefits, Council Tax Collection, Inspecting Food Premises, Complaints Systems and Total Expenditure, HMSO, London.
Audit Commission (1996c) _Local Authority Performance Indicators 1994/95_, Volume 3. Police and Fire Services, HMSO, London.
Audit Commission (1996d) _Balancing the Care Equation: Progress with Community Care_, Community Care Bulletin No. 3, Audit Commission, London.
Audit Commission (1996e) _National Picture, Local Focus: Strategy 1996_, Audit Commission, London.
Audit Commission (1996f) _Misspent Youth: Young People and Crime_, Audit Commission, London.
Audit Commission (undated) _How Effective is the Audit Commission?: Promoting Value for Money in Local Public Services_, Audit Commission, London.
Audit Commission and Social Services Inspectorate (1996) _Reviewing Social Services: An Introduction to Joint Reviews of Local Authorities', Social Services Functions by the Audit Commission and the Social Services Inspectorate_, Department of Health, London.
Baldwin, N. (1990) _The Power to Care in Children's Homes: Experiences of Residential Workers_, Gower, Aldershot.
Barclay, P. M. (1982) _Social Workers: Their Roles and Tasks_, (The Barclay Report), Bedford Square Press, London.
Barford, Roger and Warram, Corinne (1991) 'Children's Participation in Decision-Making', _Practice_, vol. 5, no. 2, pp. 93–102.
Barnes, Marian and Gerald, Wistow (1994) _Involving Carers in Planning and Review_ in Connor and Black, pp. 77–93.
Beardshaw, Veronica (1981) _Conscientious Objectors at Work: Mental Hospital Nurses – a Case Study_, Social Audit, London.
Beddoe, C. (1980) _Stress in Residential Work_, a Report to the RCA AGM 1980 by a Working Party, Residential Care Association.
Beedell, C. (1970) _Residential Life with Children_, Routledge & Kegan Paul, London.
Beeforth, M., Conlan, E., Field, V., Hoser, B. and Sayce, L. (eds) (1990) _Whose Service Is It Anyway? Users', Views on Coordinating Community Care_, Research and Development for Psychiatry, London.

Bentovim, A., Elton, A., Hildebrand, J., Tranter, M. and Vizard, E. (1988) *Child Sexual Abuse within the Family*, Wright, London.

Beresford, Peter and Croft, Suzy (1995) 'It's Our Problem Too!: Challenging the exclusion of poor people from poverty discourse', *Critical Social Policy*, issue 44/45 (Winter) pp. 75–95.

Berman, Ronald (1984) *Culture and Politics*, University Press of America, USA.

Berridge, D. (1985) *Children's Homes*, Blackwell, Oxford.

Beynon, H. (1975) *Working for Ford*, EP Publishing, Wakefield.

Blom-Cooper, Louis, Hally, Helen and Murphy, Elaine (1995) *The Falling Shadow: One Patient's Mental Health Care 1978–1993*, Duckworth, London.

Booth, T. (1985) *Home Truths: Older People's Homes and the Outcomes of Care*, Gower, Aldershot.

Bottomley, A. Keith (1994) 'Long-Term Prisoners', in Elaine Player and Michael Jenkins (eds), *Prisons After Woolf: Reform through Riot*, Routledge, London, pp. 161–77.

Brace, Sue (1994) 'Using Perspectives on Community Care Assessment', in Anne Connor and Stewart Black (eds), *Performance and Review and Quality in Social Care: Research Highlights in Social Work*, No. 20, Jessica Kingsley, London, pp. 61–76.

Brannan, C., Jones, J.R. and Murch, J.D. (1992) *Castle Hill Report: Practice Guide*, Shropshire County Council, Shrewsbury.

Braye, S. and Preston-Shoot, M. (1992) *Practising Social Work Law*, BASW/Macmillan, London.

Braye, Sheila (1994) *Safe Caring*, National Foster Care Association, London.

Brewer, C. and Lait, J. (1980) *Can Social Work Survive?*, Temple Smith, London.

Bridge Child Care Development Service (1997) *Report on Professional Judgements and Accountability in Relation to Work with the Neave Family*, carried out on behalf of Cambridgeshire County Council Social Services Department, Bridge Child Care Development Service, London.

British Association of Social Workers and Unison (undated) *Dealing with Violence and Stress in Social Services*, BASW, Birmingham.

British Association of Social Workers (BASW) (1982) *Report of the Project on Alternative Structures*, BASW, Birmingham.

British Association of Social Workers (BASW) (1997) *Whistleblowers: Guidance for Social Services on Free Expression of Staff Concerns*, BASW, Birmingham.

British Standards Institute (1987a) *British Standard (BS) 5750 Part 0: Principal Concepts and Applications*, British Standards Institute, London.

British Standards Institute (1987b) *British Standard (BS) 5750 Part 1: Specification for Design/Development, Production, Installation and Servicing*, British Standards Institute, London.

British Standards Institute (1987c) *British Standard (BS) 5750 Part 2: Specification for Production and Installation*, British Standards Institute, London.

British Standards Institute (1987d) *British Standard (BS) 5750 Part 3: Specification for Final Inspection and Test*, British Standards Institute, London.

British Standards Institute (1987e) *British Standard (BS) 5750 Part 4: A Guide to the Use of BS 5750*, British Standards Institute, London.

British Standards Institute (1987f) *British Standard (BS) 5750 Part 8: Guide to Quality Management and Quality Systems Elements for Services*, British Standards Institute, London.

British Standards Institute (1991a) *British Standard (BS) 4778: Part 2: 1991, Quality Vocabulary: Part 2: Quality Concepts and Related Definitions*, British Standards Institute, London.

British Standards Institute (1991b) *British Standard (BS) 4778: Section 3.1: 1991, Quality Vocabulary: Part 3. Availability, Reliability and Maintainability Terms: Section 3.1 Guide to Concepts and Related Definitions*, British Standards Institute, London.

British Standards Institute (1994) *British Standard (BS) EN ISO 9001: 1994, Quality Systems: Model for Quality Assurance in Design, Development, Production, Installation and Servicing,* British Standards Institute, London.

British Standards Institute (1995) *British Standard (BS) EN ISO 8402: 1995, Quality Management and Quality Assurance – Vocabulary,* British Standards Institute, London.

Buchanan, A. Wheal, A. Walder, D. Macdonald, S. and Coker, R. (1993) *Answering Back: Report by Young People Being Looked After on The Children Act 1989,* Dept of Social Work, University of Southampton, Southampton.

Bulmer, Martin (1993) 'The Social Basis of Community Care', in Joanna Bornat, Charmaine Pereira, David Pilgrim and Fiona Williams (eds), *Community Care: A Reader,* Macmillan and Open University, London, pp. 235–41.

Bulmer, Martin and Rees, Anthony M. (eds) (1996) *Citizenship Today,* UCL, London.

Cambridgeshire County Council (1997) *Bridge Report and Action Plan,* Cambridgeshire County Council, Cambridge.

Campbell, Beatrix (1989) *Unofficial Secrets: Child Sexual Abuse, The Cleveland Case,* Virago, London.

Cannan, Crescey (1994/5) 'Enterprise Culture, Professional Socialisation and Social Work Education in Britain', *Critical Social Policy,* 42 (Winter), pp. 5–19.

Care Sector Consortium (1991) *National Occupational Standards for Working with Young Children and Their Families,* HMSO, London.

Care Sector Consortium (1992) *National Occupational Standards for Care,* HMSO, London.

Carter, Neil (1989) 'Performance Indicators: "Backseat Driving" or "Hands Off" Control?', *Policy and Politics,* 17 (2), pp. 131–8 in David McKevitt and Alan Lawton (eds), *Public Sector Management: Theory, Critique and Practice,* Open University/ Sage, London, pp. 208–19.

Carter, Pam, Jeffs, Tony and Smith, Mark (eds) (1991) *Social Work and Social Welfare Yearbook 3,* Open University Press, Milton Keynes.

Cassam, Emlyn and Gupta, Himu (1992) *Quality Assurance for Social Care Agencies,* Longman, London.

Casson, Steve and George, Clive (1993) *Care Sector Quality,* Pavilion Publishing, Brighton.

Casson, Steve and George, Clive (1995) *Culture Change for Total Quality: An Action Guide for Managers in Social and Health Care Services,* Pitman, London.

Castle Priory Conference (1969) *The Residential Task in Child Care,* Conference Report, Residential Care Association.

Cavadino, M. and Dignan, J. (1992) *The Penal System: An Introduction,* Sage, London.

Cawson, P. and Martell, M. (1979) *Children Referred to Closed Units,* HMSO, London.

CCETSW (1992) *Setting Quality Standards for Residential Child Care: A Practical Way Forward,* CCETSW, London.

CCETSW (1995a) *Assuring Quality in the Diploma in Social Work – 1: Rules and Requirements for the Dip SW,* revised edition, CCETSW, London.

CCETSW (1995b) Assuring Quality in the Diploma in Social Work, CCETSW Paper 30, revised edition, CCETSW, London.

CCETSW (1995c) *Mental Health: Staff Development Issues and Strategies,* Report of a Working Conference, CCETSW Paper 19.9, CCETSW, London.

CCETSW (1996) *Assuring Quality in the Diploma in Social Work – 1: Rules and Requirements for the Dip SW,* second revision October 1996, CCETSW, London.

CCETSW (Central Council for Education and Training in Social Work) (1993) *Training for Work with Mentally Disordered Offenders,* Report of a Study of the Training Needs of Probation Officers and Social Workers, CCETSW, London.

Centre for Policy on Ageing (1984) *Home Life: A Code of Practice for Residential Care*, Centre for Policy on Ageing, London.

Challis, D. and Davies, B. (1980) 'A New Approach for Community Care with the Elderly', *British Journal of Social Work*, vol. 10, pp. 1–18.

Challis, D. and Davies, B. (1985) 'Long-Term Care for the Elderly: The Community Care Scheme', *British Journal of Social Work*, vol. 15, pp. 563–79.

Challis, D. J. and Davies, B. P. (1986) *Case Management in Community Care: An Evaluated Experiment in the Home Care of the Elderly*, Gower, Aldershot.

Chartered Institute of Public Finance and Accountancy and Audit Commission (1986) *Survey of Internal Audit in Local Government in England and Wales 1986: A Report Prepared by CIPFA and the Audit Commission*, Audit Commission, London.

Children Act (1989), HMSO, London.

Children and Young Persons Act (1969), HMSO, London.

Ciampa, Dan (1991) *Total Quality: A User's Guide for Implementation*, Addison-Wesley, London.

City of Birmingham District Council and Birmingham Area Health Authority (1976) *Joint Enquiry Arising from the Death of Neil Howlett*, Birmingham Social Services Department, Birmingham.

Clare, Anthony (1976) *Psychiatry in Dissent*, Tavistock, London.

Clarke, Alan (1994) 'Leisure and the New Managerialism', in John Clarke, Allan Cochrane and Eugene McLaughlin (eds), *Managing Social Policy*, Sage, London, pp. 163–81.

Clarke, John (ed.) (1993) *A Crisis in Care?*, Open University/Sage, London.

Clarke, John, Cochrane, Allan and McLaughlin, Eugene (1994a) 'Introduction: Why Management Matters', in John Clarke, Allan Cochrane and Eugene McLaughlin (eds), *Managing Social Policy*, Sage, London, pp. 1–11.

Clarke, John, Cochrane, Allan and McLaughlin, Eugene (eds) (1994b) *Managing Social Policy*, Sage, London.

Clifford, P., Leiper, R., Lavender, A. and Pilling, S. (1989) *Assuring Quality in Mental Health Services: The Quartz System*, Research and Development for Psychiatry (RDP) with Free Association Books, London.

Cloke, Christopher and Davies, Murray (1995) *Participation and Empowerment in Child Protection*, Pitman, London.

Clothier, Cecil, MacDonald, C. A. and Shaw, David A. (1994) *The Allitt Inquiry: Independent Inquiry Relating to Deaths and Injuries on the Children's Ward at Grantham and Kesteven General Hospital During the Period February to April 1991*, HMSO, London.

Clough, R. (1981) *Old Age Homes*, George Allen & Unwin, London.

Clough, R. (1982) *Residential Work*, Macmillan, London.

Clough, R. (1994) *Insights into Inspection: The Regulation of Social Care*, Whiting & Birch, London.

Cochrane, Allan (1994) 'Managing Change in Local Government', in John Clarke, Allan Cochrane and Eugene McLaughlin (eds), *Managing Social Policy*, Sage, London, pp. 141–62.

Cockburn, Cynthia (1978) *The Local State*, Pluto Press, London.

Cockerill, T. (1989) 'The Kind of Competence for Rapid Change', *Personnel Management*, vol. 21, no. 9, pp. 52–6.

Cohen, D. (1982) *Broadmoor*, Psychology News Press, London.

Cohen, N. (1994) 'Prejudiced Tories Attack Probation Rules', *The Independent on Sunday*, 9 September.

Cohen, S. and Taylor, L. (1978) *Prison Secrets*, Cobden Trust, London.

Cole, Andrew (1996) 'Testing a Cure for the Gripes', *Guardian Society*, 18 September, pp. 6–7.

Committee of Inquiry into the Selection, Development and Management of Staff in Children's Homes (1992) *Choosing With Care* (Warner Report) HMSO, London.

Cooper, Cathy (1997) 'Unison Fighting Replacement of Qualified Social Workers', *Community Care*, 17–23 July, p. 2.

Coote, Anna (1994) 'Performance and Quality in Public Services', in Anne Connor and Stewart Black (eds), *Performance Review and Quality in Social Care*, Jessica Kingsley, London, pp. 187–99

Cornish, D. B. and Clarke R. V. G. (1975) *Residential Treatment and its Effects upon Delinquency*, Home Office, HMSO, London.

Corrigan, Paul and Leonard, Peter (1978) *Social Work Practice Under Capitalism: A Marxist Approach*, Macmillan, London.

Coulshed, Veronica (1990) *Management in Social Work*, Macmillan, London.

Criminal Justice Act (1991), HMSO, London.

Cutler, Tony and Waine, Barbara (1994) *Managing the Welfare State: The Politics of Public Sector Management*, Berg, Oxford.

Darvill, Giles and Smale, Gerald (eds) (1990) *Partners in Empowerment: Networks of Innovation in Social Work*, London, NISW.

Davies, Anne (1992) *Exploring Competence in Registration, Inspection and Quality Control*, CCETSW, London.

Davies, B. and Durkin, M. (1991) 'Skill, Competence and Competences in Youth and Community Work', *Youth and Policy*, 34, pp. 1–11.

Davies, D. and Challis, B. (1986) *Matching Resources to Needs in Community Care*, Gower, Aldershot.

Davies, L. (1982) *Residential Care: A Community Resource*, Heinemann, London.

Davies, N., Lingham, R., Prior, C. and Sims, A. (1995) *Report of the Inquiry into the Circumstances Leading to the Death of Jonathan Newby on 9th October 1993 in Oxford*, Oxfordshire Health Authority, Oxford.

De Maria, William and Cyrell, Jan (1996) 'Behold the Shut-eyed Sentry! Whistleblower Perspectives on Government Failure to Correct Wrongdoing', *Crime, Law and Social Change*, 24, pp. 151–66.

Deming, W. Edwards (1986) *Out of the Crisis* Cambridge University Press, Cambridge.

Department of Health (1989a) *Caring for People in the Next Decade and Beyond: Policy Guidance*, HMSO, London.

Department of Health (1989b) *Working for Patients: The Health Service: Caring for the 1990s*, HMSO, London.

Department of Health (1990a) *Caring for Quality: Guidance for Standards for Residential Homes for Elderly People*, HMSO, London.

Department of Health (1990b) *Caring for Quality: Guidance for Standards for Residential Homes for People with a Physical Disability*, HMSO, London.

Department of Health (1991a) *Implementing Community Care: Purchaser, Commissioner and Provider Roles*, HMSO, London.

Department of Health (1991b) *Welfare of Children and Young People in Hospital*, HMSO, London.

Department of Health (1991c) Patterns and Outcomes in Child Placement: Messages from Current Research and their Implications, HMSO, London.

Department of Health (1991d) *The Children Act 1989 Guidance and Regulations*, 10 volumes, HMSO, London.

Department of Health (1992a) *Committed to Quality: Quality Assurance in Social Services Departments*, HMSO, London.

Department of Health (1992b) *Review of Health and Social Services for Mentally Disordered Offenders and Others Requiring Similar Services* (Chairman Dr John Reed), final summary report, Cmnd 2088, HMSO, London.

Department of Health (1992c) *The Health of the Nation: A Strategy for Health in England*, Cm 1986, HMSO, London.

Department of Health (1992d) *Guidance on Standards for the Residential Care Needs of People with Learning Disabilities/Mental Handicap*, HMSO, London.

Department of Health (1992e) *Guidance on Standards for the Residential Care Needs of People with Specific Mental Health Needs*, HMSO, London.

Department of Health (1993) *Legal Powers in the Care of Mentally Ill People in the Community*, Report of the Internal Review, Department of Health, London.

Department of Health (1995) *Child Protection: Messages from Research*, HMSO, London.

Department of Health and Home Office (1995) *Mentally Disordered Offenders: Inter-Agency Working*, HMSO, London.

Department of Health/Social Services Inspectorate (1988) *Towards a Climate of Confidence: Report of a National Inspection of Management Arrangements for Public Sector Residential Care for Elderly People*, HMSO, London.

Department of Health/Social Services Inspectorate (1989) *Homes are For Living In*, HMSO, London.

Department of Health/Social Services Inspectorate (1991a) *Purchase of Service: Practice Guidance and Practice Material for Social Services Departments and Other Agencies*, HMSO, London.

Department of Health/Social Services Inspectorate (1991b) *Children in the Public Care: A Review of Residential Child Care*, (The Utting Report), HMSO, London.

Department of Health/Social Services Inspectorate (1991c) *Practitioners' Guide to Care Management and Assessment*, HMSO, London.

Department of Health/Social Services Inspectorate (1991d) *Inspecting for Quality: Guidance on Practice for Inspection Units in Social Services Departments and Other Agencies: Principles, Issues and Recommendations*, HMSO, London.

Department of Health/Social Services Inspectorate (1991e) *Complaints About the Social Services Department: Ideas for Practice Booklet for Clerks, Receptionists and Telephonist*, HMSO, London.

Department of Health/Social Services Inspectorate (1991f) *The Right to Complain: Practice Guidance on Complaints Procedures in Social Services Departments*, HMSO, London.

Department of Health/Social Services Inspectorate (1993a) *Diversification and the Independent Residential Care Sector: A Manual for Providers of Residential Care Homes*, HMSO, London.

Department of Health/Social Services Inspectorate (1993b) *The Inspection of the Complaints Procedures in Local Authority Services Departments*, HMSO, London.

Department of Health/Social Services Inspectorate (1993c) *Planning for Permanence? An Inspection of Adoption Services in Three Northern Local Authorities*, Department of Health, London.

Department of Health/Social Services Inspectorate (1993d) *Occupational Therapy – the Community Contribution: Report on Local Authority Occupational Therapy Services*, Department of Health, London.

Department of Health/Social Services Inspectorate (1993e) *Raising the Standard: The Second Annual Report of the Chief Inspector, Social Services Inspector 1992/93*, HMSO, London.

Department of Health/Social Services Inspectorate (1993f) *Evaluating Performance in Child Protection: A Framework for the Inspection of Local Authority Social Services Practice and Systems*, HMSO, London.

Department of Health/Social Services Inspectorate (1993g) *Corporate Parents: Inspection of Residential Child Care Services in Eleven Local Authorities, November 1992 to March 1993*, Department of Health, London.

Dews, V. and Watts, J. (1995) *Review of Probation Officer Recruitment and Qualifying Training* (Dews Report), HMSO, London.

DHSS and Advisory Council on Child Care (1970) *Care and Treatment in a Planned Environment*. A Report on the Community Homes Project, HMSO, London.

DHSS (1972) *Management Arrangements for the Re-organised National Health Service*, HMSO, London.

Department of Health and Social Security (1974) *Revised Report of the Working Party on Security in NHS Psychiatric Hospitals* (Glancy Report), DHSS, London.

DHSS (1978) *Review of the Mental Health Act 1959*, Cmnd 7320, HMSO, London.

DHSS (1980) *Report of the Review of Rampton Hospital,* (Chairman Sir John Boynton) Cmnd 8073, London, HMSO.

DHSS (1981) *Control and Discipline in Community Homes: A Report of a Working Party*, DHSS, London.

DHSS (1983) *The NHS Management Inquiry* (Griffiths Report), HMSO, London.

DHSS (1985) *Social Work Decisions in Child Care: Recent Research Findings and their Implications*, HMSO, London.

DHSS (1988) *Community Care: An Agenda for Action,* (Griffiths Report) HMSO, London.

DHSS (1995) *Report of a Regional Meeting at Haigh Hall on 29th November 1984* Implementation of the Mental Health Act 1983 'The Way Forward', DHSS/SSI North West Region.

DHSS and Welsh Office (1988) *Working Together: A Guide to Arrangements for Inter-Agency Co-operation for the Protection of Children from Abuse*, HMSO, London.

DHSS Development Group, Social Work Service, Welsh Office (1990) *Working Together for Children and Their Families*. Report of a Project Undertaken with South Glamorgan County Council, HMSO, London.

DHSS Social Services Inspectorate (1986) *Inspection of Community Homes*, DHSS, London.

Directors of Social Work in Scotland (1992) *Child Protection Policy, Practice and Procedure: An Overview of Child Abuse Issues and Practice in Social Work Departments in Scotland*, HMSO, Edinburgh.

Disability Discrimination Act (1995) HMSO, London.

Disabled Persons (Services, Consultation and Representation) Act 1986, HMSO, London.

Dobson, Roger (1996) 'The Suffering and the Shame', *Independent on Sunday*, 7 April, p. 5.

Dominelli, Lena (1996) 'Deprofessionalising Social Work: Equal Opportunities, Competences and Postmodernism', *British Journal of Social Work*, no. 26, pp. 153–75.

Dominelli, Lena, Jeffers, Lennie, Jones, Graham, Sibanda, Sakhile and Williams, Brian (1995) *Anti-Racist Probation Practice*, Arena, Aldershot.

Donzelot, J. (1979) *The Policing of Families*, Hutchinson, London.

Doray, Bernard (1988) *From Taylorism to Fordism: A Rational Madness*, Free Association Books, London.

Drummond, Helga, (1993) *The Quality Movement*, Kogan Page, London.

Educational Broadcasting Services Trust (1992) *More Than Meets the Eye: Observing Quality in Residential Homes*, Department of Health, London.

Elcock, H. (1993) 'Local Government', in D. Farnham and S. Horton (eds), *Managing the New Public Services*, Macmillan, London, pp. 150–71.

Elliott, Michele (ed.) (1993) *Female Sexual Abuse of Children: The Ultimate Taboo* Longman, Harlow.

Ernst and Young Quality Improvement Consulting Group (1993) *Total Quality: A Manager's Guide for the 1990s*, Kogan Page, London.

Etzioni, A. (1969) *The Semi Professions and Their Organization: Teachers, Nurses and Social Workers*, Free Press, New York.

Everitt, Angela (1990) 'Will Women Managers Save Social Work?', in Pam Carter, Tony Jeffs and Mark K. Smith (eds), *Social Work and Social Welfare Yearbook 2, 1991*, Open University Press, Buckingham, pp. 134–48.

Everitt, Angela and Hardiker, Pauline (1996) *Evaluating for Good Practice*, BASW/Macmillan, London.

Fair Employment (Northern Ireland) Act, (1989), HMSO, London.

Farnham, David and Horton, Sylvia (1993a) 'The New Public Service Managerialism: An Assessment' in David Farnham and Sylvia Horton (eds) (1993b) *Managing the New Public Services*, pp. 237–54.

Farnham, David and Horton, Sylvia (eds) (1993b) *Managing the New Public Services*, Macmillan, London.

Foucault, M. (1981) 'Questions of Method: An Interview with Michel Foucault', *Ideology and Consciousness*, 8, pp. 3–14.

Franklin, Bob (ed.) (1986) *The Rights of Children*, Blackwell, Oxford.

Franklin, Bob and Parton, Nigel (1991) *Social Work, the Media and Public Relations*, Routledge, London.

Franks Committee (1972) *The Departmental Committee on Section 2 of the Official Secrets Act 1911*, 4 volumes, HMSO, London.

Freeman, Richard (1993) *Quality Assurance in Training and Education: How to Apply BS5750 (ISO 9000) Standards*, Kogan Page, London.

Frost, N. and Stein, M. (1992) 'Empowerment and Child Welfare', in J. C. Coleman and C. Warren-Anderson (eds), *Youth Policy in the 1990s: The Way Forward*, Routledge, London, pp. 161–71.

Frost, Nick and Stein, Mike (1989) *The Politics of Child Welfare: Inequality, Power and Change*, Harvester Wheatsheaf, London.

Gambe, David, Gomes, Jenny, Kapur, Vijay, Rangel, Moira and Stubbs, Paul (1992) *Improving Practice with Children and Families: A Training Manual*, Northern Curriculum Development Project, CCETSW, Leeds.

General Social Services Council Action Group Final Report (1993) National Institute for Social Work, London.

George, Mike (1995) 'Rules of Engagement', *Community Care*, 7–13 September, pp. 16–17.

Gerth, H. H. and Mills, C. W. (1948) (translated and edited) *From Max Weber: Essays in Sociology*, New York.

Gibbons, J., Conroy, S. and Bell, C. (1995) *Studies in Child Protection: Development After Physical Abuse in Early Childhood*, HMSO, London.

Gibbs, Ian and Sinclair, Ian (1992) 'Consistency: A Pre-Requisite for Inspecting Old People's Homes?', *British Journal of Social Work*, 22, pp. 535–50.

Goffman, Erving (1967) *Asylums: Essays on the Social Situation of Mental Patients and Other Inmates*, Harmondsworth, Penguin.

Goffman, Erving (1968) *Stigma: Notes on the Management of Spoiled Identity*, Penguin, Harmondsworth.

Goldacre, Michael, Seagroat, Valerie and Hawton, Keith (1994) *Suicide After Discharge from Psychiatric Inpatient Care*, University of Oxford, Oxford

Golding, Peter and Middleton, Sue (1982) *Images of Welfare: Press and Public Attitudes to Poverty*, Martin Robertston, Oxford.

Gostin, Larry *A Human Condition* MIND Special Report; 1977.

Gottesmann, M. (ed.) *Residential Child Care: An International Reader*, Whiting & Birch, London, pp. 138–56.

Gray, A. and Jenkins, W. (1983) *Policy Analysis and Evaluation in British Government*, RIPA, London.

Gulbenkian (1993) *One Scandal Too Many – The Case for Comprehensive Protection for Children in All Settings*, Report of a Working Group Convened by the Gulbenkian Foundation, Calouste Gulbenkian Foundation, London.

Gutch, R. (1996) 'No Pay, No Say? No Way', *The Guardian* Guardian Society, 13 March, pp. 6–7.

Hadley, R. and Clough, R. (1996) *Care in Chaos: Frustration and Challenge in Community Care*, Cassell, London.

Hadley, R., Cooper, M., Dale, P. and Stacey, G. (1987) *A Community Social Worker's Handbook*, Tavistock, London.

Hall, P., Land, H., Parker, R. and Webb, A. (1975) *Change, Choice and Conflict in Social Policy*, Heinemann, London.

Harland, Tom (1993) 'Managing Quality the BS 5750 Way', *Yorkshire Executive*, May–July, pp. 49–50.

Harris, Robert J., Barker, Mary W., Reading, Paul, Richards, Margaret and Youll, Penny (1985) *Educating Social Workers*, Association of Teachers in Social Work Education (ATSWE), Leicester.

Hawes, J. M. (1991) *The Children's Rights Movement: A History of Advocacy and Protection*, Twayne Publishers, Hall & Co., Boston.

Hayek, F. (1960) *The Constitution of Liberty*, Routledge & Kegan Paul, London.

Hayman, Vic (1993) 'Re-Writing the Job: A Sceptical Look at Competences', *Probation Journal*, December, pp. 180–3.

Henkel, Mary (1994) 'Performance Review and the Managerial Revolution', in Connor and Black, pp. 9–19.

Hill, A. (1980) 'How the Press Sees You', *Social Work Today*, vol. 11, no. 36, 20 May 1980, pp. 19–20.

Hill, S. G. (1979) 'Independent Inquiries – Their Role and Effect', pp. 35–41 in *After Normansfield*, Report of a Day Conference, Institute of Health Service Administrators, London.

Hirst, Judy (1995) 'Minimum Standard Bearers', *Community Care*, 20–26 July, issue 1078, p. 24.

HM Treasury (1991) *Competing for Quality; Buying Better Public Services*, White Paper, CM 1730, HMSO, London.

Home Office (1967) *Extracts from a Handbook for the New Civil Servant*, Home Office, London.

Home Office (1969) *People in Prison*, HMSO, London.

Home Office (1971) *Job Appraisal Review*, Establishment and Organisation Department, Home Office, London.

Home Office (1973) *Report on the Work of the Prison Department*, 1972, Cmnd 5375, HMSO, London.

Home Office (1977) *Prisons and the Prisoner*, HMSO, London.

Home Office (1986) *Criminal Justice: A Working Paper*, Home Office, London.

Home Office (1987) *Special Units for Long Term Prisoners: Regimes, Management and Research. A Report by the Research and Advisory Group on the Long Term Prison System*, HMSO, London.

Home Office (1988a) *National Standards for Community Service Orders: First Draft*, HMSO, London.

Home Office (1988b) *Bail Accommodation and Secure Bail Hostels*, Consultation Paper, Home Office, London.

Home Office (1988c) *Punishment, Custody and the Community*, Cm 424, HMSO, London.

Home Office (1988d) *Private Sector Involvement in the Remand System*, Cm 434, HMSO, London.

Home Office (1989a) *Management of Vulnerable Prisoners Working Group Report*, Cm 835, HMSO, London.

Home Office (1989b) *Prison Sanitation: Proposals for the Ending of Slopping Out*, Report by Her Majesty's Chief Inspector of Prisons, HMSO, London.

Home Office (1989c) *National Standards for Community Service Orders*, HMSO, London.

Home Office (1990a) *Crime, Justice and Protecting the Public*, cm 965, HMSO, London.

Home Office (1990b) *The Practice of Young Offender Throughcare by the Probation Service in Four Young Offender Institutions and Six Probation Areas*, HM Inspectorate of Probation, London.

Home Office (1990c) *Report of the Parole Board 1989*, HMSO, London.

Home Office (1991a) *Custody, Care and Justice: The Way Ahead for the Prison Service in England and Wales*, Cm 1647, HMSO, London.

Home Office (1991b) *Management of the Prison Service: Report by Admiral Sir Raymond Lygo KCB*, HMSO, London.

Home Office (1991c) *Treatment Programmes for Sex Offenders in Custody: A Strategy*, Home Office, London.

Home Office (1991d) *The Control Review Committee, 1984: Implementation of the Committee's Recommendations*, Directorate of Custody, Prison Service Headquarters, London.

Home Office (1991e) 'Projections of Long Term Trends in the Prison Population to 1999', *Home Office Statistical Bulletin*, 19/91, Home Office, London.

Home Office (1991f) *HIV/AIDS A Multidisciplinary Approach in the Prison Environment*, Directorate of Prison Medical Services, London.

Home Office (1991g) *Regimes for Women*, HM Prison Service, London.

Home Office (1991h) *Caring for Drug Users – A Multidisciplinary Resource Pack for People Working with Drug Users*, Directorate of Prison Medical Services, London.

Home Office (1991i) *Contracting for Prison Health Services: A Consultation Paper*, Directorate of Prison Medical Services, London.

Home Office, Department of Health and Welsh Office (1992) National Standards for the Supervision of Offenders in the Community, Home Office, London.

Home Office (1993) *Vision and Values*, Prison Department, London.

Home Office (1994) *Three Year Plan for the Probation Service 1994–1997*, Home Office, London.

Home Office (1995) *Strengthening Punishment in the Community*, (Green Paper), Home Office, London.

Home Office/Department of Health and Social Security (1974) *Interim Report of the Committee on Mentally Abnormal Offenders*, Cmnd 5678, HMSO, London.

Home Office/Department of Health and Social Security (1975) *Report of the Committee on Mentally Abnormal Offenders*, Cnd 6244, (Butler Report), HMSO, London.

House of Commons (1992) *Report of the Inquiry into the Removal of Children from Orkney in February 1991*, House of Commons ([HC]); 195; 1992–93, London.

Howe, E. (1992) *The Quality of Care*, A Report of the Residential Staff Inquiry, Local Government Management Board, Luton.

Hudson, Barbara L., Cullen, Rachel and Roberts, Colin (1993) *The Allitt Inquiry*, Independent inquiry Relating to Deaths and injuries on the Children's ward at Grantham and Kesteven General Hospital during the Period February to April 1991, HMSO, London.

Humberside County Council (undated) *Care of Elderly People in Residential Homes: Handbook. A Code of Good Practice*, Humberside.

Institute of Health Service Administrators (1979) *After Normansfield*, Report of a day Conference held in the Jarvis Hall of the Royal Institute of British Architects, London, on 13 July 1979, Institute of Health Service Administrators, London.

Issitt, Mary and Woodward, Maureen (1992) 'Competence and Contradiction', in Pam Carter, Tony Jeffs and Mark K. Smith (eds), *Changing Social Work and* Welfare, Open University Press, Buckingham, pp. 40–54.

Jacob, Joseph M. (1994) 'Lawyers Go to Hospital', in *Public Law*, Summer, pp. 255–81, in David McKevitt and Alan Lawton (1994) (eds) *Public Sector Management: Theory, Critique and Practice*, Open University/Sage, London, pp. 128–44.

James, A., Brooks, T. and Towell, D. (1992) *Committed to Quality: Quality Assurance in Social Service Departments*, HMSO, London.

James, Ann (1994) 'Reflections on the Politics of Quality', in Anne Connor and Stewart Black (eds), *Performance Review and Quality in Social Care*, Jessica Kingsley, London, pp. 200–14.

James, Ann (1994) *Managing to Care: Public Services and the Market*, Longman, London.

Jeffs, Tony and Smith, Mark K. (eds) *Changing Social Work and* Welfare, Open University Press, Buckingham, pp. 40–54.

Jeffs, Tony and Smith, Mark K. (eds), *Social Work and Social Welfare Yearbook 3 1991*, Open University Press, Milton Keynes, pp. 178–93.

Jillings, John, Tunstill, Jane and Smith, Gerrilyn, (1996) *Report on Abuse in Children's Homes in Clwyd* (unpublished report).

Jones, C. (1993) 'Distortion and Demonisation: The Right and Anti-Racist Social Work Education', *Social Work Education*, 12 (12), pp. 9–16.

Jones, C. (1996a) 'Regulating Social Work: A Review of the Review', in S. Jackson and M. Preston-Shoot (eds), *Social Work Education in a Changing Policy Context* Whiting and Birch, London, pp. 30–42.

Jones, C. (1996b) 'Anti-Intellectualism and the Peculiarities of Social Work Education', in N. Parton (ed.), *Social Theory, Social Change and Social Work*, Routledge, London, pp. 56–65.

Jones, Chris (1989) 'The End of the Road? Issues in Social Work Education', in P. Carter, T. Jeffs and M. Smith (eds), *Social Work and Social Welfare Year Book*, Open University Press, Buckingham, pp. 140–9.

Jones, Kathleen (1975) *Mental Health and Social Policy*, Routledge & Kegan Paul, London.

Jones, Maxwell (1968) *Social Psychiatry in Practice* Penguin, Harmondsworth.

Jones, Richard (1996) *Mental Health Manual*, 5th edn, Sweet & Maxwell, London.

Kahan, B. (1991) 'Residential Care and Education in Great Britain', in M. Gottesmann (ed.), *Residential Child Care: An International Reader*, pp. 138–56 Whiting & Birch, London, pp. 138–56.

Kanter, Rosabeth Moss and Summers, David V. (1994) 'Doing Well While Doing Good: Dilemmas of Performance Measurement in Nonprofit Organizations and the Need for a Multiple-Constituency Approach', in W. W. Powell (ed.) (1987) *The Non-Profit Sector: A Research Handbook,* Yale University Press, New Haven, CT.

Kelly, Aidan (1991) 'The "New", Managerialism in the Social Services', in Pam Carter, Tony Jeffs and Mark K. Smith (eds), *Social Work and Social Welfare Yearbook 3 1991*, Open University Press, Milton Keynes, pp. 178–93.

Kelly, Des and Warr, Bridget (eds) (1992) *Quality Counts*, Whiting & Birch and Social Care Association, London.

Kelly, Des, Payne, Chris and Warwick, John (1990) *Making National Vocational Qualifications Work for Social Care*, London, National Institute for Social Work/ Social Care Association, London.

Kempe, C. Henry *et al.* (1962) 'The Battered Child Syndrome', *Journal A.M.A.*, 7 July 1962, 181, 1, pp. 17–24.

Kemshall, H. (1993) 'Quality: Friend or Foe?', *Probation Journal*, March, pp. 13–20.

Kendrick, Andrew and Fraser, Sandy (1992) 'Summary of the Literature Review', Appendix B, in Scottish Office (1992) *Another Kind of Home: A Review of Residential Child Care*, Social Work Services Inspectorate for Scotland, HMSO, London, pp. 100–28.

Kerruish, Alison and Smith, Helen (1993) *Developing Quality Residential Care: A User-Led Approach*, Pitman, London.

Kirkpatrick, Ian and Lucio, Miguel Martinez (eds) (1995) *The Politics of Quality in the Public Sector*, Routledge, London.

Kitchener, Martin and Whipp, Richard (1995) 'Quality in the Marketing Change Process: The Case of the National Health Service', in Ian Kirkpatrick and Miguel Martinez Lucio (eds) (1995) *The Politics of Quality in the Public Sector*, Routledge, London, pp. 190–211.

Knapp, M. (1984) 'The Three "E"'s', *Community Care*, 20 September, pp. 14–16.

Langan, Mary and Clarke, John (1994) 'Managing in the Mixed Economy of Care', in John Clarke, Allan Cochrane and Eugene McLaughlin (eds), *Managing Social Policy*, Sage, London, pp. 73–92.

Lawson, Alan and Coffin, Nicola (1996) 'Social Services Complaints Procedures: the Perspectives of Users and Staff', *Social Services Research*, No. 4.

Le Grand, Julian and Bartlett, Will (eds) (1993) *Quasi-Markets and Social Policy*, Macmillan, London.

Leckie, Tom (1994), 'Quality Assurance and Social Work', in Connor and Black, pp. 125–37

Leicestershire County Council and Area Health Authority (Teaching) (1980), *Carl Taylor: Report of an Independent Inquiry*, Leicestershire County Council, Leicester.

Levy, Allan and Kahan, Barbara (1991) *The Pindown Experience and the Protection of Children*, The Report of the Staffordshire Child Care Inquiry 1990, Staffordshire County Council, Stafford.

Lewis, Jane and Glennerster, Howard (1996) *Implementing the New Community Care*, Open University Press, Buckingham.

Ling, Tom (1994) 'The New Managerialism and Social Security', in John Clarke, Allan Cochrane and Eugene McLaughlin (eds), *Managing Social Policy*, Sage, London, pp. 32–56.

Littlewood, P. and Kelly, B. (1986) *After Release: A Report on the Processes Surrounding the Release of Young People from the Ogilvie Wing Secure Unit, and Their Perception of these Processes*, Report to the Social Work Services Group, Sociology Department, University of Glasgow.

Local Authorities Social Services Act (1970), HMSO, London.

Local Government Act (1988), HMSO, London.

Local Government Act (1992), HMSO, London.

Local Government Act (1972), HMSO, London.

Local Government Finance Act (1982), HMSO, London.

Lynch G. and Pope B. (1990) *Involving Clients and Staff in the Development of Quality Assurance Systems: Social Services and Quality Assurance*, Social Information Systems, Manchester.

Mangham, I. L. and Silver, M. S. (1986) *Management Training: Context and Practice*, Economic and Social Research Council (ESRC) and Department of Trade and Industry (DTI), London.

Manning, B. (1996) 'Change for the Better' *Community Care* 31 October–6 November, pp. 6–7.

Manning, Bernadette and Casson, Steve (1997) *Total Quality in Child Protection – A Guide for Managers*, Russell House, Lyme Regis.

Marsden, David (1990) 'The Meaning of Social Development' in Marsden, David and Oakley, Peter (ed) (1990) *Evaluating Social Development Projects*, Oxfam, Oxford, pp. 1–17.

Marsden, David and Oakley, Peter (eds) (1990) *Evaluating Social Development Projects*, Oxfam, Oxford.

Marsden, David, Oakley, Peter and Pratt, Brian (1994) *Measuring the Process: Guidelines for Evaluating Social Development*, Intrac Publications, Oxford.

Marsh, Peter and Triseliotis, John (1996) *Ready to Practise? Social Workers and Probation Officers: Their Training and First Year in Work*, Avebury, Aldershot.

Martin, J. P. (1984) *Hospitals in Trouble*, Blackwell, Oxford.

Mattingley, M. A. (1981) 'Occupational Stress for Group Care Personnel', in F. Ainsworth and L. C. Fulcher (eds), *Group Care for Children: Concepts and Issues*, Tavistock, London.

Mawby, R., Fisher C. and Hale, J. (1979) 'The Press and Karen Spencer', *Social Work Today*, vol. 10, no. 22, 30 January, pp. 13–16.

Mawby, R. I., Fisher C. J. and Park, A. (1979) 'Press Coverage of Social Work', *Policy and Politics*, vol. 7, no. 4, pp. 357–76.

McClay, Brian (1994) 'Putting Complaints Procedures Into Effect', in A. Connor and S. Black (eds), *Performance Review and Quality in Social Care*, Jessica Kingsley, London, pp. 153–65.

McKevitt, David and Lawton, Alan (1994) (eds) *Public Sector Management: Theory, Critique and Practice*, Open University/Sage, London.

Mental Health Act (1959), HMSO, London.

Mental Health Act (1983), HMSO, London.

Mental Health Commission, (1995) *The Sixth Biennial Report 1993–1995*, HMSO, London.

Miller, Stewart and Peroni, Francesca (1992) 'Social Politics and the Citizen's Charter', in Nick Manning and Robert Page, *Social Policy Review 4*, Social Policy Association, London, pp. 242–60.

Millham, S. Bullock, R. and Hosie, K. (1978) *Locking Up Children: Secure Provision with the Child-Care System*, Saxon House, Farnborough.

Millham, S., Bullock, R. and Cherrett, P. (1975) *After Grace – Teeth! A Comparative Study of the Residential Experience of Boys in Approved Schools*, Human Context Books, London.

Millham, S., Bullock, R. and Hosie, K. (1980) *Learning to Care: The Training of Staff for Residential Social Work with Young People*, Gower, Farnborough.

Millham, S., Bullock, R., Hosie, K. and Haak, M. (1986) *Lost in Care: The Problems of Maintaining Links between Children in Care and their Families,* Gower, Aldershot.

Mitchell, S. and Tolan, F. (1994) 'Performance Review Through Inspection and Monitoring by Central Government', in Connor and Black, pp. 20–30.

Moore, Wendy (1996) 'Return of the Soundbite King', *The Guardian: Society*, 6 March, p. 9.

Morris, Jenny (1993) *Pride Against Prejudice: Transforming Attitudes to Disability*, Women's Press, London.

Moss, Peter and Melhuish, Edward (1991) *Current Issues in Day Care for Young Children*, HMSO, London.

Murphy, E. (1991) *After the Asylums*, Faber, London.

National Association of Health Authorities and Trusts (1985) *Registration and Inspection of Nursing Homes: A Handbook for Health Authorities,* National Association of Health Authorities and Trusts, London.

National Association of Health Authorities and Trusts (1991) *Care of People with a Terminal Illness,* National Association of Health Authorities and Trusts, London.

National Audit Office (1988) *Quality of Clinical Care in National Health Service Hospitals,* Paper 736, House of Commons, London.

National Audit Office (1992) Report by the Comptroller and Auditor General, *Health Services for Physically Disabled People Aged 16 to 64,* HMSO, London.

National Children's Home (1992) *Report of the Committee of Inquiry Into Children and Young People Who Sexually Abuse Other Children,* National Children's Home, London.

National Committee of Further and Higher Education (1997) *Higher Education in Learning Society: Report of the National Committee,* (Dearing Report), Stationery Office, London.

National Consumer Council and National Institute for Social Work (1988) *Open to Complaints: Guidelines for Social Services Complaints Procedures,* National Consumer Council, London.

National Health Service (1972) *Report of the Committee of Inquiry into Whittingham Hospital,* Cmnd 4861, HMSO, London.

National Health Service (NHS) and Community Care Act (1990), HMSO, London.

National Health Service Management Executive (NHSME) (1993) *Guidance for Staff on Relations with the Public and the Media,* Department of Health, London.

Nellis, M. (1995) 'Probation Values for the 1990s', *The Howard Journal,* vol. 34 no. 1, (Feb.) p. 23, pp. 19–45.

Newman, Janet (1994) 'The Limits of Management: Gender and the Politics of Change', in John Clarke, Allan Cochrane and Eugene McLaughlin (eds), *Managing Social Policy,* Sage, London, pp. 182–209.

NHS Executive/Department of Health (1994) *Introduction of Supervision Registers for Mentally Ill People from 1, April, 1994,* Health Service Guidelines HSG (94)5.

NHSTD (1993) *Developing Managers for Health and Social Care: Building Strategies for Shared Management Development using HSSM: Managers and Trainers Guide,* Briston, NHSTD.

NISW (1988a) *Residential Care: The Research Reviewed* (Wagner Report, Vol. 1), HMSO, London.

NISW (1988b) *Residential Care: A Positive Choice* (Wagner Report Vol. II), HMSO, London.

Nokes, P. (1967) *The Professional Task in Welfare Practice,* Routledge & Kegan Paul, London.

Nolan, Lord (1995) *First Report of the Committee on Standards in Public Life,* Nolan Report, HMSO, London.

Norfolk County Council and Area Health Authority (1975) *Report of the Review Body Appointed to Enquire into the Death of Stephen Meurs,* Norfolk County Council, Norwich.

Oakeshott, Michael (1962) 'Rationalism in Politics', in Michael Oakeshoot, *Rationalism in Politics and Other Essays,* Methuen, London.

Oakland, John S. (ed.) (1989) *Total Quality Management,* Heinemann, London.

Oldfield, Mark (1994) 'Talking Quality, Meaning Control: McDonald's, the Market and the Probation Service', *Probation Journal,* December, pp. 186–92.

Oliver, Michael (1990) *The Politics of Disablement,* Macmillan, Basingstoke.

Ollier, Gerard (1991) *Will NVQs Reach Small Work Units?,* Care Sector Consortium Voluntary Organisations Group, London.

Omachonu, U. K. and Ross, J. E. (1994) *Principles of Total Quality,* Kogan Page, London.

Open Learning Foundation, National Health Service Training Directorate and The Open University (1994) *Health and Social Services Management Programme: Management Education Scheme by Open Learning*, Open University, Milton Keynes.

Page, R. and Baldock, J. (eds) (1990) *Social Policy Review 6*, Social Policy Association, Canterbury.

Page, R. and Clarke, G. A. (eds) (1977) *Who Cares? Young People in Care Speak Out*, National Children's Bureau, London.

Parker, Roy (1988) 'Residential Care for Children', in NISW (1988a) *The Research Reviewed*, pp. 57–124.

Parsloe, Phyllida (1990) 'Future of Social Work Education: Recovering from Care for Tomorrow', in Pam Carter, Tony Jeffs and Mark K. Smith (eds), *Social Work and Social Welfare Yearbook 2 1990*, Open University Press, Milton Keynes, pp. 197–210.

Parton, N. (1991) *Governing the Family*, Macmillan, London.

Parton, Nigel (1991) *Governing the Family: Child Care, Child Protection and the State*, Macmillan, London.

Patients Association (undated) *NHS Complaints Procedures: A Guide for Patients*, Patients Association, London.

Peters, T. J. and Austin, N. (1985) *A Passion for Excellence: The Leadership Difference*, Collins, London.

Peters, Thomas J. (1988) *In Search of Excellence: Lessons from America's Best-Run Companies*, Harper & Row, New York.

Petrie, C. (1980) *The Nowhere Boys*, Saxon House, Farnborough.

Petrie, Steph (1995) *Day Care Regulation and Support: Local Authorities and Day Care under the Children Act 1989*, Save the Children, London.

Peyer, A., Eaton, L., Black, D., Clough, M., Learmont, D. and Tait, F. (1982) *Child Abuse: A Study of Inquiry Reports 1973–1981*, HMSO, London.

Phillips, Ceri, Palfrey, Colin and Thomas, Paul (1994) *Evaluating Health and Social Care*, Macmillan, London.

Phillips, M. (1979) 'Social Workers and the Media: A Journalist's View', *Social Work Today*, vol. 10, no. 22 (30 September) p. 22.

Phillipson, C., Biggs, S. and Kingston, P. (1995) *Elder Abuse in Perspective*, Open University Press, Buckingham.

Player, Elaine and Jenkins, Michael (eds) (1994a) 'Introduction', in Elaine Player and Michael Jenkins (eds), *Prisons After Woolf: Reform through Riot*, Routledge, London, pp. 1–28.

Player, Elaine and Jenkins, Michael (eds) (1994b) *Prisons After Woolf: Reform through riot*, Routledge, London.

Politt, C. (1988) 'Bringing Consumers Into Performance Measurement: Concepts, Consequences and Constraints', *Policy and Politics*, 16 (2), pp. 77–87.

Pollitt, Christopher and Baichaert, Geert (1995) (eds) *Quality Improvement in European Public Services: Concepts, Cases and Commentary*, Sage, London.

Prime Minister and the Chancellor of the Duchy of Lancaster (1995) *The Citizen's Charter: The Facts and Figures*, A Report to mark four years of the Charter Programme, Cm 2970, HMSO, London.

Prime Minister's Office (1991) *The Citizen's Charter: Raising the Standard*, White Paper, Cm 1599, HMSO, London.

Pringle, K. (1996), 'Men Challenging Gender Oppression on Social Work Programmes in Higher Education: A Framework for Action', unpublished paper, Sunderland.

Pugh, G. (1988) *Services for Under Fives: Developing a Co-ordinated Approach*, National Children's Bureau, London.

Race Relations Act (1976), HMSO, London.

Rae, Malcolm A. (1993) *Freedom to Care: Achieving Change in Culture and Nursing Practice in a Mental Health Service*, Ashworth Hospital.

Raynor, Peter (1996) 'Effectiveness Now: A Personal and Selective Overview', in Jill McIvor (ed.), *Working with Offenders*, Jessica Kingsley, London, pp. 182–93.

Raynor, Peter, Smith, David and Vanstone, Maurice (1994) *Effective Probation Practice*, BASW/Macmillan, Basingstoke.

Reason, P. and Rowan, J. (eds) (1981) *Human Inquiry: A Sourcebook of New Paradigm Research*, John Wiley, Chichester.

Registered Homes Act (1984), HMSO, London.

Registration of Homes (Amendment) Act (1991), HMSO, London.

Report of Committee on Local Authority and Allied Personal Social Services (1968) (Seebohm Report), Cmnd 3703, HMSO, London.

Ritchie, J. H., Dick, D. and Lingham, R. (1994) *The Report of the Inquiry Into the Care and Treatment of Christopher Clunis*, HMSO, London.

Robb, Barbara (1966) *Sans Everything: A Case to Answer*, Allen & Unwin, London.

Roberts, M. (1980) 'Giving the Public the Right Image', *Community Care*, no. 308 (27 March) pp. 16–17.

Rodway, Simon and Rea Price, John (1996) 'Tireless Campaigner for Children's Needs', Obituary for Baroness Lucy Faithfull, *The Guardian*. 14 March.

Rogers, A., Pilgrim, D. and Lacey, R. (1993) *Experiencing Psychiatry: Users', Views of Services*, Macmillan and MIND, London.

Rojek, C., Peacock, G. and Collins, S. (1988) *Social Work and Received Ideas*, Routledge, London.

Rose, Nicholas (1995) 'Whistleblowing – Time for a Change', *New Law Journal Practitioner*, January, pp. 113–15.

Royston, Stephen (1996) 'Quality Controllers', *Community Care*, 1120, 16–22 May.

Salaman, G., Adams, R. and O'Sullivan, T. (1994) *Managing Personal and Team Effectiveness Book 1: Managing Competently*, Health and Social Services Management Programme, Open University, Milton Keynes, pp. 29–38.

Sale, Diana (1990) *Quality Assurance*, Macmillan, London.

Sang, Bob, Lambley, Sharon and Rush, Howard (1993) *Achieving Quality Management Development for Community Care*, Centre for Business Research, University of Brighton.

Sargeant, Tony, et al., (1992) 'Field Support Workers', feasibility study for the Care sector Consortium, Manchester Polytechnic.

Schon, Donald A. (1991) *The Reflective Practitioner: How Professionals Think in Action*, Avebury, Aldershot.

Scottish Home and Health Department (1985) *Report of the Review of Suicide Precautions at HM Detention Centre and HM Young Offenders Institution, Glenochil*, HMSO, London.

Scottish Office (1990) *Another Kind of Home: A Review of Residential Child Care*, HMSO, Edinburgh.

Scottish Office (1991) *Discussion Paper: Improving Quality Assurance in Community Care*, Scottish Office, Edinburgh.

Scull, A. (1977) *Decarceration: Community Treatment and the Deviant: A Radical View*, Prentice-Hall, Englewood Cliffs, New Jersey.

Secretaries of State for Wales, Scotland and Northern Ireland (1989) *Community Care in the Next Decade and Beyond*, HMSO, London.

Secretary of State for Social Services (1974) *Report of the Committee of Inquiry into the Care and Supervision Provided in Relation to Maria Colwell*, HMSO, London.

Secretary of State for Social Services (Department of Health and Social Security) (1980) *The Report of the Committee of Inquiry into the Case of Paul Steven Brown*, Cmnd 8107, HMSO, London.

Secretary of State for Social Services (1975) *Report of the Committee of Inquiry into the Provision and Co-ordination of Services to the Family of John George Auckland*, HMSO, London.

Senate Select Committee on Public Interest (1994) *Whistleblowing In the Public Interest*, 1070–1131 August 1994 Senate Printing Unit, Canberra, Australia.

Shaw, Ian (1995) 'The Quality of Mercy: The Management of Quality in the Personal Social Services', in Ian Kirkpatrick and Miguel Martinez Lucio (eds), *The Politics of Quality in the Public Sector*, Routledge, London, pp. 128–50.

Simm, Michael (1995) 'Aiming High', *Community Care*, 2–8 November, issue 1093, pp. 16–19.

Simpkin, Mike (1979) *Trapped within Welfare*, Macmillan, London.

Sinclair, Ian and Gibbs, Ian (1996) *Quality of Care in Children's Homes*, Social Work Research and Development Unit Working Paper Series B. No. 3, University of York, York.

Smale, Gerald, Tuson, Graham with Biehal, Nina and Marsh, Peter (1993) *Empowerment, Assessment, Care Management and the Skilled Worker*, NISW Practice and Development Exchange, HMSO, London.

Smith, David (1995) *Criminology for Social Work*, BASW/Macmillan, London.

Snow, C. P. (1954) *The New Men*, Penguin, Harmondsworth.

Snow, C. P. (1964) *The Corridors of Power*, Penguin, Harmondsworth.

Social Services Inspectorate (1987) *From Home Help to Home Care: An Analysis of Policy, Resourcing and Service Management*, HMSO, London.

Social Services Inspectorate (1988a) *Managing Policy Change in Home Help Services*, HMSO, London.

Social Services Inspectorate (1988b) *Protecting Children: A Guide for Social Workers Undertaking a Comprehensive Assessment*, HMSO, London.

Social Services Inspectorate (1989a) *Managing Home Care in Metropolitan Districts*, HMSO, London.

Social Services Inspectorate (1989b) *Sign Posts: Leading to Better Services for Deaf–Blind People* Department of Health, London.

Social Services Inspectorate (1990) *Inspecting Home Care Services: A Guide to the SSI Method*, HMSO, London.

Social Services Inspectorate (1991) *Hear Me: See Me*, Department of Health, London.

Social Services Inspectorate (1992) *Concern for Quality: The First Annual Report of the Chief Inspector Social Services Inspector 1991/92*, HMSO, London.

Social Services Inspectorate (1993a) *Standards for the Residential Care of People with Mental Disorders*, HMSO, London.

Social Services Inspectorate (1993b) *No Longer Afraid – The Safeguard of Older People in Domestic Settings*, HMSO, London.

Social Services Inspectorate (1993c) *Developing Quality Standards for home support services*, HMSO, London.

Social Services Inspectorate (1993d) *Raising the Standard: The Second Annual Report of the Chief Inspector Social Services Inspectorate 1992/3*, HMSO, London.

Social Services Inspectorate (1993e) *Report of an Inspection of Management and Provision of Social Work in the Three Special Hospitals, July–September 1993*, Department of Health, London.

Social Services Inspectorate (1993f) *Whose Life is it Anyway? A Report of an Inspection of Services for People with Multiple Impairments*, Department of Health, London.

Social Services Inspectorate (1994a) *Putting People First: The Third Annual Report of the Chief Inspector Social Services Inspector 1993/94*, HMSO, London.

Social Services Inspectorate (1994b) *Responding to Youth Crime: Findings from Inspections of Youth Justice Services in Five Local Authority Social Services departments*, HMSO, London.
Social Services Inspectorate (1995) *Partners in Caring: The Fourth Annual Report of the Chief Inspector Social Services Inspectore*, 1994/95, HMSO, London.
Social Services Inspectorate (1996) *Almost Half*, Department of Health, London.
Social Work Service (1983) Castle Priory Conference, London, DHSS.
Social Worker 2 in the Lucie Gates Case (1983) 'Savaged by the Press', *Community Care*, no. 445, 13 January 1983, pp. 16–17;
Sone, Kendra (1994) 'A Safe Haven', *Community Care* 1–7 September, no. 1032, pp. 6–7.
Sone, Kendra (1995) 'Whistle Down the Wind', *Community Care*, 1075, 6–12 July, pp. 16–17.
Sparrow, P. R. and Bognano, M. (1993) 'Competency Requirement Forecasting: Issues for International Selection and Assessment', *International Journal of Selection and Assessment*, vol. 1, no. 1, pp. 50–8.
Spencer, J. (1995) 'A Response to Mike Nellis: Probation Values for the 1990s', *The Howard Journal*, vol. 34, no. 4 (Nov.).
Stein, M. and Carey, K. (1986) *Leaving Care*, Blackwell, Oxford.
Stevens, Andy (ed.) (1993b) *Back from the Wellhouse: Discussion Papers on Sensory Impairment and Training in Community Care*, CCETSW, Paper 32.1, CCETSW, London.
Stevenson, O. (1994) 'Social Work in the 1990s: Empowerment – Fact or Fiction?', in R. Page and J. Baldock (eds), *Social Policy Review 6*, Social Policy Association, Canterbury.
Stewart, J. K., Yea, M. D. and Brown, R. J. (1989) 'Changing Social Work Roles in Family Centres: A Social Psychological Analysis', *British Journal of Social Work*, vol. 20, issue 24, no. 3, pp. 45–64.
Street, D. Vinter, R. D. and Perrow, R. C. (1966) Organization for Treatment: A Comparative Study of Institutions for Delinquents, Free Press, New York.
Stroud, John (1973a) 'Residential Care', in John Stroud (ed.) (1973b).
Stroud, John (ed.) (1973b) *Services for Children and Their Families: Aspects of Child Care for Social Workers*, Pergamon, Oxford.
Swain, John, Finkelstein, Vic, French, Sally and Oliver, Mike (eds) (1992) *Disabling Barriers – Enabling Environments*, Open University and Sage, London.
Taylor, Laurie, Lacey, Ron and Bracken, Dennis (1980) *In Whose Best Interests? The unjust Treatment of Children in Courts and Institutions*, Cobden Trust, London.
Thornton, D., Curran, L., Grayson, D. and Holloway, V. (1984) *Tougher Regimes in Detention Centres: Report of an Evaluation by the Young Offender Psychology Unit*, HMSO, London.
Thorpe, David and Thorpe, Suzanne (1992) *Monitoring and Evaluation in the Social Services*, Pavilion Publishing, Brighton.
Thorpe, David H. (1994) *Evaluating Child Protection*, Open University Press, Buckingham.
Tichy, N. M. (1983) *Managing Strategic Change: Technical, Political and Cultural Dynamics*, John Wiley, Chichester.
Timms, N. (1991) 'A New Diploma for Social Work or Dunkirk as Total Victory', in P. Carter, T. Jeffs and M. K. Smith (eds), *Social Work and Social Welfare Yearbook 3 1991*, Open University Press Milton Keynes, pp. 205–14.
Tomlinson, David F. (1993) *No Longer Afraid: The Safeguard of Older People in domestic Settings*, HMSO, London.
Townsend, P. (1962) *The Last Refuge: A survey of Residential Institutions and Homes for the Aged in England and Wales*, Routledge & Kegan Paul, London.

Treasury and Cabinet Office (1992) *Efficiency and Effectiveness in the Civil Service*, Cmnd 8616, HMSO, London.

Treasury, The (1968) *The Civil Service: 1: Report of the Committee, 1966–68*, HMSO, London.

Triseliotis, John and Marsh, Peter (1996) *Readiness to Practise: The Training of Social Workers in Scotland and Their First Year in Work*, The Scottish Office Central Research Unit, Edinburgh.

Tuckman, A. (1992) 'Out of the Crisis: Quality, TQM and the Labour Process', Paper given at Annual Conference on the Organisation and Control of the Labour Process, UMIST, April, 1992.

Tuckman, A. (1994a) 'The Yellow Brick Road: Total Quality Management and the Restructuring of Organizational Cultures', *Organization Studies*, 15, issue 5 (Summer) pp. 727–51.

Tuckman, A. (1994b) 'Ideology, Quality and TQM', in H. Willmott and A. Wilkinson (eds), *Making Quality Critical: New Perspectives on Organizational Change*, Routledge, London.

United Kingdom Central Council for Nursing, Midwifery and Health Visiting (UKCC) (1992) *Code of Professional Conduct*, 3rd edn, United Kingdom Central Council for Nursing, Midwifery and Health Visiting (UKCC), London.

Utley, Alison (1997) 'Flood Warning: Prepare to be Sued by Students', *Times Higher Education Supplement*, 14 February, p. 4.

Vickers, Lucy (1995) 'Whistleblowing and Freedom of Speech in the NHS', *New Law Journal Practitioner*, 18 August, pp. 1257–8.

Walby, Sylvia and Greenwell, June (1994) 'Managing the National Health Service', in John Clarke, Allan Cochrane and Eugene McLaughlin (eds), *Managing Social Policy*, Sage, London, pp. 57–72.

Walker, D. (1976) 'Are Social Workers Badly Treated by the Newspapers?', *Social Work Today*, vol. 7, no. 9 (5 August) pp. 292–3.

Walmsley, J., Reynolds, J. Shakespeare, P. and Wolfe, R. (eds) (1992) *Health, Welfare and Practice, Reflecting on Roles and Relationships*, Open University and Sage.

Walter, J. A. (1978) *Sent Away: A Study of Young Offenders in Care*, Saxon House, Farnborough.

Warlingham Park Hospital Inquiry (1976) *report of the Committee of Inquiry*, Croydon Area Health Authority, Croydon.

Warner, Norman (1994) *Community Care: Just a Fairy Tale?*, Carers National Association, London.

Watts, Janet (1996) 'Listen to the Children', *The Guardian* Guardian Society, 13 March, pp. 2–3.

Webb, D. (1990–1) 'Puritans and Paradigms: A Speculation on the Form of New Moralities in Social Work', *Social Work and Social Sciences Review*, 2 (2), pp. 146–59.

Webb, D. (1996) 'Regulation for Radicals: The State, CCETSW and the Academy', in N. Parton (ed.), *Social Theory, Social Change and Social Work*, Routledge, London.

Welsh Office (1991) *Charter for Patients in Wales*, Welsh Office, Cardiff.

Westman, David (1992) *Whistleblowing: The Law of Retaliatory Discharge*, BNA Books, Washington.

Williams, G. and Macreadie, J. (1992) *Ty Mawr Community Home Inquiry*, Gwent County Council.

Wilson, Julian (1996) 'Power Games', *Community Care*, 9–15 May, issue 1119, pp. 22–3.

Winn, Liz (ed.) (1992) *Power to the People: The Key to Responsive Services in Health and Social Care*, King's Fund, London.

Winner, Mary (1992) *Quality Work with Older People: Developing Models of Good Practice.* Improving Social Work Education and Training 12, CCETSW, London.

Woolf, Rt Hon. Lord Justice and Tumin, His Hon. Judge S. (1991) *Prison Disturbances April 1990: Report of an Inquiry.* Cm 1456, HMSO, London.

Working Group on Organisational and Management Problems of Mental Illness Hospitals (1978, but undated) *Organisational and Management Problems of Mental Illness Hospitals*, Department of Health and Social Security, London.

Wrigley, Leonard and McKevitt, David (1994) 'Professional Ethics, Government Agenda and Differential Information', in David McKevitt and Alan Lawton (1994) (eds), *Public Sector Management: Theory, Critique and Practice*, Open University/Sage, London, pp. 71–84.

Young, R. (1979) 'Social Workers and the Media: A Social Services View', *Social Work Today*, vol. 10, no. 22 (30 January) pp. 10–11.

Zeithaml, V. A., Parasuraman, A. and Berry, L. L. (1990) *Delivering Quality Service*, Free Press, New York.

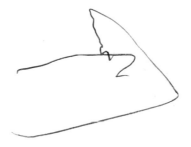

Index